25 TOP METAL SONGS

TAB+ = TAB + TONE + TECHNIQUE

This is not your typical guitar tab book. In the new *Tab+* series from Hal Leonard, we provide you guidance on how to capture the guitar tones for each song as well as tips and advice on the techniques used to play the songs.

Where possible, we've confirmed the gear used on the original recordings via new and previously published interviews with the guitarists, producers, and/or engineers. Then we make general recommendations on how to achieve a similar tone, based on that info.

Some of the songs herein will be easy to play even for advanced beginner players, whereas others present a much greater challenge. In either case, we've identified key techniques in each song that should help you learn the song with greater ease.

ISBN 978-1-4768-1337-0

HAL•LEONARD®
CORPORATION
7777 W. BLUEMOUND RD. P.O. BOX 13819 MILWAUKEE, WI 53213

Visit Hal Leonard Online at
www.halleonard.com

25 TOP METAL SONGS

Performance Notes 3

Ace of Spades 16
MOTÖRHEAD

Afterlife 23
AVENGED SEVENFOLD

Am I Evil? 34
METALLICA

Blackout 43
SCORPIONS

Breaking the Law 53
JUDAS PRIEST

Chop Suey! 58
SYSTEM OF A DOWN

Cowboys from Hell 65
PANTERA

Down with the Sickness 73
DISTURBED

Evil 81
MERCYFUL FATE

Freak on a Leash 101
KORN

Hangar 18 109
MEGADETH

Iron Man 122
BLACK SABBATH

Laid to Rest 128
LAMB OF GOD

The Last in Line 136
DIO

Madhouse 147
ANTHRAX

Mr. Crowley 152
OZZY OSBOURNE

Psychosocial 161
SLIPKNOT

Pull Me Under 171
DREAM THEATER

Raining Blood 189
SLAYER

Roots Bloody Roots 195
SEPULTURA

Sober 202
TOOL

Tears Don't Fall 211
BULLET FOR MY VALENTINE

Thunder Kiss '65 224
WHITE ZOMBIE

The Trooper 235
IRON MAIDEN

Unsung 245
HELMET

Guitar Notation Legend 253

PERFORMANCE NOTES TAB. TONE. TECHNIQUE.
By Michael Mueller

"ACE OF SPADES"
Motörhead

Led by bassist Lemmy Kilmister, Motörhead combined the heavy sounds of Black Sabbath with the fury of British punk to craft a unique brand of heavy metal that would become the progenitor of 1980s speed metal and thrash. The title track of their 1980 release *Ace of Spades* has become the band's signature song and a heavy metal anthem for the ages.

TONE

Guitarist "Fast Eddie" Clarke used a 1970s Fender Stratocaster outfitted with a DiMarzio humbucking pickup (X2N) in the bridge and a DiMarzio single-coil (possibly SDS-1) in the neck position. He plugged into Marshall plexi heads run through Marshall 4x12 cabs.

Use a solidbody guitar with a humbucking pickup in the bridge for this track. Plug into a British-type tube amp, such as a Marshall, Laney, or Orange. Dial in a fair amount of gain or consider using a distortion pedal. The only effect needed here is that you "feel the need, the need for speed."

TECHNIQUE

The tempo on this track is a blistering 282 bpm, but don't let that scare you, as the rhythms are primarily quarter- and eighth-note driven, so it's sort of like playing a more typical rock tune at 140 bpm, only with eighth- and 16th-note rhythms as the basis. In fact, seeing as many metronomes don't go up to 282, you may be forced to practice the tune at "half-time," where you'll read quarter notes as eighths and eighths as 16ths.

Beginning in bar 9 of the Bridge, you'll play eight measures of octaves. Be sure to mute the string between the octave notes with the underside of your index finger.

"AFTERLIFE"
Avenged Sevenfold

Even though Avenged Sevenfold formed in 1999 in the midst of nü metal and its accompanying dearth of guitar pyrotechnics, guitarists Synyster Gates and Zacky Vengeance brought '80s-style shred fire to modern metal. By the time of their 2007 self-titled release, the duo's twin-guitar attack, replete with incendiary harmonized lines and sweep picking, had a huge hand in bringing guitar soloing glory back to the front lines of modern metal.

TONE

Both Gates and Vengeance used custom Schecter guitars equipped with Seymour Duncan Invader humbucking pickups and Floyd Rose tremolo systems. They plugged into Bogner Uberschall heads run through Bogner cabs loaded with 30-watt Celestions. There is a fair amount of compression going on as well.

To get this sound, use a guitar equipped with humbuckers in both the bridge and the neck positions, plugged into a high-gain amp, such as a Bogner or a modern Marshall (Gates and Vengeance currently use Marshall JVM models). For the lead lines, add a compressor pedal for extra sustain, and believe it or not, an overdrive pedal (with the gain off) for extra boost and pick definition.

TECHNIQUE

Gates and Vengeance's guitar parts are not for the faint of fretting. The harmonized lines require a good amount of technical proficiency, so your best approach is to attack them at slower tempos using a metronome, gradually getting up to tempo. The opening riff (Riff A) features some pretty large-interval slides—hitting the wrong target notes here would be catastrophic, so spend some time on your "muscle memory" for these big moves.

In bars 9–12 of the solo, Gates draws on his inner John Petrucci (Dream Theater), firing off alternate-picked quasi-chromatic lines interspersed with sweep picking attacks including unusual (bars 11–12) chord fingerings. Again, it's important to work these up to speed using a metronome to achieve a clean attack, rather than sounding the lowest and highest notes of the arpeggio with a raking sound in between.

"AM I EVIL?"

Metallica

Metallica's fantastic 1983 cover of this Diamond Head tune first appeared as the B-side to the "Creeping Death" single in 1984. It was later included on 1998's *Garage, Inc.*, as well as the Elektra Records re-issue of *Kill 'Em All*.

TONE

Hammett used his 1974 Gibson Flying V plugged into Marshall 100-watt heads and Marshall 4x12 cabs, with an Ibanez TS-808 Tube Screamer providing extra boost. Similarly, Hetfield used an Epiphone Flying V (with Gibson truss rod cover) plugged into a ProCo Rat pedal run into a Jose Arredondo–modded Marshall SLP through a Marshall 4x12 cab with 65-watt Celestions.

Likewise, you'll certainly want to use a humbucker-equipped solidbody guitar plugged into a high-gain tube amp. If you're using a modern model, like the new Marshalls, a Mesa/Boogie, or a Bogner, you won't need the distortion or overdrive pedal in front of the amp, though you may want a clean boost for the solo. Remember, too, that this was recorded before the band went to the "scooped EQ" tone, so be sure to keep some mids in your tone.

TECHNIQUE

"Am I Evil?" is an early showcase of guitar techniques that would largely define thrash metal guitar: palm-muted gallops, Phrygian-inspired harmony, and blistering solos. But interestingly, the solo finds much of its inspiration in Eddie Van Halen. The legato shred-fest at 1:24 requires a fairly simple technique, but at 232 bpm, you've got your work cut out for you. Use your index and pinky fingers for the two fretted notes in each triplet (same goes for the similar technique later in the song), and strive for clean execution and equal volume across all the notes.

The Guitar Solo opens in B minor pentatonic, then goes to the EVH well for a B Mixolydian-based line in measure 3 (a classic Eddie-style phrase), before returning to B minor. At measure 13, Hammett channels his inner Jimmy Page for a lightning-fast pull-off lick in E Dorian. Unless you've got a strong and fast pinky finger, you may find it easiest to use your ring finger on the 15th fret, middle finger on 14, and your index on 12.

"BLACKOUT"

Scorpions

Although "The Zoo," from 1980's *Animal Magnetism*, brought much-deserved attention to the Scorpions, it was their 1982 release *Blackout*, featuring the title track and hit "No One Like You," that put the Teutonic titans on the heavy metal map in the U.S., setting the table for the band's superstardom to come with 1984's *Love at First Sting*.

TONE

Guitarist Rudolf Schenker, as usual, used his trusted Gibson Flying V, whereas lead guitarist Matthias Jabs preferred his 1963 Fender Strat outfitted with a Bill Lawrence L90 pickup and a Floyd Rose. Both guitarists plugged into Marshall JCM 800 2210 heads through Marshall 4x12 cabs.

Whether you go Flying V, super-Strat, Explorer, or whatnot, as long as you've got a humbucking pickup in the bridge position and a floating tremolo system, you'll be fine. A Marshall-type tube amp is your best bet, set for a fairly saturated "crunch" sound. Using a master-volume model or distortion channel, try the gain around 6–7 and give the mids a boost.

TECHNIQUE

The rhythm guitar is pretty much Schenker's patented root–5th–octave power chords and the solo rather stock minor pentatonic material, but it's the attack that gives "Blackout" its character. Jabs, in particular, both in his rhythm riffs and fills and in his solo embarks on a pinch harmonic (labeled "P.H." in the tab) rampage. To properly execute a pinch harmonic, hold the pick close to the tip, and allow your thumb to touch the string immediately after striking the string.

In bar 3 of the solo, you'll encounter a series of 16th-note pull-offs in 12th position. The easiest way to play this lick is to bar your index finger across the top three strings at the 12th fret, then use your pinky finger at the 17th fret of the E string, your ring finger at the 15th fret of the B string, and your middle finger at the 14th fret of the G string.

"BREAKING THE LAW"
Judas Priest

On the strength of the singles "Living After Midnight" and "Breaking the Law," Judas Priest with their 1980 release *British Steel* brought the aggressive and largely underground nascent heavy metal scene screaming into the mainstream, paving the way for the New Wave of British Heavy Metal, which would also bring acts like Iron Maiden and Def Leppard to the fore.

TONE

Guitarist Glenn Tipton used his 1978 Fender Strat with two DiMarzio humbuckers and a Kahler floating tremolo system, whereas his battery mate K.K. Downing favored a Gibson Flying V. Both guitarists plugged into 50- and 100-watt non-master volume Marshall heads, run through Marshall cabs.

You'll certainly want a guitar equipped with a bridge-position humbucker, be it an SG, Flying V, Les Paul, or super-Strat for this tune. A British-style tube amp (Marshall, Orange, Laney) is your best bet. Non-master volume heads need to be run incredibly loud to generate the gain heard on this track, so if you have one, consider using a classic distortion pedal instead, to save your (and your neighbor's or audience's) ears. If you've got a two-channel amp with gain and master volume controls, start with the gain around 6 and adjust from there.

TECHNIQUE

The main riff is brilliant in its simplicity and should be easy even for a beginner. When the Verse begins, be sure to really dig in on the muted strums. These aren't just rhythm scratches but rather a full-on and intentional effect. Use your fret hand to mute the strings, but be sure you don't allow any harmonics to ring out.

In bars 13–16 of the Interlude, you'll find the harmonic divebombs, but you also hear motorcycle and siren sounds, which you can mimic using your whammy bar and harmonics. Try hitting the natural harmonic above the 7th fret on the 2nd string, and manipulate the bar to create a siren-type sound.

Post-interlude, the main riff is harmonized in octaves. If you're the only guitarist or you want your other guitarist to play the underlying rhythm guitar, you can use a harmonizer pedal set for an octave above, or conversely you can play the upper octave part and use an octave pedal to sound the lower voice.

"CHOP SUEY!"
System Of a Down

As nü metal grew in popularity in the late 1990s and early 2000s, the genre soon became diluted with drop-tuned, pseudo-rap-metal wannabes. System of a Down was most certainly not one of them. A true standout of the era, SOAD brought influences as wide-ranging as Frank Zappa and Rush to their brand of metal, as their 2001 release *Toxicity* and its breakthrough hit "Chop Suey!" so perfectly shows.

TONE

In a 2001 interview with Guitar One, Malakian said he used Gibson Les Pauls and SGs, outfitted with Gibson humbucking pickups, for the *Toxicity* sessions. He plugged into a combination of three amps: Mesa/Boogie Triple Rectifier, Marshall, and a Carvin (using just the Boogie in live settings).

Malakian gets a tight, thick distortion just going guitar-to-amp, and you should do the same. A Boogie (Mark IV, Dual or Triple Rectifier) is preferable to really nail it, though a modern Marshall (JVM, JCM 2000) or similar high-gain amp will get you there as well. Use a humbucker-equipped axe with heavy strings to accommodate the ultra-low tuning.

TECHNIQUE

The song's main distorted riff (Rhy. Fig. 2) and its verse riff (Rhy. Fig. 3) comprise alternating power chords, mostly a half step apart. The best way to attack these are to fret the lower of each alternating pair with your index finger, and the chord a half step higher with your middle finger. The lone exception is beats 3–4 of measure 2 in the main riff, where the D5 and C5 are a whole step apart. There you'll use your index on the C5 and ring finger on the D5. These parts require crisp and precise rhythm, best achieved with steady up-and-down strokes from your picking hand.

Malakian loves to use alternative stringed instruments in place of effects, to create interesting textures. Likewise, if you really want to mix things up on your version of this song, substitute a mandolin for the clean-toned electric guitar (Gtr. 3) on the tremolo picking parts. Keep in mind, however, that a mandolin is tuned in 5ths (G–D–A–E, low to high), so you'll have to determine the proper fingerings.

"COWBOYS FROM HELL"
Pantera

Grunge and female singer-songwriter scenes may have dominated the early to mid-1990s, but metal was far from dormant. Fueled by "Dimebag" Darrell Abbott's pulverizing riffs, blazing solos, and screaming harmonics, Texas quartet Pantera stood unmatched as the preeminent metal band of the era.

TONE

Dime used his Dean ML (lightning bolt paint job) equipped with Bill Lawrence L500XL pickups (with the "hot blade" of the bridge humbucker reversed so it faced the neck). He plugged into solid-state Randall RG100ES and RG100HT heads and cabs. A key ingredient to his signature tone was that he used an MXR 6-band EQ set for a mid boost (frown face), when was then fed into a Furman PQ4 EQ that scooped the previously boosted mids and boosted the lows and highs (smiley face).

If you really want to cop Dime's tone, look no further than the Krank Krankenstein. Even though Dime never actually used them (he was working with Krank on them at the time of his murder), they were built with Dime's input and feedback and do indeed generate that "mosquito-ey" buzzsaw distortion for which Dime's known. Plug a humbucker- and floating tremolo–equipped solidbody into that puppy, "krank" it up, and go. And don't forget the phaser for the open-E chug that kicks off the tune.

TECHNIQUE

The solo features many of Dime's most signature moves. In bar 5, Dime debuts the "Dime scale," which is his version of the "EVH scale" (Eddie Van Halen). Essentially, it's a non-scalar finger pattern meant to get you from point A to point B in cool fashion. It should be obvious that you'll use your index, middle, and pinky fingers for this one, then use the same fingers for the "stretch" legato licks in bars 7–8. Showing a knack for thematic development, in bars 10 and 12 Dime reprises the tritone move he introduced in bars 2 and 4. This then leads to the quasi-chromatic (G–A–B♭–B–B♭–A) blues lick in bar 13. An alternate way of playing this lick is to keep it all on one string, using all four fret-hand fingers and playing the B note at the 16th fret of the 3rd string.

"DOWN WITH THE SICKNESS"
Disturbed

Fueled by guitarist Dan Donegan's pummeling riffs and singer David Draiman's now-famous stutter assaults, Disturbed blasted onto the scene in 2000 with chest-rattling single "Stupify" [sic], and then showed they were here to stay with the follow-up title-track single, "Down with the Sickness."

TONE

Donegan currently has endorsement deals with Schecter guitars and Randall amps. Back in 2000, he was getting that huge metal tone via a Paul Reed Smith singlecut through a Mesa/Boogie Triple Rectifier.

One of the keys to Donegan's sound is a tight and thick low end. Using drop tunings, as he does here (drop D, down a half step: D♭–A♭–D♭–G♭–B♭–E♭), every attack of a low-register power chord should rattle the room. You'll need a solidbody guitar equipped with humbucking pickups—more PRS or Les Paul than super-Strat style. Then, plug into a high-gain tube amp with the gain cranked up quite high (around 7–8). Make sure you don't venture into the "mushy" tone zone—you still want an edge to it.

TECHNIQUE

One key element of this—and many other Disturbed tunes—is the tight 16th-note rhythms. It's not syncopation, per se, but those 16th rests are so imperative it sort of feels like it. Be sure to go through the rhythms slowly and work up to speed, keeping them crisp throughout.

One technical challenge is Donegan's harmonic stabs found in bars 4 and 12 of the Verse and on beat 3 of each bar in the Chorus. In all instances, your fret hand will be in 2nd position, with your index finger fretting power chords on the lowest two strings, so you'll need to use your pinky finger to "fret" the harmonics. Additionally, it may take some practice to make the jump from the lowest two strings to the 2nd and 3rd strings with your picking hand with consistent accuracy. Again, start slow, making sure your rhythm is spot on and that the harmonics ring clearly, as they are absolutely key to the tune.

"EVIL"

Mercyful Fate

Mercyful Fate, with their Gothic tendencies and obsession with the occult, is one of the earliest cornerstones of the northern European death and black metal scene. Although singer King Diamond received the spotlight for his incredible range and banshee wails, guitarists Hank Shermann and Michael Denner proved a more than capable twin-guitar attack. "Evil," the track featured here, comes from the band's 1983 debut, *Melissa*.

TONE

Shermann used Fender Stratocasters plugged into vintage Marshall JMP non-master volume heads cranked for max gain, as well as an Ibanez Tube Screamer for that squawky mid-boost. Denner preferred a Gibson Flying V, likewise plugged into vintage non-master volume Marshall heads and cabs.

If you're in a two-guitar band, it makes sense for you and the other guitar player to use similarly equipped guitars: single-coil and humbucker. If your amp has a separate distortion channel with master volume, try setting the gain around 5–6. You also may want to try a mid-boost, first via the amp EQ, or alternatively using an EQ pedal. Finally, there is some studio-added delay on certain parts of this tune, so you'll want a delay pedal set for dotted eighth-note regeneration with four repeats for those sections.

TECHNIQUE

There's quite a bit of syncopation happening in this track, so be vigilant with your rhythms. In bar 11 of the Intro, where the main Verse riff is first introduced, dig the 16th–dotted eighth rhythm on the G5 chord—it's essential that you're not late on the attack here.

The song goes through several key changes, beginning in E minor, then D minor, then B minor, then C♯ minor, and back to B minor to cap it off. Though many of the lines played here contain what are now considered "stock" scale-based metal licks, it's interesting to note not only that Shermann and Denner "play the changes" but also the preponderance of the Dorian mode intermingled throughout with Aeolian, or natural minor. And it doesn't seem accidental, as the duo are careful not to play Dorian's major 6th over the III chord (e.g., in the key of E minor, they'll play the Dorian C♯ over an E5–G5 progression, but when a C5 appears, they switch to the Aeolian mode with a C natural as the 6th).

"FREAK ON A LEASH"

Korn

Korn turned the post-grunge world on its ear with their brand of quirky and abstract yet brutal blend of metal and hip-hop. *Follow the Leader*, which features this track, marked the band's commercial breakthrough, reaching the top of the charts in 1998.

TONE

A central component of the band's sound was guitarists James "Munky" Shaffer and Brian "Head" Welch's use of Ibanez UV7 and K7 seven-string guitars, often tuned down a whole step so that the seventh string sounded a thundering low A. In the studio, the pair played through combinations of Mesa/Boogie Triple Rectifiers, Bogners, and Rivera Boneheads, through various Marshall and Rivera 4x12 cabs.

To replicate the tone, a seven string tuned down a whole step is your best bet. The range in this song goes from low B♭ up to the high E at the 12th fret of the 1st string, so you could also tune your six-string to match the pitches of strings 7–2 of a seven-string, down a whole step (A–D–G–C–F–A), and then adjust your fingerings accordingly. For example, the note at the 12th fret of the 1st string will now be played at the 19th fret.

Plug into a modern high-gain amp, such as a Boogie, Bogner, Randall, or Marshall JVM series, with the gain set high (around 8) and the bass control cranked up with the mids and treble a little past half. You're also going to need a Digitech Whammy pedal for this track, as well as a delay pedal set for dotted eighth-note regeneration with three repeats and a chorus pedal set for plenty of swirl. Copying the effects spot on may be an exercise in futility, but with some experimentation, you'll find sounds that work great on this track.

TECHNIQUE

Most of the parts here are fairly simple to play—the tough part is dialing in the sounds. But when you get to the Interlude, the Gtr. 2 part is played with heavy 16th-note syncopation, exploiting the minor 2nd interval to great effect. Be sure to count each beat here in 16th-note subdivisions (one-ee-and-uh, two-ee-and-uh, etc.), to make sure you're nailing the rhythm.

"HANGAR 18"
Megadeth

Dave Mustaine has burned through a lot of high-caliber guitarists in Megadeth, but none is more identified with the band than Marty Friedman, whose exotic and incendiary lines graced Megadeth's most successful releases: *Rust in Peace* and *Countdown to Extinction*. "Hangar 18," a song about the famously mysterious Area 51, proves the perfect showcase for Friedman's otherworldly chops.

TONE

When Friedman joined the band and entered the studio to record *Rust in Peace*, Mustaine had his tech put together an identical guitar rig for his thrash Padawan consisting of a VHT 2150 power amp, a Bogner Triple Giant preamp, and Marshall cabs loaded with four 75-watt Celestions. Additionally, they used Tubeworks and Marshall preamps for some of the solos. Mustaine used his Jackson King V, while Friedman employed his trusted and newly painted black Jackson Kelly #1.

Because of the high F♯ notes in one of the late solos, you'll need a 24-fret guitar equipped with a humbucking pickup in the bridge position. Pair that with a high-gain tube amp such as a Bogner, Marshall JVM series, or Engl, making sure to have a good mid boost, either via the amp EQ or possibly through a pedal like the Ibanez Tube Screamer (with the gain set to "0").

TECHNIQUE

The first Interlude opens with some smooth, well-executed sweep arpeggios courtesy of Friedman. For this particular finger shape, you can play the 15th-fret D note either with your ring finger or with your middle finger. The latter requires you to bounce between the 4th and 2nd strings with that finger in rapid succession but also increases the probability of playing it as cleanly and evenly as Friedman does. In bar 16, Gtr. 4 descends in a sequence of fours. On the second 16th note of beat 3, try playing that E note (9th fret, 3rd string) at the 14th fret of the 4th string; this will keep you in a comfortable finger pattern.

The fourth Guitar Solo (Mustaine) requires a huge stretch from the 14th to the 21st fret. This is pretty easy on the top three strings, but once you get down to the bottom three, it becomes taxing on your fret hand. You'll either want to "high-strap" it or rest your guitar on a raised knee, to help facilitate the stretch and avoid injury to your wrist. Alternatively, you may consider using tapping on the 21st-fret notes. You won't be able to reproduce it note-for-note, but at that speed, it's not necessary.

"IRON MAN"
Black Sabbath

Talk about "heavy metal!" From the eerie low-E bends to Ozzy Osbourne's guttural declaration to perhaps the greatest heavy guitar riff of all time, "Iron Man" set the bar for all metal to follow. Taken from the band's second album, *Paranoid*, this track gets its title from the first time Ozzy heard the riff, saying it sounded "like a big iron bloke walking about."

TONE

Iommi gets his classic Sabbath tone from a 1965 Gibson SG Special with a P-90 pickup in the bridge and a custom-wound John Birch Simplux P-90–style single coil in the neck position. The SG is plugged into a Laney Supergroup amp (all controls on "10") through Laney 4x12 cabs loaded with 25-watt Goodman speakers. He also placed a Dallas Arbiter Rangemaster Treble Boost in line. The Orange amps famously seen in the "Iron Man" video were just for the shoot.

A P-90–equipped axe is ideal, though a Les Paul–type with humbuckers will also suffice. Just make sure the headstock angle allows for a full-step bend of the low E string behind the nut. Plug that into a British-style tube amp like a Laney, Orange, or Marshall, but avoid any highly saturated "modern" metal tones. With today's amps, you won't need a treble boost.

TECHNIQUE

For years, the opening low-E bend was one of the more mysterious techniques in metal guitar history, but Iommi set it straight in a 1997 interview with *Guitar World*. "I raise and lower the pitch of the open low E note by pressing down on that string behind the nut with the index finger of my fretting hand. At the same time, I also fret the E note at the 2nd fret on the D string with my little finger and let it ring," he says. "I pluck the E note on the D string with my middle finger (picking hand) as I pick the low E with the plectrum; this is known as hybrid picking."

"LAID TO REST"
Lamb of God

The early Oughties saw many metal bands crash onto the scene, many only to burn out after a few years. Lamb of God, however, led by the dual-guitar carnage of Willie Adler and Mark Morton, has become one of the top-drawing metal bands of the past decade. "Laid to Rest," from the band's 2004 breakthrough album Ashes of the Wake, is a prime example of the group's pummeling sound and killer riffs.

TONE
Morton plugged a custom Jackson guitar (which would later become his signature MM1 model), loaded with Seymour Duncan humbucking pickups, into a pair of Mesa/Boogie Mark IV heads run through Mesa/Boogie 4x12 cabs loaded with Celestion Vintage 30 speakers. On one Mark IV, the mids are scooped, and on the other, boosted. Adler used a Framus Diablo Custom outfitted with humbucking pickups, and also plugged into Mesa/Boogie Mark IV heads and 4x12 cabs.

Similarly, you'll want to use a humbucking-equipped solidbody like a Jackson or Adler's new signature ESP Eclipse models. Plug into a high-gain amp such as a Mesa/Boogie Mark IV or Mark V, Engl, Bogner, or Marshall Vintage Modern series. Given the high level of gain you'll be using, you might want to consider a noise suppressor such as the Boss NS-2 or a Rocktron Hush unit.

TECHNIQUE
Overall, the key to playing this song is tight rhythm. The tune is in 6/8 (six eighth notes per bar), but the pulse is felt as two beats of triplets (One–two–three–Four–five–six). Throughout, the band engages in highly syncopated unison rhythms, so it's essential that you nail them.

If you have trouble stretching to the C note on the 3rd string (17th fret) in the second bar of Riff B (Verse), you could play it at the 13th fret of the 2nd string, but I encourage you to play it as transcribed. Conversely, in bars 3–4 of Riff D, heard in the final Verse, you may find it much easier to play the Eb note on the 4th string at the 1st fret rather than on 6th fret, 5th string as written.

"THE LAST IN LINE"
Dio

Ronnie James Dio was—and very well may forever be—the greatest heavy metal singer of all time. As a bonus, he had a knack for hiring really, really good guitarists, including Vivian Campbell, who played on this stellar title track from Dio's 1984 album The Last in Line.

TONE
Campbell used a Charvel Strat with a bridge-position Seymour Duncan humbucking pickup and a Floyd Rose. This was plugged into a Marshall JCM 800 head and a Marshall 4x12 cab with 75-watt Celestions. Campbell pushed the front of the amp with a Boss SD-1 Super Overdrive.

Given the whammy maneuvers in "The Last in Line," you'll want a solidbody guitar equipped with a floating trem and a bridge-position humbucker. Some form of Marshall or similar Brit-style tube amp with a fair amount of gain (but not overly saturated) is your ticket, along with an overdrive (e.g., Boss SD-1, Tube Screamer) or even clean boost or EQ to provide extra oomph in the solo.

TECHNIQUE
For the classically-influenced fingerstyle Intro, use your thumb for all the 5th-string notes, your index on the 3rd, middle on the 2nd, and ring on the 1st. Then comes the power- and sus-chord–fueled Interlude. Here, you may want to play the full barre-chord versions of these dyads; that is, for the Dsus4, play a D major barre chord at the 5th fret, placing your pinky on the suspended G note (8th fret, 2nd string), then removing it to play the D major chord.

For the cool arpeggio section in bars 8–9, play the opening Em shape with your pinky, middle and index fingers on strings 5, 4, and 3, respectively. For the C/E that follows, shift up to play the 5th-string E with your ring finger, while your index finger bars the 4th and 3rd strings at the 5th fret. For the Em7 that follows, hold the C/E shape, but place your pinky finger on the D note (7th fret, 3rd string). In bar 17, you might want to jack up a 1-1/2-step bend from the 17th fret, rather than the 2-1/2 step whopper at the 15th fret, depending on the radius of your fretboard. For example, on a Fender Strat, the top string frets out on bends at just about 1-1/2 steps.

"MADHOUSE"

Anthrax

Anthrax rocked just as hard as the other three members of the "Big Four" (Metallica, Megadeth, Slayer) in the 1980s, and in fact became de facto leaders of the speed metal movement as those other bands became more accessible. "Madhouse" is from the band's 1985 release, *Spreading the Disease*, an all-time classic thrash album.

TONE

Scott Ian plugged his 1983 Jackson Randy Rhoads V into a Marshall JCM 800 2203 head run through a Marshall 4x12 cab. He says the key to his tone, though, was a TC Electronic Booster/Distortion pedal placed in line, which gave him the edge and low end without being too fuzzy. Dan Spitz also used a Jackson Rhoads V, loaded with a single Jackson humbucker in the bridge and equipped with a Floyd Rose trem. Like Ian, he plugged into a Marshall JCM 800 2203 head and Marshall cab.

The Marshall JCM 800 2203 was pretty much a defining tone of early thrash, usually with a boost or overdrive slamming the front of the amp, so that's a great place to start for getting this tone. Many of today's high-gain tube amps will get you there without the extra boost, but be sure you maintain that "edgy" tone. You'll need a solidbody guitar with a bridge-position humbucker and a floating trem as well.

TECHNIQUE

As with most thrash tunes, the first key technique is to really dig in with your pick attack throughout. That being said, let's take a look at the hip but tricky main riff (Riff A). After attacking it with several fingerings, I found that fretting all the 5th-string notes with my ring finger and 6th-string notes with my middle finger yielded the cleanest attack and best set up the return to the E5 power chord.

The other potential challenge in this tune comes in bars 2 and 6 of Riff B, where you've got to execute the E–F trill on the 4th string using your fret hand's ring (3rd fret) and middle (2nd fret) fingers. Most guitarists play trills exclusively with their index fingers serving as "anchor," so this is a curveball of sorts. You might want to make an exercise of playing trills with all combinations of fingers.

"MR. CROWLEY"

Ozzy Osbourne

Ozzy Osbourne is yet another metal singer who's been blessed to work with some of the greatest guitarists of all time, including the late, great Randy Rhoads, who played on this track from 1981's *Blizzard of Ozz*. Rhoads had said that "Mr. Crowley" was his favorite solo he ever recorded. We couldn't agree more!

TONE

His 1970s Gibson Les Paul Custom was Rhoads's weapon of choice for this track. He plugged into a Marshall JMP Super Lead Plexi with Marshall 4x12 cabs loaded with Altec speakers, for a brighter sound. His effects included a variety of MXR pedals (Distortion+, Stereo Flanger, Stereo Chorus, Analog Delay), Korg and Roland tape echoes, a Crybaby wah pedal, and his secret weapon: an MXR 10-band EQ pedal.

To cop this sound, you'll need an axe with a bridge-position humbucker, preferably a Les Paul–style guitar or a Jackson Rhoads V. Plug it into a high-gain distortion pedal, like the MXR Distortion+, and a chorus pedal to fatten the tone (not a "swirly" chorus, though). The 10-band EQ is actually quite key to Rhoads's tone, if you can swing it. Otherwise, keep your bass low, a good mid-boost, and fairly neutral treble for EQ. If you happen to have an Electro-Harmonix POG or POG2, you can create a very credible organ sound for the Intro.

TECHNIQUE

Rhoads primarily relies on D minor and minor pentatonic scales, with the occasional ♭5th (A♭) tossed in for chromatic appeal. But at bar 7 of the Outro Solo, the C♯ (7th of D) makes the first of many appearances, indicating a switch to the D Hungarian minor scale (D–E–F–G♯–A–B♭–C) and a pronounced neoclassical vibe.

In the Interlude, each two-bar phrase begins on the second 16th note of beat 2; be sure you maintain that 16th rest and don't rush it. For the trilled section beginning in bar 9 of the Outro Solo, use your first and second fingers for all the trills. Then, for the three-notes-per-string legato ascent in bar 13, use your index, middle, and pinky fingers for every three-note pattern.

"PULL ME UNDER"
Dream Theater

With their landmark 1992 release, *Images and Words*, along with its lead single "Pull Me Under," Dream Theater turned the prog-metal world on its head and established a new bar for total-band musicianship and technical proficiency—one that the band has only continued to raise in the 20 years since.

TONE

John Petrucci used his custom Ibanez "Picasso" guitar loaded with DiMarzio Tone Zone (bridge) and Humbucker from Hell (neck) pickups. He plugged into Mesa/Boogie Quad and the Triaxis preamps into a Mesa Power amp, run through Mesa/Boogie 4x12 cabs. He also used a Roland Jazz Chorus for clean tones.

If you've got bucks to spare, pick up an Ernie Ball Music Man JP signature model and a Mesa/Boogie Mark IV (or Mark V) along with a Boogie 4x12. The Boogie is pretty essential to Petrucci's tone (you can even get his amp settings from his web site), but any decent super-Strat with humbucking pickups in the bridge and neck and a Floyd Rose trem should do the trick. You'll also want a slight chorus effect on the clean parts.

TECHNIQUE

With 17 pages of Petrucci prowess, where to begin? First, Petrucci's time is impeccable, so play through these challenging parts with a metronome, to ensure precise rhythm, gradually speeding it up until you play at tempo.

Here are a few specific things to watch for: Petrucci uses all downstrokes for the 16th-note power-chord rhythms in the Interludes—it's fast, but possible. In the Pre-Chorus and behind the Keyboard Solo, he uses some really cool chord voicings that require in some cases substantial stretches while allowing for open, ringing strings. This is a signature Petrucci move, so it's worth spending some time on these and trying them in various areas of the neck, if you're going to play other Dream Theater material. Finally, try to adhere to strict alternate picking on single-note lines, as Petrucci does. It will help to keep things clear and consistent.

"PSYCHOSOCIAL"
Slipknot

By the time of their 2008 release, *All Hope Is Gone* (from which this track is taken), the Iowa nonet Slipknot had become one of the biggest heavy metal bands on the planet. While their studio albums are rife with pulverizing riffs from guitarists Jim Root and Mick Thomson, it's the band's inimitable and mesmerizing live show that converts even the casual metal fan.

TONE

Root used his trusty Fender Flathead Telecaster equipped with an EMG-81 in the bridge and an EMG-60 in the neck, plugged into Orange Rockerverb heads and run through Orange, Diezel, and Bogner cabs. Thomson used his custom Ibanez MTM-1 model, also equipped with the EMG-81 and EMG-60 pickups, and plugged into a Rivera Knucklehead KR7 head through Rivera 4x12 cabs loaded with 100-watt Celestions.

To emulate the Slipknot tone, use a solidbody guitar equipped preferably with active humbuckers (EMG, Seymour Duncan Blackouts) and plugged into a high-gain tube amp with the gain set at 8 or higher and a generous amount of bass in the EQ. Your guitar will need heavy-gauge strings (Root and Thomson use D'Addario .011–.058) to accommodate the ultra-low tuning of this tune: Drop-D, down 2-1/2 steps (low to high: A–E–A–D–F♯–B). Alternatively, you could play the tune on the lowest six strings of a seven-string guitar, dropping the low B one step, to A, and the 3rd string (G) a half step, to F♯, to maintain the fingerings in the transcriptions.

TECHNIQUE

Slipknot is one of the rare metal bands that can both jackhammer away on 16th-note rhythms (Intro) one minute and settle into a hypnotic eighth-note groove the next, with equal credibility. As such, your main focus here is on rhythm. Be sure to use a metronome to develop an airtight attack throughout. Thomson and Root shred through their solos, but they're mostly pattern-based, so look for those familiar shapes and work them up to tempo. Finally, in bar 7 of the first solo, there's a footnote for the Whammy pedal setup. If you don't have a Whammy pedal, don't worry about it. It's very subtle and not at all essential. You can just play the notes in traditional fretted fashion.

"RAINING BLOOD"
Slayer

Slayer! Led by the always pummeling and sometimes twisted riffing of Kerry King and Jeff Hanneman, Slayer's 1986 release *Reign in Blood*, featuring the classic "Raining Blood" shown here, ranks as one of the most important and influential thrash albums of all time.

TONE
The Slayer tone is raw and bludgeoning. King played an ESP equipped with a DiMarzio Mega Drive humbucker in the bridge, plugged into a Marshall JCM 800 through a Marshall 4x12 cab loaded with Celestion Vintage 30s. He also placed a Boss RGE 10-band EQ in line for extra mid boost. Likewise, Hanneman used the same rig, only he plugged a B.C. Rich Bich into it.

To capture this brutal sound, use a solidbody guitar equipped with humbucking pickups and a floating trem, like the ESP 25th Anniversary Reign in Blood model. The Marshall JCM 800 is one of the defining tones of thrash, so that's preferable, but any high-gain tube amp (Engl, Rivera, Mesa/Boogie Rectifier series) will suffice. Another key element, and one thrash guitarists should have on their pedalboard anyway, is an EQ pedal. MXR makes a signature Kerry King 10-band EQ (MXR KFK1), or you can go with the venerable BOSS GE-7. Set the EQ for a mid-boost (frown shape).

TECHNIQUE
The tempos here, particularly the double time section prior to the first Verse, are plain relentless. That section comprises two three-note patterns pedaled against an open low E. Use your pinky, middle, and index fingers for the A–G–F♯ (5–3–2) pattern and your pinky, ring, and index fingers for the B♭–A–G (6–5–3) pattern. You're nearly tremolo picking this section, but if you listen closely, you can hear all the notes, so start slowly and build up to that insane speed to keep it as clean as possible. Do the same for all the various riffs.

In the Outro, one guitar will cover the tremolo picking while the other produces miscellaneous whammy bar effects. Use the natural harmonics at the 5th and 7th frets for most of these, shaking the bar till it begs for mercy. It's also not a bad place to add some insane shred lines—the more chaotic, the better!

"ROOTS BLOODY ROOTS"
Sepultura

Led by singer/guitarist Max Cavalera, Sepultura combined punk, hardcore, and their native Brazilian music to form a unique blend of heavy metal world music that also made them one of the most distinctive metal bands of the 1990s. "Roots Bloody Roots" is from their 1996 album, *Roots*, their final release with Cavalera at the helm.

TONE
According to an interview with *Guitar Shop*, Cavalera used a Gibson SG, with only the bottom four strings present. Those were downtuned 2-1/2 steps, to B–E–A–D. He plugged into Marshall heads and cabs, with a custom "bigger Muff" distortion pedal built by Richard Kaplan (owner of Indigo Ranch Studios). Lead guitarist Andreas Kisser used his reliable Jackson Randy Rhoads V loaded with Seymour Duncan PAF humbuckers and plugged into a Mesa/Boogie Triaxis preamp through a Mesa 500 Strategy power amp.

You'll need heavy-gauge strings to avoid floppy strings in this tuning. Cavalera and Kisser used .013–.056. If you've got a seven-string, you can use the bottom six strings, downtuning the 3rd string from G, to F♯, to maintain the fingerings in the tab. Plug into a high-gain tube amp such with the gain cranked up. You might consider adding a fuzz effect for the E–F single-note main riff, for extra body. You'll also need a wah pedal and a delay pedal (set for whole note regeneration, one repeat) for the solo.

TECHNIQUE
It doesn't get much simpler than an E–F single-note riff, but with some mild syncopation, man does it groove! Add Kisser's similar motif on the top two strings using major 7ths (D♯ and E, respectively), and you've got a classic example of well-executed metal dissonance. Mind your rhythms in both parts.

Bars 1–2 of the solo feature unison bends executed in concert with a wah pedal. Start in the toe-up position, and gradually push down till you hit the desired frequency and leave it there for the rest of bar 1, then repeat for bar 2. Beginning in bar 5, you'll need a Floyd Rose–style whammy bar. Use the 20th-fret high C as indicated for bars 5–6. Following that, you can either try to replicate the part as written, or use your ear and a sense of adventure to create your own part over bars 7–8.

"SOBER"
Tool

Combining the angst of the popular grunge movement, the raw brutality and dark themes of heavy metal, and the intelligence and complexity of progressive rock, Tool crafted a unique sound and style that has been often imitated but never duplicated. "Sober" was not only the first single from the band's 1993 album, *Undertow*, but also the track that launched them into mainstream.

TONE
Guitarist Adam Jones is an avowed devotee of the Gibson Les Paul Custom Silverburst, which is the axe, loaded with Seymour Duncan humbuckers, that he used to record this track. He plugged into a 1976 non-master–volume Marshall Super Bass modded to Super Lead specs, which was run through a Marshall 4x12 cab.

On subsequent albums, Jones began blending amp sounds in the studio, using Diezel VH4, Bogner Uberschall, Mesa/Boogie Dual Rectifier, and Rivera Knucklehead models, among others. You really can't go wrong with any of these choices (or a high-gain Marshall) when trying to cop Jones's tone. You'll want to use a Les Paul or similarly humbucking-equipped guitar as well. Additionally, you'll need a delay pedal set for eighth-note regeneration (400 ms rate) with one repeat and a flanger set with a fairly fast rate mid-depth for the watery effect heard in the Verse.

TECHNIQUE
Octaves are an essential part of 1990s metal, but Jones adds his own wrinkle: allowing the string between the octave notes—in this case, D—to ring freely. To do so, you'll need to arch your index finger considerably while fretting the A string, thus allowing the open D to ring. The same arching technique applies to the dyads (fretted note and open D) heard throughout the Verse section.

While we're on the octaves topic, you'll see that Jones bends an octave shape in bar 2 of the Interlude. To achieve this bend, pull the strings downward (toward the floor), rather than pushing up; this will give you the leverage you need.

"TEARS DON'T FALL"
Bullet for My Valentine

Bullet for My Valentine is a melodic metalcore quartet hailing from Wales. Led by the blistering fretwork of guitarists Michael Paget and Matthew Tuck, BFMV quickly rose through the ranks, becoming a top festival draw and leader of the metalcore movement. "Tears Don't Fall" was the fourth single from the band's 2006 release, *The Poison*.

TONE
Tuck used a Jackson Randy Rhoads V (RR1) through a Peavey 5150 II (or 6505), whereas Paget used an ESP Dave Mustaine Flying V loaded with Seymour Duncans run through a Mesa/Boogie Triple Rectifier. Both used a Roland JC-120 for clean tones, which presumably provided the slight chorusing effect in the Intro, and T.C. Electronic delays.

Use a solidbody guitar, ideally a Flying V type, equipped with humbuckers. You'll want to plug into a harmonically rich amp with natural compression such as Peavey's 6505+ or a Mesa/Boogie Rectifier model. Be sure to dial in lots of gain. For the main clean-toned riff, you can apply really light chorusing or leave it dry. Your delay should be set for quarter note regeneration (rate = 370ms), with five repeats. You'll also need a wah pedal, such as the Dunlop Slash model that Paget uses.

TECHNIQUE
Play the opening riff with your index on the root and your ring finger on the 5th of each power chord. Use your pinky to hit the natural F (6th) on beat 3 of bar 2. For the F5 chord on strings 4–2 in Rhy. Fig. 1, be sure to bar strings 3–2 at the 5th fret with your ring finger, so all you need do is lift your pinky from the 6th-fret F on beats 1–2 of bar 2, and then replace it for beats 3–4. Riff C will require a sound ear to hit those quarter-note bends. To practice hitting that note reliably, play the A note at the 7th fret, then the B♭ at the 8th fret. Keeping those two sounds in mind bend the 7th-fret A until you reach the midway point. Use the original recording as a guide as well.

The first Guitar Solo is a barn burner, but it's all based in A minor pentatonic sequences. Work on those sequences slowly until you can play each at tempo, then just string them together.

"THUNDER KISS '65"

White Zombie

Combining elements of traditional metal, industrial, and the sounds of grisly horror, White Zombie simultaneously raised the fear factor mastered by Alice Cooper, Kiss and Mötley Crüe while creating metal you could actually dance to. Though leader Rob Zombie would later find his "dark soul mate" in guitarist John 5, this track, as well as all of *La Sexorcisto: Devil's Music, Vol. 1*, features original guitarist Jay Yuenger, aka J.

TONE

J. used his "STP" guitar, a Charvel 6 in which he placed an EMG 81 humbucker in the bridge and an EMG single-coil in the neck. He also got rid of the mini-toggles and installed a Gibson 3-way pickup selector switch. He plugged into a Marshall JCM 800 run through a Marshall 4x12 cab, placing a ProCo Rat distortion pedal and a wah pedal in line.

Likewise, a humbucker-equipped super-Strat into a high-gain tube amp will cop this tone. Though J. gets plenty of gain, it's not oversaturated—at least on the rhythm guitars—so keep it down around 6. J. is pretty freewheeling with regard to the wah pedal in the solo, and so should you. For bends, start in the toe up position, and gradually press the pedal down as you bend the string.

TECHNIQUE

It's not often a simple low-E pedal becomes an identifiable riff, but with the cool, syncopations here, that's exactly what it is, with the G and F♯ 3rds dyads merely capping it off. Pay close attention to the rhythm; playing along with the original track should make it pretty easy. Throughout the Verse, J. plays E minor pentatonic–based fills behind the vocal, and you should be familiar with these patterns, if not the licks themselves. There are also a lot of unison bends on the 3rd and 2nd strings. Strive for in-tune bends here; practice bending the 3rd-string note to match the stationary 2nd-string note until the movement is ingrained in your "muscle memory."

"THE TROOPER"

Iron Maiden

Led by singer Bruce Dickinson's soaring vocals and the relentless twin-guitar attack of Dave Murray and Adrian Smith, Iron Maiden has become arguably the most influential heavy metal band in history. "The Trooper" is an all-time metal classic from the band's 1983 landmark release *Piece of Mind*.

TONE

According to a 1983 *Guitar World interview*, Murray used his 1957 Fender Strat, equipped with a DiMarzio humbuckers (Super Distortion bridge, PAF neck). He ran through three MXR pdeals—a 10-band EQ, a Distortion Plus, and a Phase Shifter—and a Dunlop Crybaby wah pedal, then into Marshall JCM 800 2204 50-watt heads run through Marshall 4x12 cabs loaded with 65-watt Celestions. Smith used either a Gibson SG or an Ibanez Destroyer, plugged into an Ibanez Tube Screamer, MXR Micro Amp, and BOSS chorus and flanger pedals, also into 50-watt Marshall JCM 800 heads and cabs.

A key element of Maiden's tone is a solid mid-boost. Plug a humbucker-equipped solidbody into a classic British-style tube amp, such as a Marshall or Laney, and then use the onboard EQ to dial in plenty of mids. If you have an outboard EQ, such as the MXR 10-band or a BOSS GE-7, start with a "frown"-shaped curve and tweak it from there. For the subtle flanger part at the end of each verse, set your rate and depth quite low, for just a hint of the effect.

TECHNIQUE

The F♯–G trills in the main riff are simple enough, but it may take a few runs through to be comfortable playing them in time. Use your index and middle fingers to play these.

Murray and Smith work so well together because they bring complementary skills to the stage. The lick in bars 5–7 is classic Murray, as is the legato pull-off lick repeated over bars 9–11. For Smith, who is much more a blues-based metal guitarist, it's more than just playing stock licks. One of his favorite moves the bend-and-release, often on 5ths and 6ths, as in bars 12–15 of the second Guitar Solo. Bending to pitch is key to Smith's "singing" sound, so make sure you're hitting those notes.

"UNSUNG"
Helmet

Helmet mastermind Page Hamilton is quite the jazz aficionado, even having studied the art form in New York City in the late 1980s. But while there, he became intrigued with the alternative and post-punk scenes, and soon began writing music that fused that raw power and aggression with the complexities of the jazz style—and Helmet was born. "Unsung," which is more of a grunge rocker in the style of Soundgarden, appears on the Helmet's 1992 release, *Meantime*.

TONE

Hamilton used an ESP Horizon to record the Meantime album, whereas rhythm guitarist Peter Mengede used Gibson guitars. In an 1992 interview with Guitar World, Hamilton says both he and Mengele used Yamaha GEP-50 effects processors, essentially using the stock "Heavy Metal" setting, for their main "crunch" sound. For power, Hamilton used a combination of Marshall JCM 800 2204S and Orange heads fed into Orange 4x12 cabs.

These days, Hamilton still uses the ESP Horizon, though it's now a signature model, so a similar super-Strat model will do. He also now uses Fryette amps (formerly VHT). Likewise, you'll want a high-gain tube amp, such as the Fryette, Marshall JVM, or even an Orange Rockerverb, with the gain set to high (around 8)

TECHNIQUE

Hamilton's drop-D tuning makes easy, single-finger barre work of the power chords here, but later in the tune, he adds open strings to the shape. This not only introduces jazzier sounds but also requires a switch from a single-finger barre to fretting the strings with individual fingers. For example, in bar 13 of the Chorus, play the Cmaj7(no 3rd) chord with your middle, ring, and pinky fingers at the 10th fret of the 6th, 5th, and 4th strings, respectively. Doing so will allow you to easily use your index finger on the 3rd string for the Aadd9 chord in bar 15, all while allowing the appropriate open strings to ring out. The Outro features even more of these chords, and some will require other fingerings. Just be sure the notes all ring out clearly.

Ace of Spades

Words and Music by Ian Kilmister, Edward Clarke and Philip Taylor

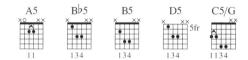

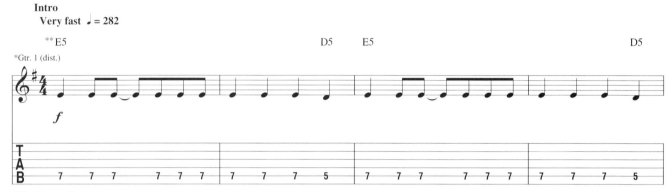

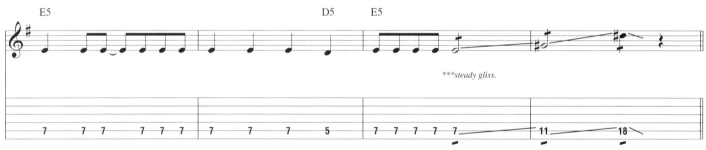

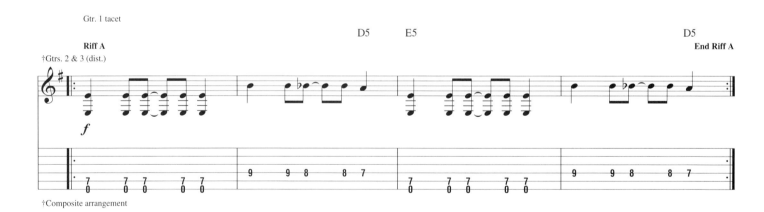

G5

1. If you like to gam - ble, __ I tell you I'm __ your man. __ You
2. Play - ing for the high one, __ I danc - in' with the dev - il.
3. Push - ing up the an - te, __ I know you've got to see me. __

win some, lose some, __ it's all the same _____ to me. _____
Go - in' with the flow, it's all a game _____ to me. _____
Read 'em and weep, the dead man's __ hand _____ a - gain. _____

Gtrs. 2 & 3: w/ Riff A (2 times)   2nd time, Gtr. 4: w/ Fill 1

E5   D5   E5   D5

Gtr. 4 (dist.)

f

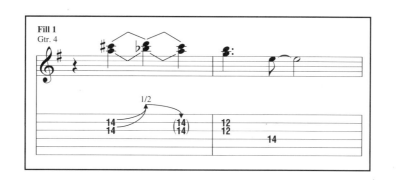

Fill 1
Gtr. 4

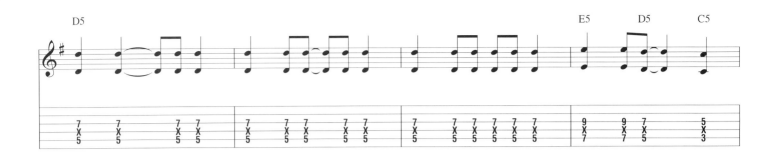

And don't for - get the Jok - er.

(cont. in slashes)

(cont. in slashes)

Guitar Solo

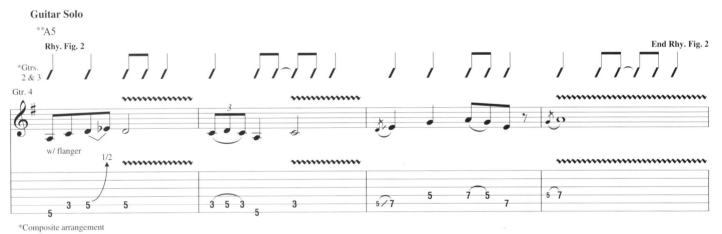

*Composite arrangement

**See top of first page of song for chord diagrams pertaining to rhythm slashes.

Afterlife

Words and Music by Matthew Sanders, James Sullivan, Brian Haner, Jr. and Zachary Baker

*Strings arr. for gtr.
**Chord symbols reflect implied harmony.
***Composite arrangement

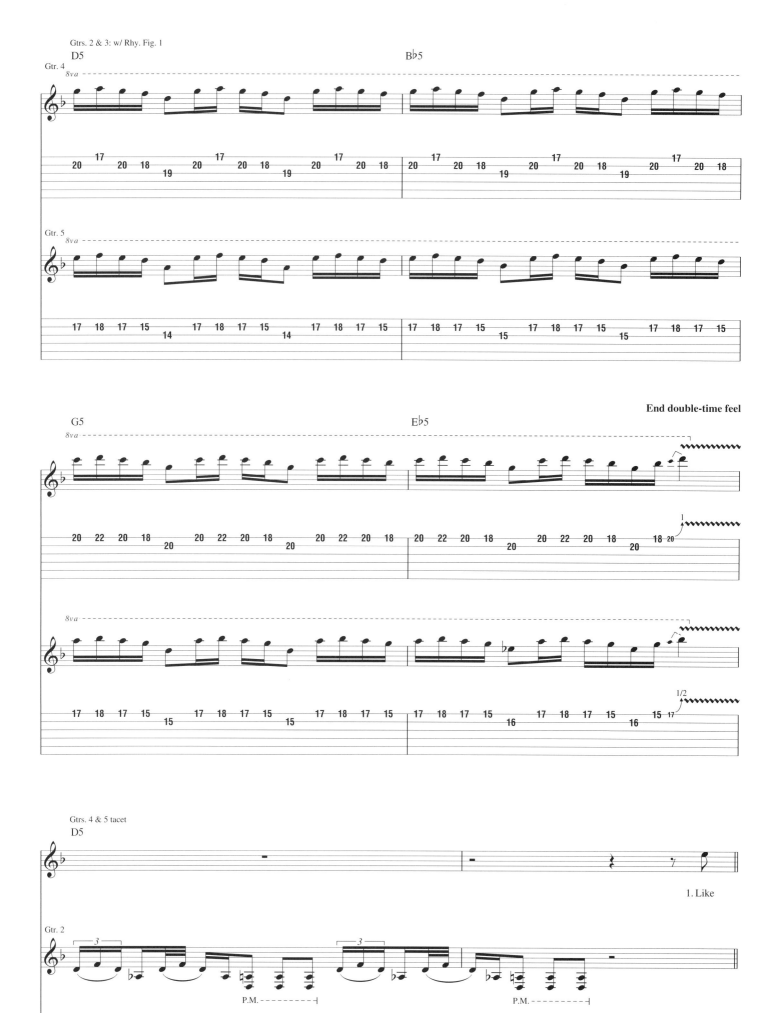

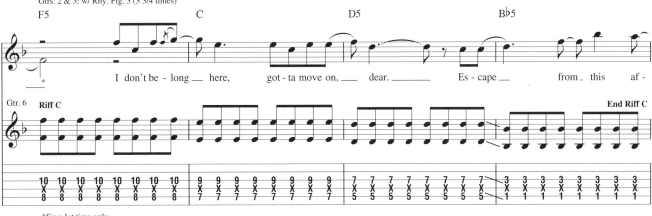

*Sing 1st time only.

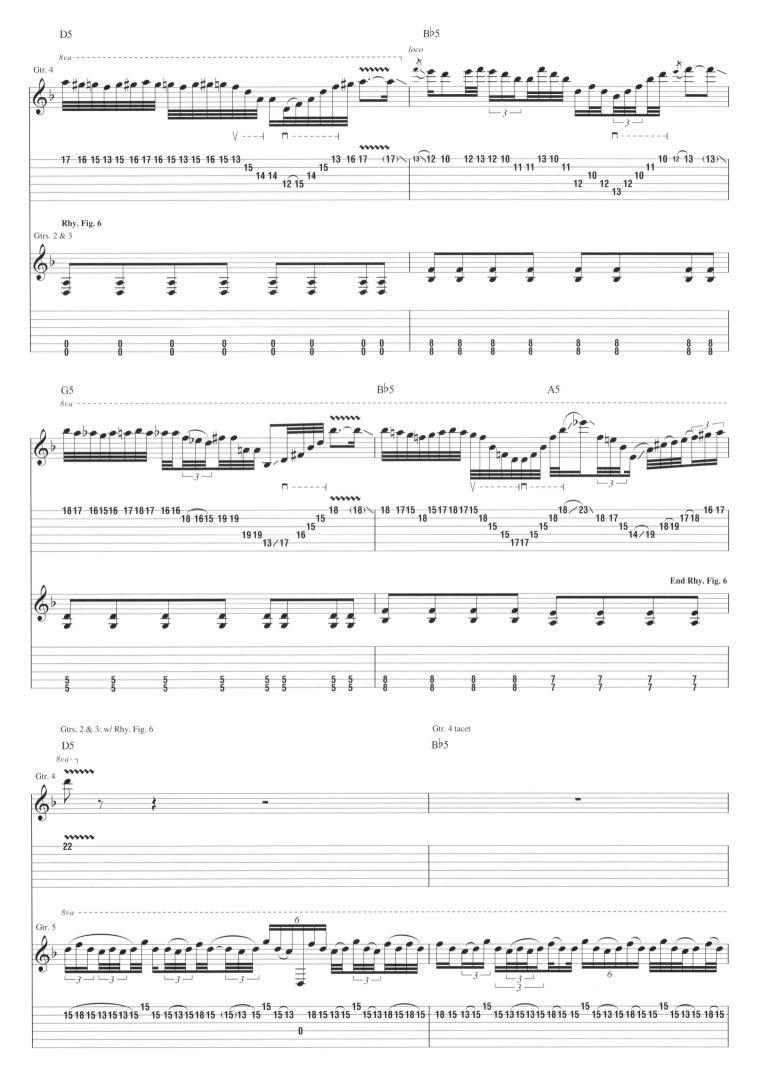

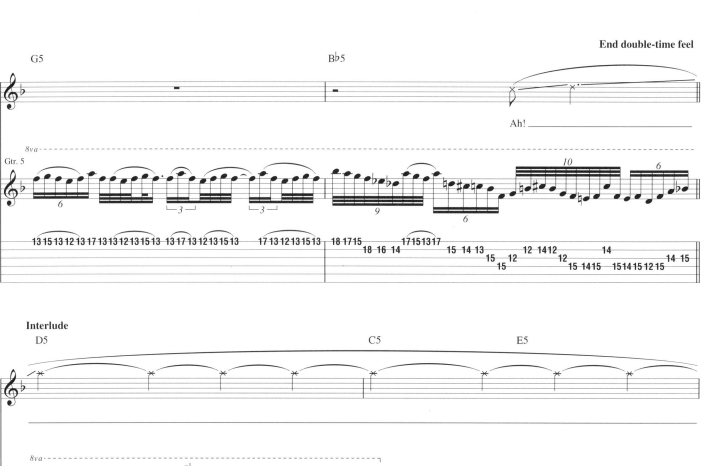

Interlude

from Metallica - *Garage Inc.*

Am I Evil?

Words and Music by Sean Harris and Brian Tatler

Very fast ♩ = 232

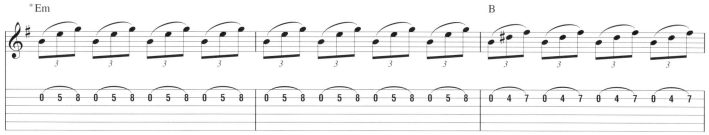

*Chord symbols reflect implied harmony.

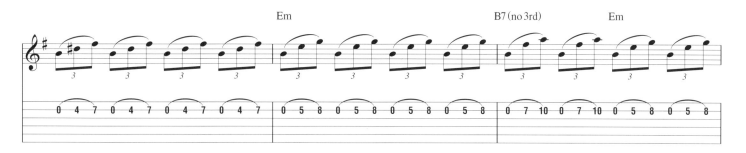

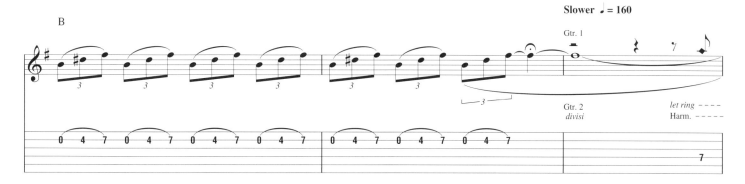

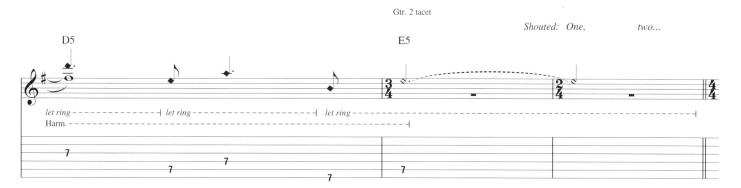

Half-time feel

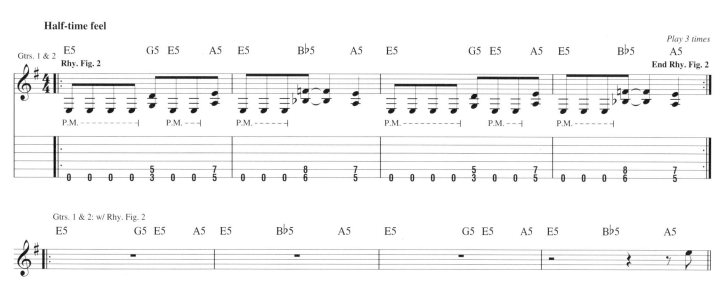

35

Gtrs. 1 & 2: w/ Rhy. Fig. 7 (10 times)

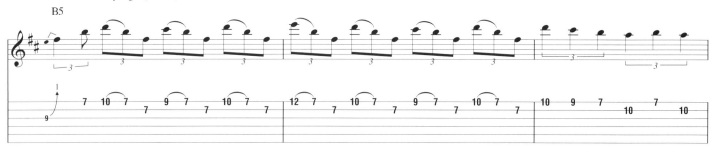

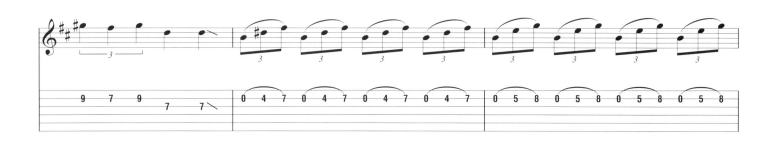

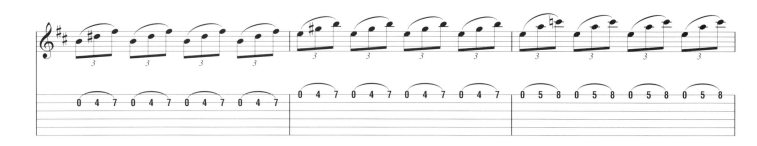

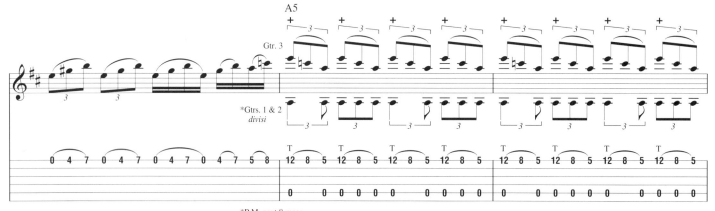

*P.M. next 8 meas.

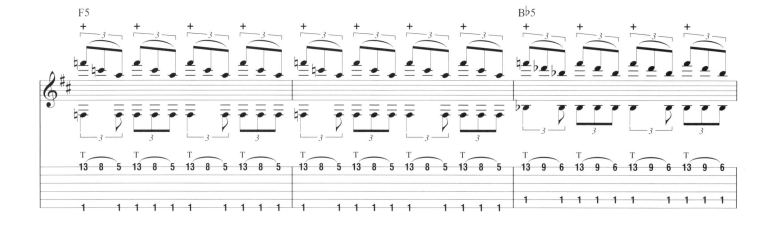

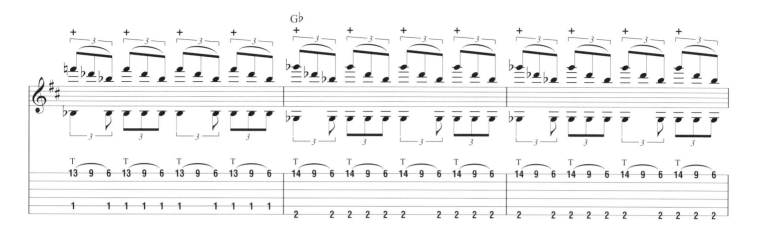

Gtrs. 1 & 2: w/ Rhy. Fig. 7 (10 times)

B5

Gtr. 3

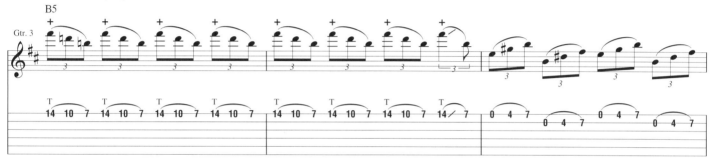

Gtrs. 1 & 2: w/ Rhy. Fig. 8 (4 times)

E5

steady gliss.

Blackout

Words and Music by Herman Rarebell, Klaus Meine, Rudolf Schenker and Sonja Kittelsen

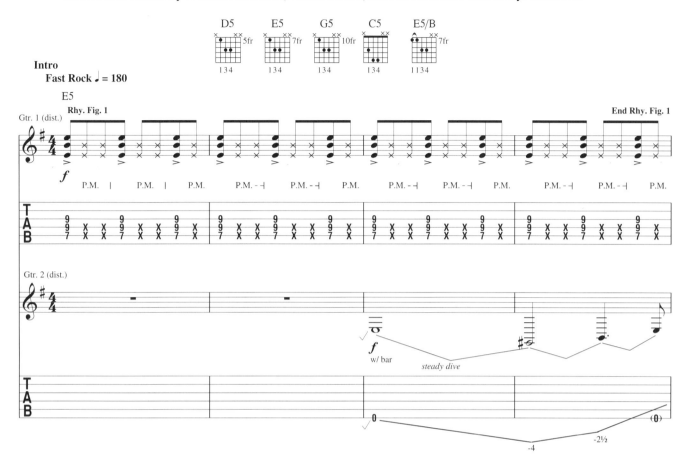

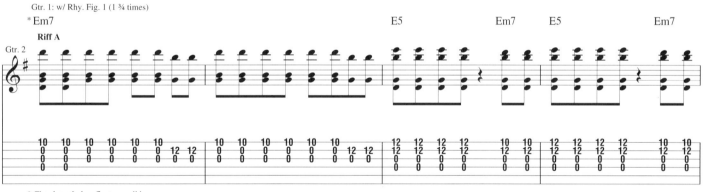

* Chord symbols reflect overall harmony.

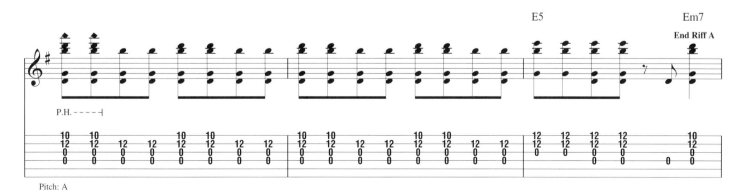

Pitch: A

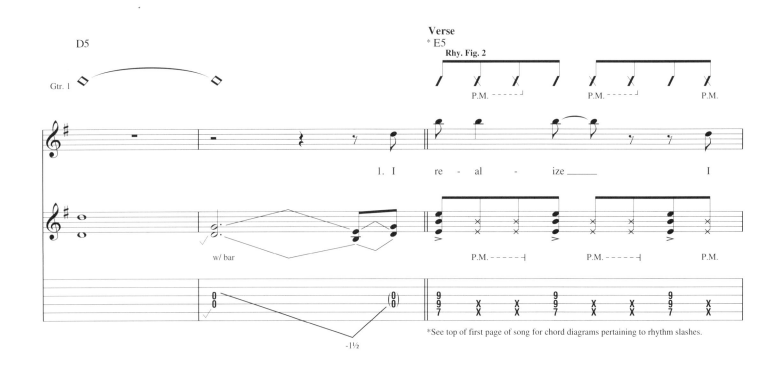

*See top of first page of song for chord diagrams pertaining to rhythm slashes.

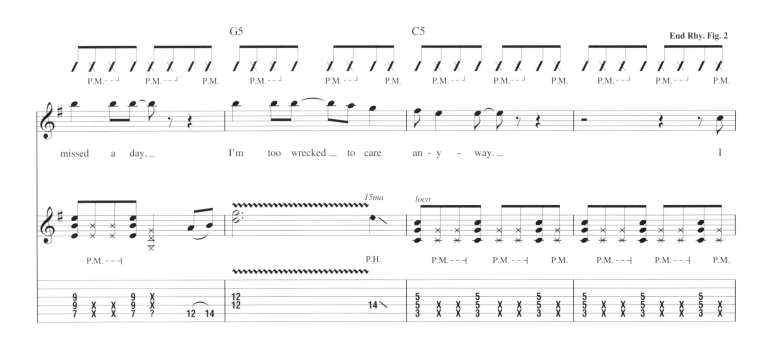

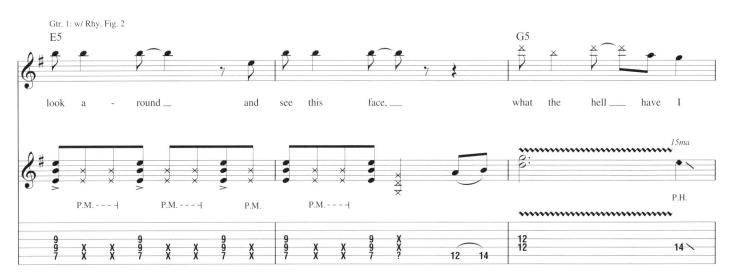

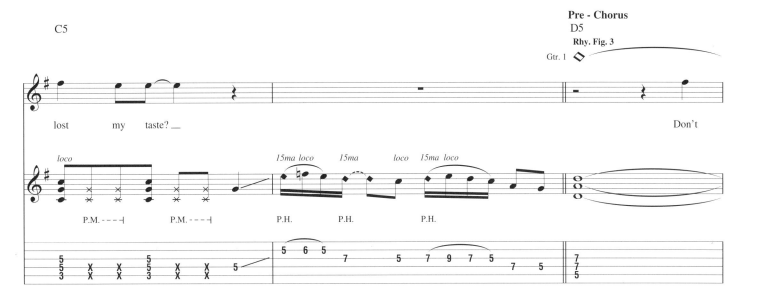

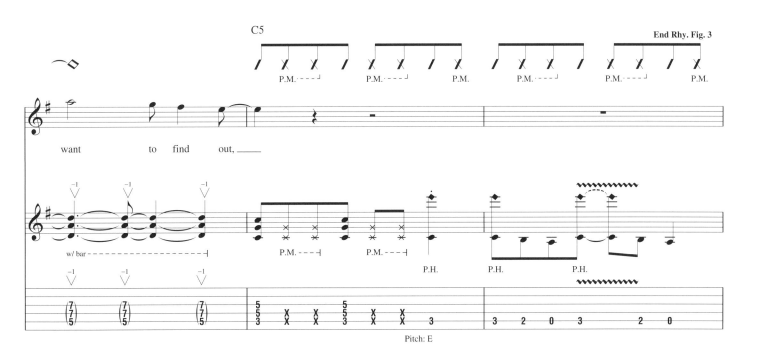

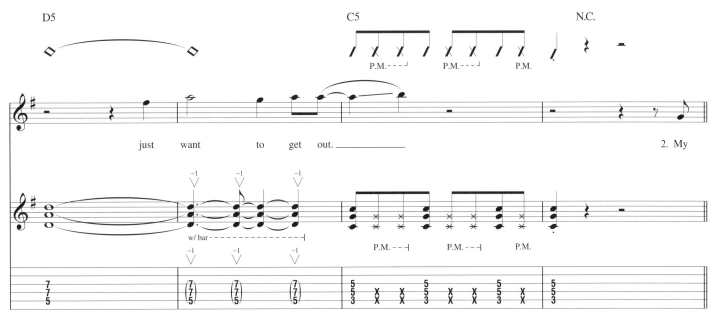

Verse

Gtr. 1: w/ Rhy. Fig. 2 (2 times)

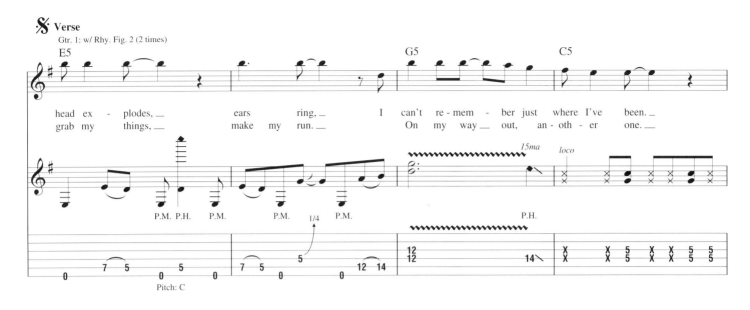

head ex — plodes, — ears ring, — I can't re — mem — ber just where I've been. —
grab my things, — make my run. — On my way — out, an — oth — er one. —

Pitch: C

2nd time, Gtr. 2: w/ Fill 1

Last thing — I re — call, —
Would like to know — be — fore I stop,

2nd time, Gtr. 2: w/ Fill 2

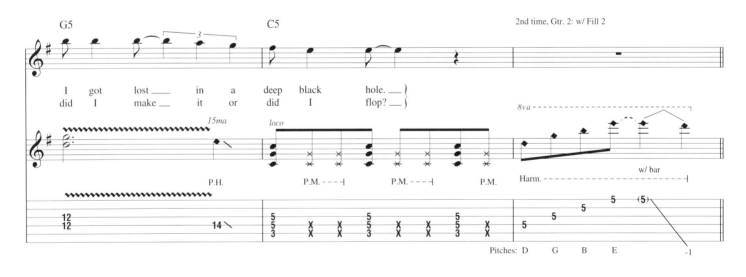

I got lost — in a deep black hole. —)
did I make — it or did I flop? —)

Pitches: D   G   B   E

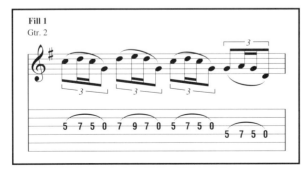

Fill 1
Gtr. 2

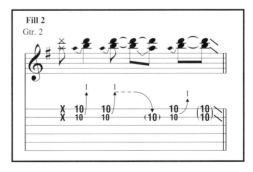

Fill 2
Gtr. 2

46

Pre - Chorus

Gtr. 1: w/ Rhy. Fig. 3

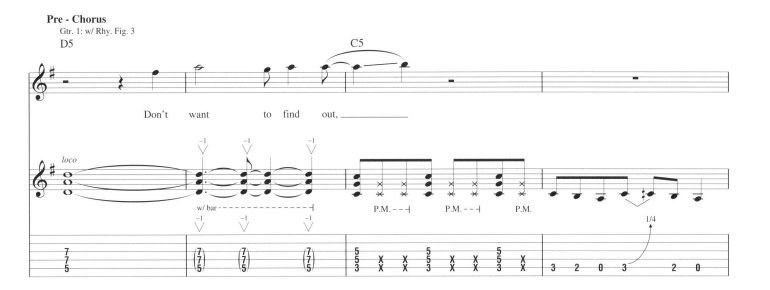

Don't want to find out, ___

Chorus

To Coda ⊕

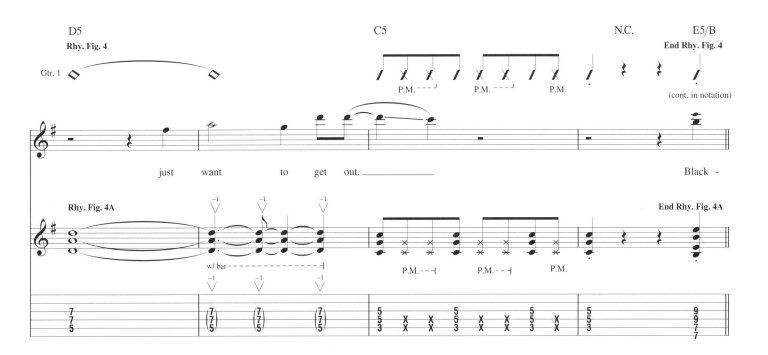

just want to get out. ___ Black -

out. I real - ly had a black - out. Black -

* Composite arrangement

** Chord symbols reflect implied harmony.

Guitar Solo

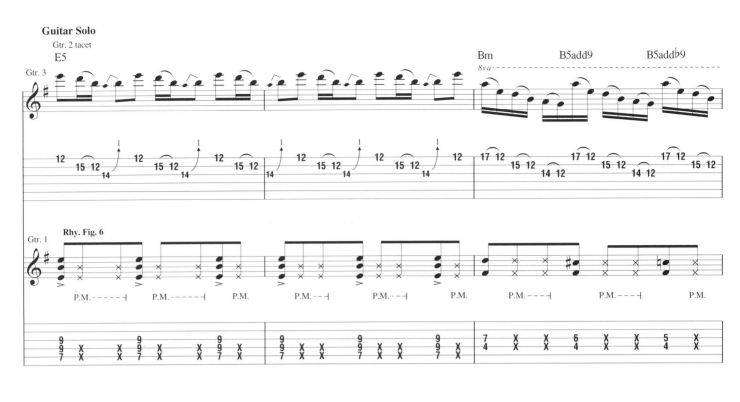

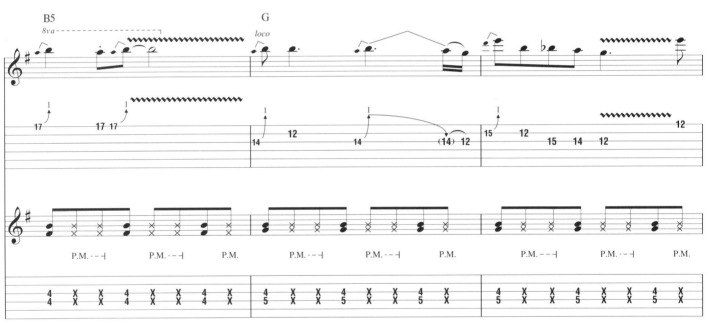

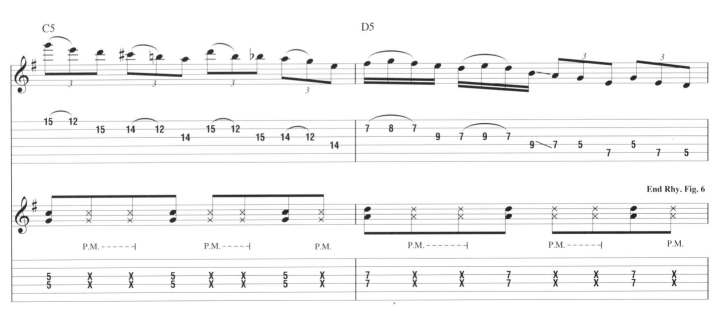

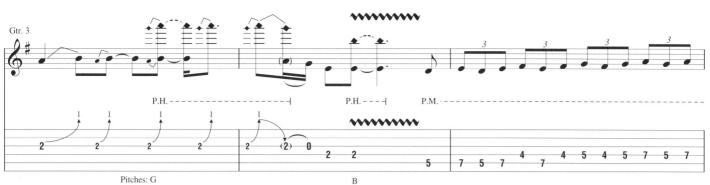

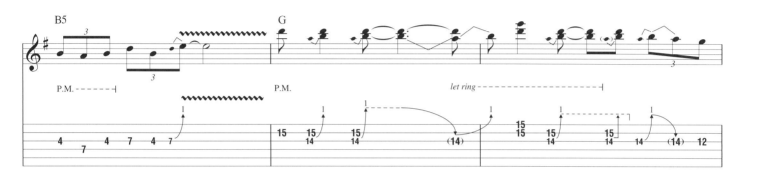

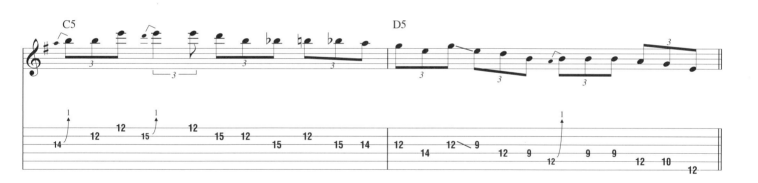

Pre - Chorus
Gtr. 1: w/ Rhy. Fig. 3

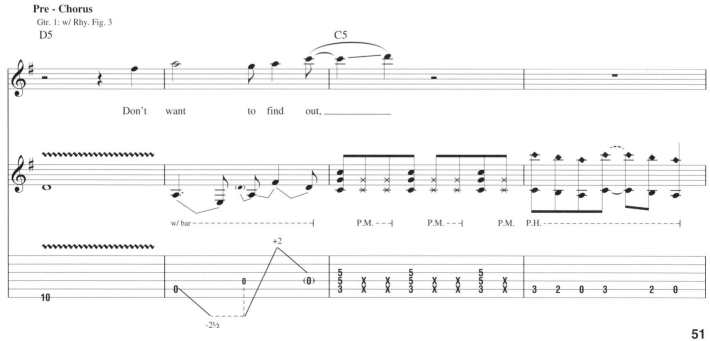

Don't want to find out, _____

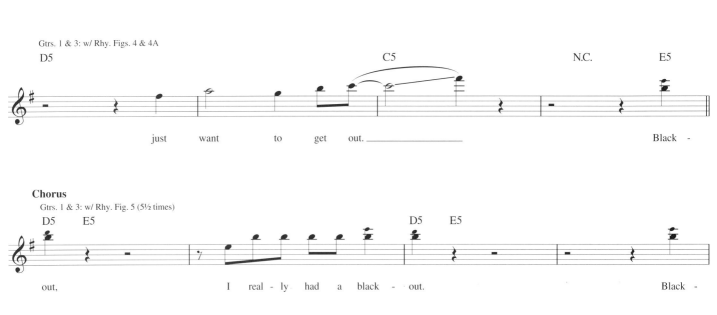

Gtrs. 1 & 3: w/ Rhy. Figs. 4 & 4A

just want to get out. _____ Black-

Chorus

Gtrs. 1 & 3: w/ Rhy. Fig. 5 (5½ times)

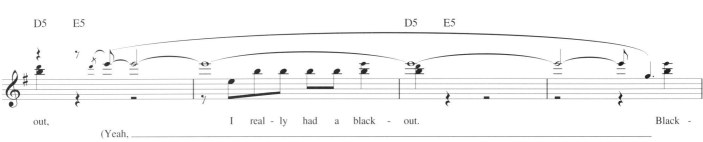

out, I real-ly had a black-out. Black-

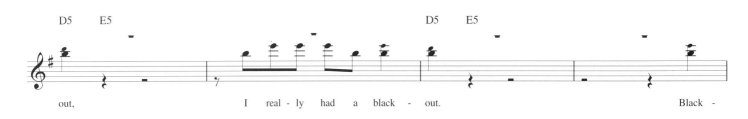

out, I real-ly had a black-out. Black-
(Yeah, _____

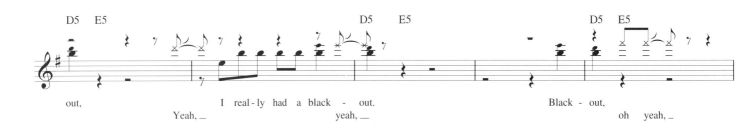

out, I real-ly had a black-out. Black-

out, I real-ly had a black-out. Black-out,
Yeah, __ yeah, __ oh yeah, __

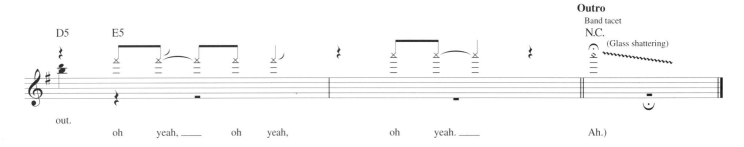

black-out. oh yeah, __ oh yeah, oh yeah, Black-
oh yeah,

Outro
Band tacet
N.C.
(Glass shattering)

out.
oh yeah, __ oh yeah, oh yeah. ___ Ah.)

Breaking the Law

Words and Music by Glenn Tipton, Rob Halford and K.K. Downing

Intro

Moderately fast ♩ = 162

*Chord symbols reflect implied harmony.
**Composite arrangement

Verse

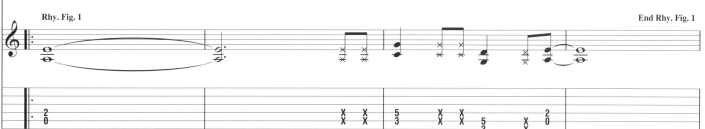

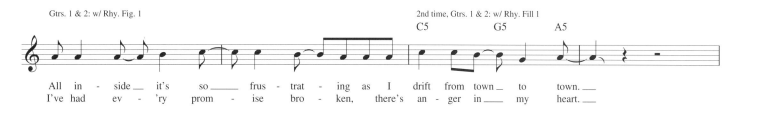

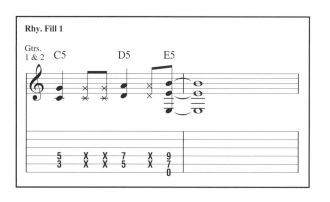

Feel as though no-bod-y cares.___ if I live___ or die,_____
You don't know___ what it's like.___ You don't have___ a clue.___

Gtrs. 1 & 2

fdbk.

so I might___ as well___ be-gin___ to put some ac-tion in my life.___
If you did,___ you'd find___ your-selves___ do-ing the same thing, too.___

2nd time, Gtr. 5: w/ Fill 2

Chorus
Gtrs. 1 & 2 tacet

A5

Break-ing the law,___ break-ing the law.___ Break-ing the law,___ break-ing the law.___

*Gtrs. 3 & 4 (dist.)

P.M.------------------------- P.M.-------------------------

*Composite arrangement

1.

Break-ing the law,___ break-ing the law.___ Break-ing the law,___ break-ing the law.___

P.M.------------------------- P.M.-------------------------

Fill 2
Gtr. 5 (dist.)

**Vol. swell

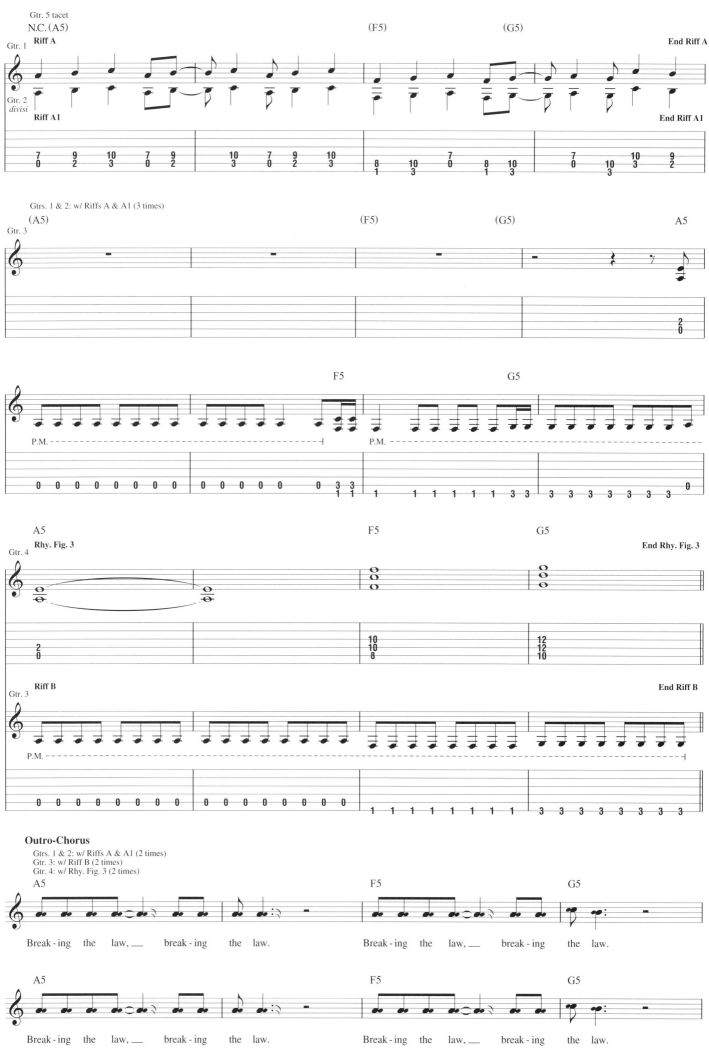

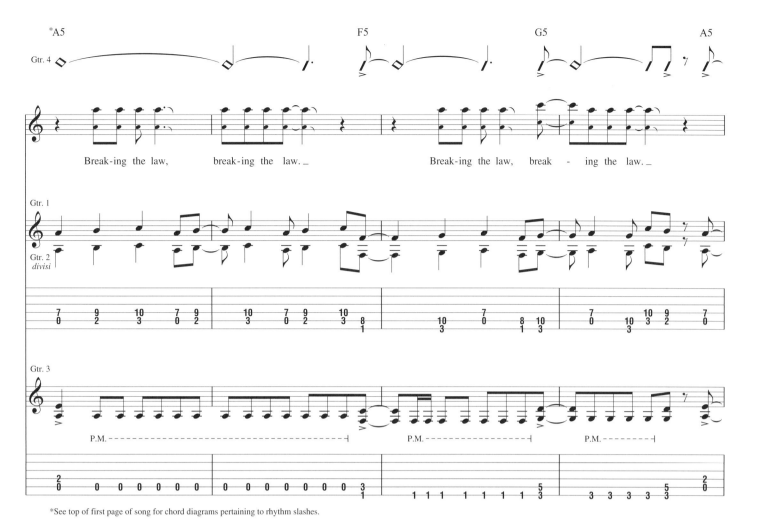

*See top of first page of song for chord diagrams pertaining to rhythm slashes.

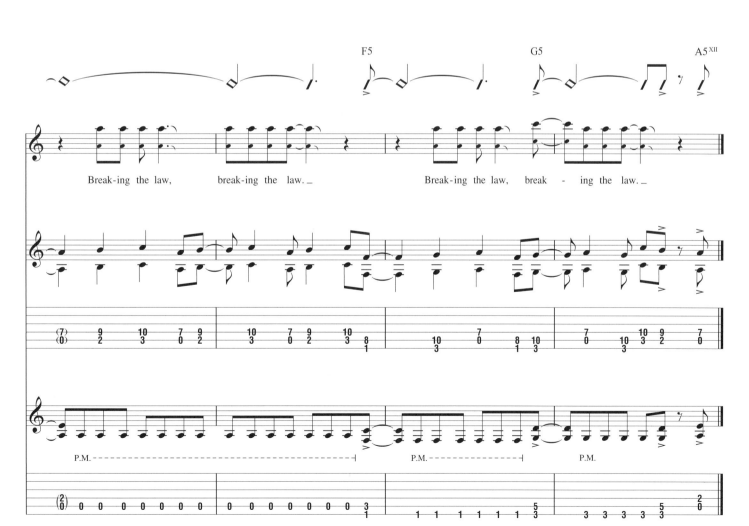

Chop Suey!

Words and Music by Daron Malakian and Serj Tankian

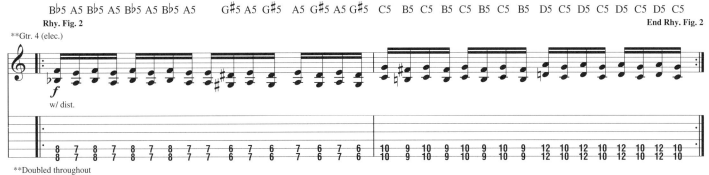

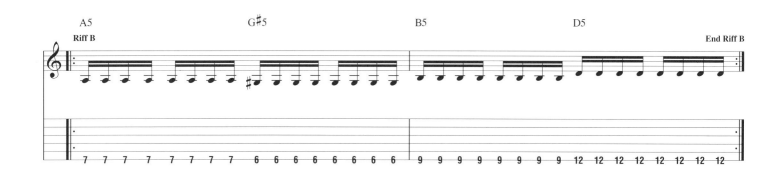

Verse

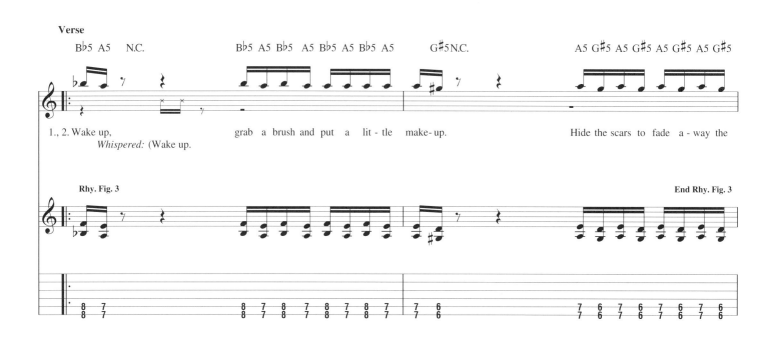

1., 2. Wake up,   grab a brush and put a lit - tle make-up.   Hide the scars to fade a - way the

Whispered: (Wake up.

Gtr. 4: w/ Rhy. Fig. 3 (3 times)

shake - up.   Why'd you leave the keys up - on the ta - ble?   Here you go, cre - ate an - oth - er

Hide the scars to fade a - way the...)

fa - ble,   you want - ed to. Grab a brush and put a lit - tle make-up,   you want - ed to. Hide the scars to fade a - way the

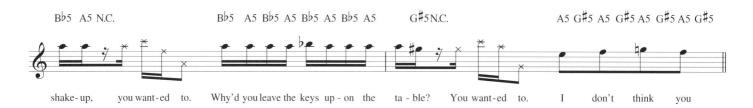

shake-up,   you want-ed to. Why'd you leave the keys up - on the ta - ble? You want-ed to. I don't think you

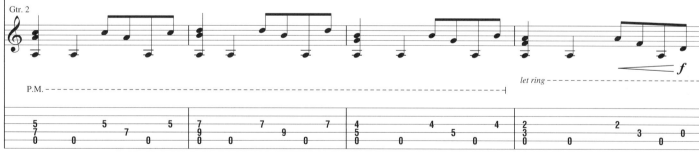

B♭5 A5 B♭5 A5 B♭5 A5 B♭5 A5 G♯5 A5 G♯5 A5 G♯5 A5 G♯5 C5 B5 C5 B5 C5 B5 C5 B5 D5 C5 D5 C5 D5 C5 D5 C5
2.
Gtr. 3: w/ Riff A (1 3/4 times)
Gtr. 5: w/ Riff C1 (1 1/4 times)
B♭5 A5 B♭5 A5 B♭5 A5 B♭5 A5 B♭5 A5 B♭5 A5 B♭5 A5 B♭5 A5 Am
Rah! die
Gtrs. 2 & 4
P.M.
F6add♯4 Cmaj7(no3rd) F Am
in my self - right - eous su - i - cide.
P.M.
let ring
F6add♯4 Cmaj7(no3rd) Fmaj7
I cry when an - gels de - serve to die.
Gtr. 2
Gtr. 3
Gtr. 2 divisi
let ring
let ring
Gtr. 5

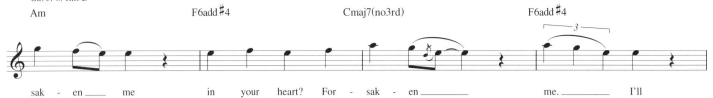

sak - en ___ me   in your heart?   For - sak - en _____ me. _____ I'll

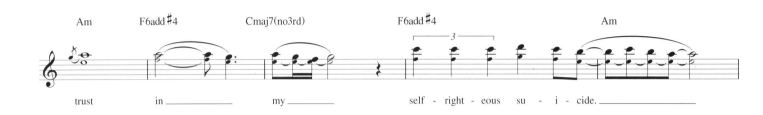

trust   in _____ my _____ self - right - eous su - i - cide. _____

I _____ cry _____ when an - gels de - serve to die _____ in _____

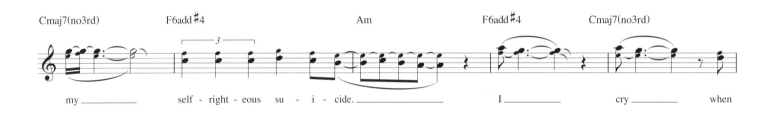

my _____ self - right - eous su - i - cide. _____ I _____ cry _____ when

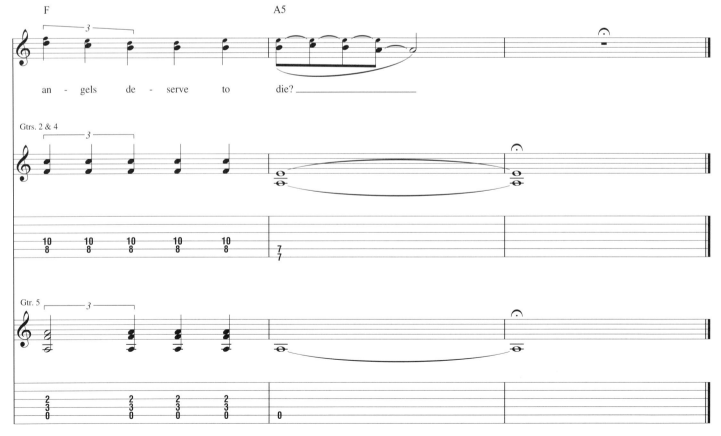

an - gels de - serve to die? _____

Cowboys from Hell

Words and Music by Vince Abbott, Darrell Abbott, Rex Brown and Phil Anselmo

Gtr. 3 tacet

Em7

Gtr. 4

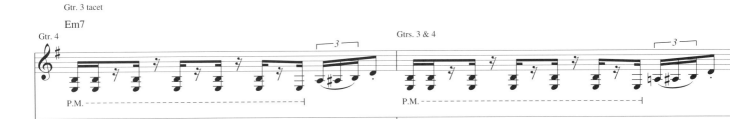

Screamed: Oh, *come on!*

Riff D

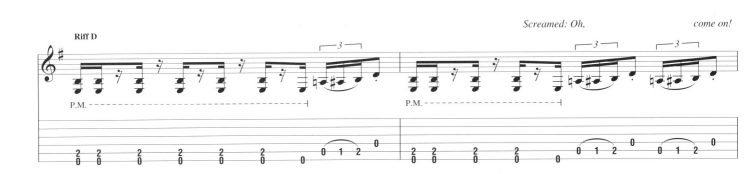

End Riff D

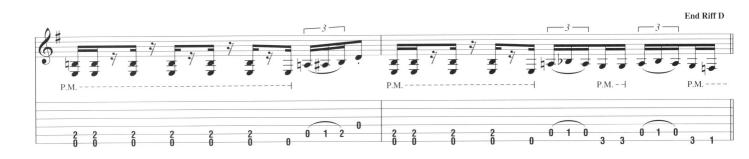

Verse

E5

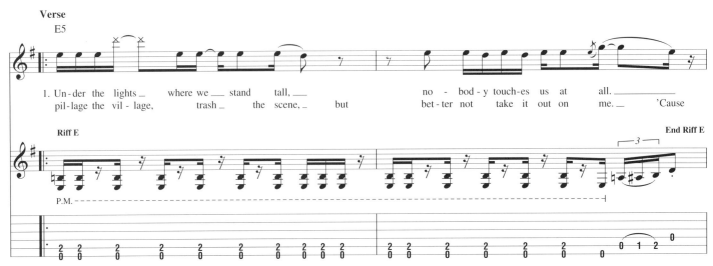

1. Un-der the lights___ where we___ stand tall,___   no - bod-y touch-es us at___ all.___

pil-lage the vil - lage, trash___ the scene,___ but   bet - ter not take it out on me.___ 'Cause

Riff E   **End Riff E**

66

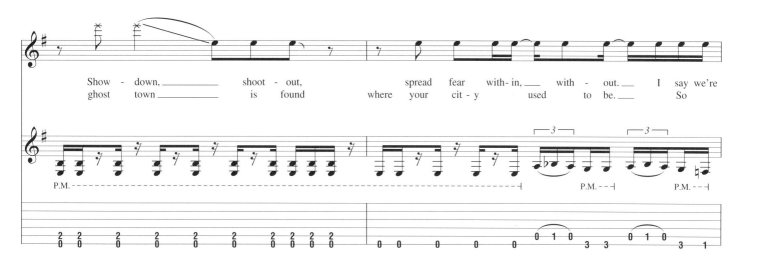

Show - down, _____ shoot - out, _____ spread fear with- in, ___ with - out. ___ I say we're
ghost town _____ is found where your cit - y used to be. ___ So

Gtrs. 3 & 4: w/ Riff E

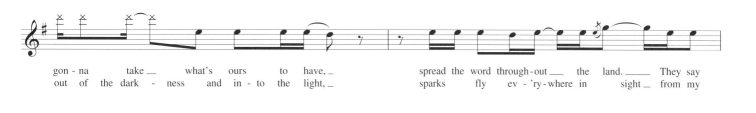

gon - na take __ what's ours to have, __ spread the word through-out __ the land. ___ They say
out of the dark - ness and in - to the light, __ sparks fly ev - 'ry-where in sight __ from my

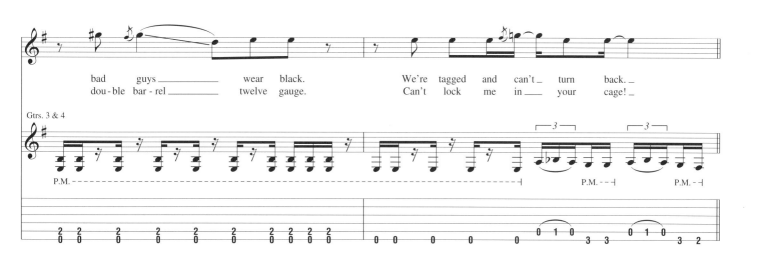

bad guys _____ wear black. We're tagged and can't turn back. __
dou - ble bar - rel _____ twelve gauge. Can't lock me in __ your cage! __

Gtrs. 3 & 4

Pre-Chorus

G5   Ab5   G5   Bb5   A5   G#5

You see us com - in' and you al - to - geth - er run for cov - er. ___

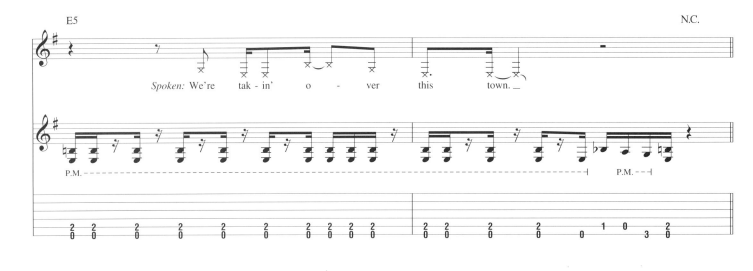

Spoken: We're tak - in' o - ver this town. __

% Chorus

1st & 3rd times, Gtrs. 3 & 4: w/ Riff C (2 times)
2nd time, Gtrs. 3 & 4: w/ Riff C (1 3/4 times)

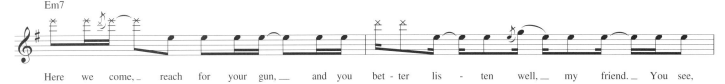

Here we come, __ reach for your gun, __ and you bet - ter lis - ten well, __ my friend. __ You see,

it's been slow __ down be - low. __ Aimed at you, _____ we're the cow - boys from hell. __

Deed is done, __ a - gain we won. __ Ain't talk - in' no __ tall tales, _____ friend. __ 'Cause,

1.

To Coda 1 ✦

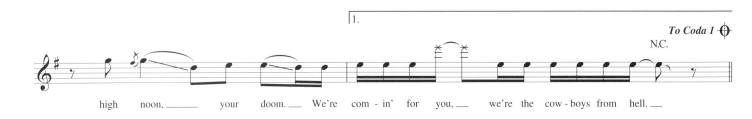

high noon, _____ your doom. __ We're com - in' for you, __ we're the cow - boys from hell. __

Interlude

Gtr. 4: w/ Riff D   Gtr. 3: w/ Riff D (last 5 meas.)

See here!

2. Oh, _____

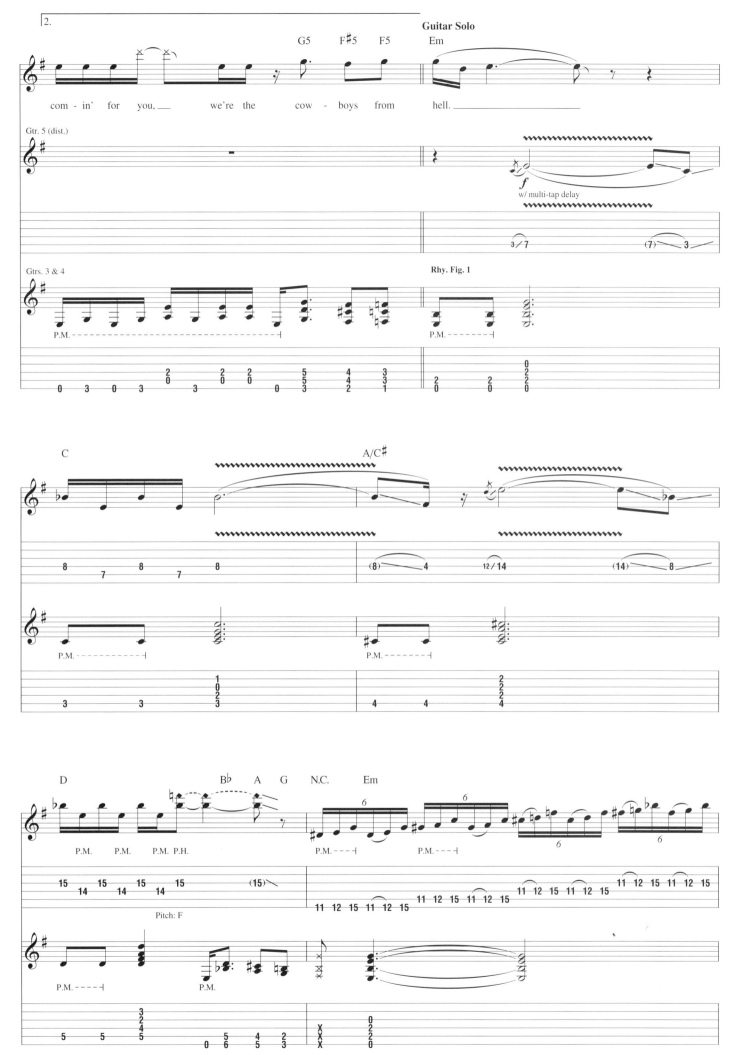

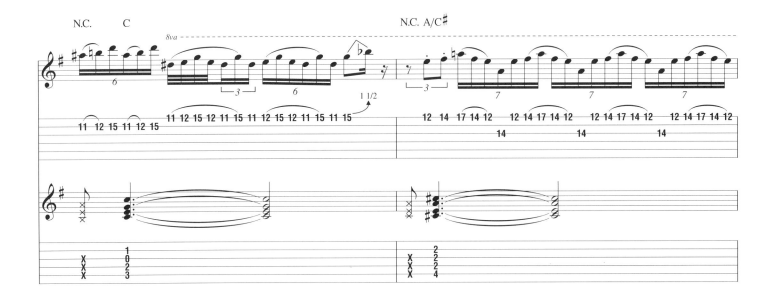

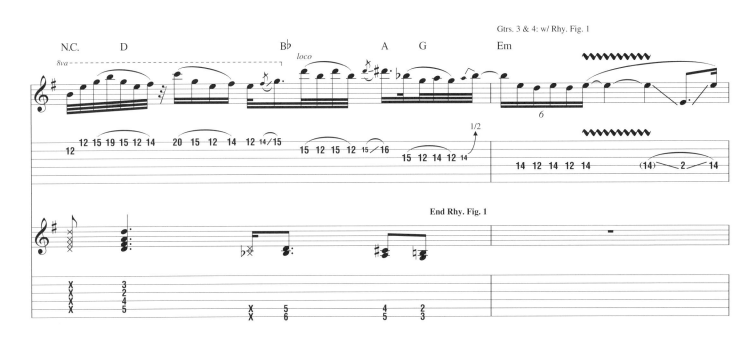

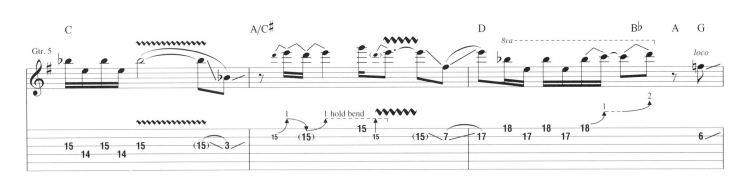

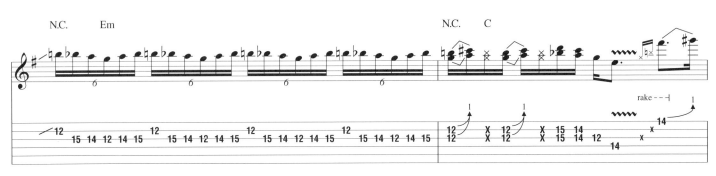

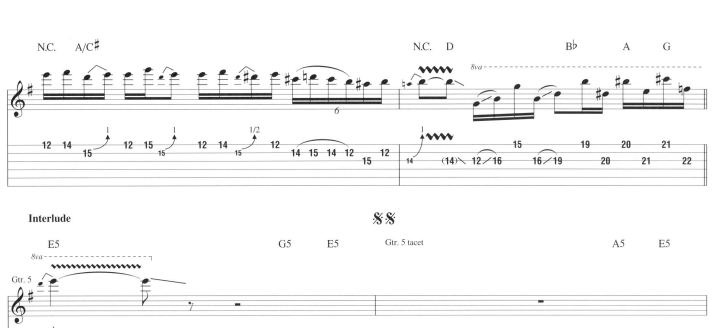

Interlude

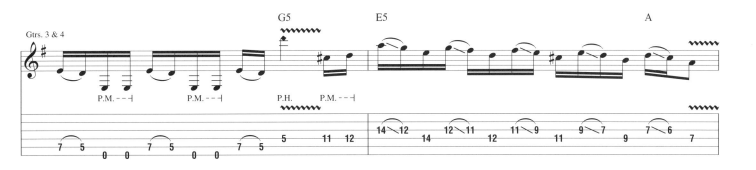

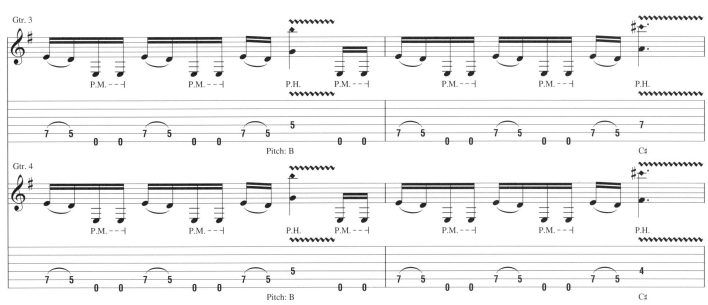

from Disturbed - *Sickness*

Down with the Sickness

Words and Music by Mike Wengren, Dan Donegan, Dave Draiman and Steve Kmak

Drop D tuning, down 1/2 step:
(low to high) D♭-A♭-D♭-G♭-B♭-E♭

Intro
Moderately slow ♩ = 90

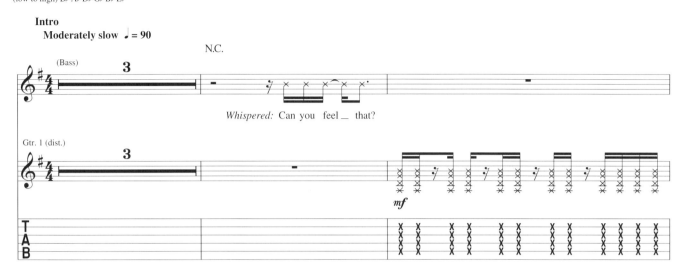

Whispered: Can you feel __ that?

Ah, shit. __

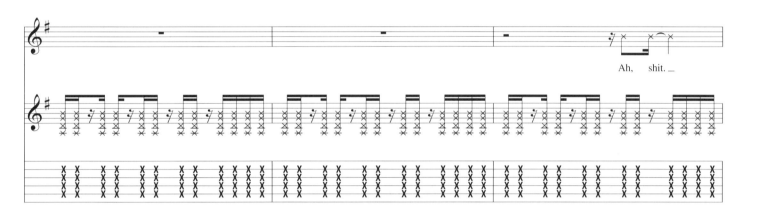

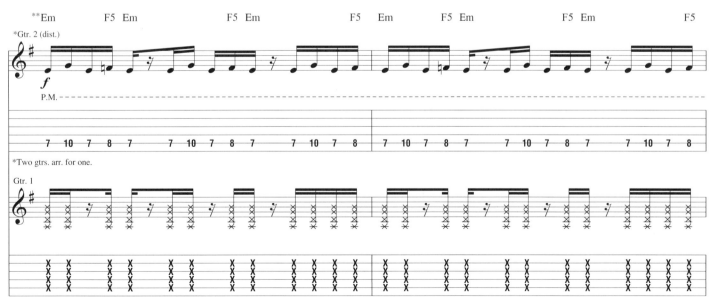

*Two gtrs. arr. for one.

**Chord symbols reflect implied harmony.

74

Outro-Chorus

Get up, come on, get down _ with the sick - ness. _ Get up, come on, get down _ with the sick - ness. _

Rhy. Fig. 3

End Rhy. Fig. 3

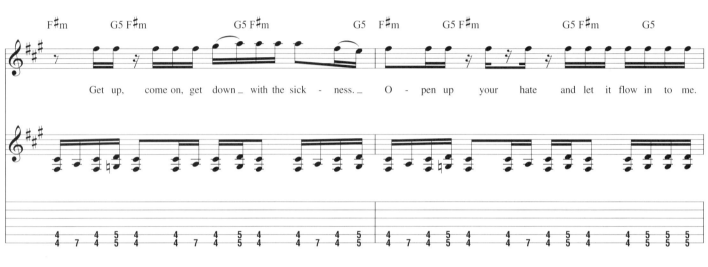

Get up, come on, get down _ with the sick - ness. _ O - pen up your hate and let it flow in to me.

Gtr. 2: w/ Rhy. Fig. 3

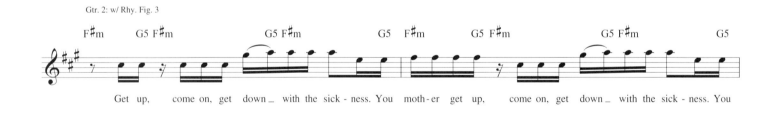

Get up, come on, get down _ with the sick - ness. You moth - er get up, come on, get down _ with the sick - ness. You

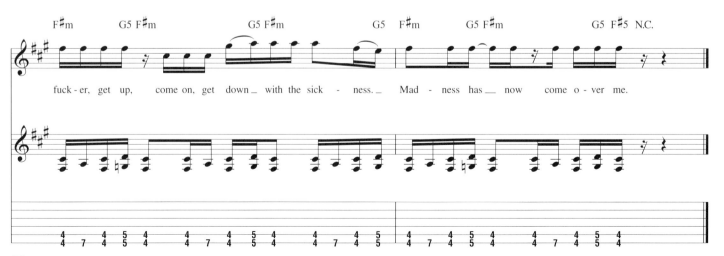

fuck - er, get up, come on, get down _ with the sick - ness. _ Mad - ness has _ now come o - ver me.

Evil

Words and Music by Kim Petersen and Hank Sherman

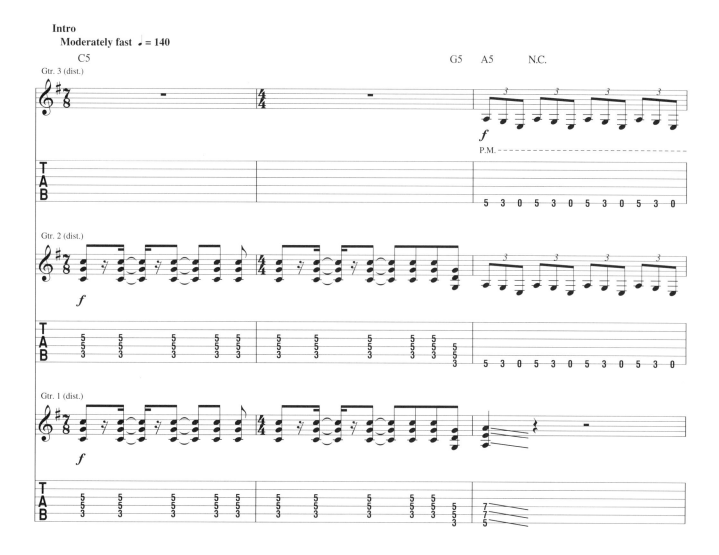

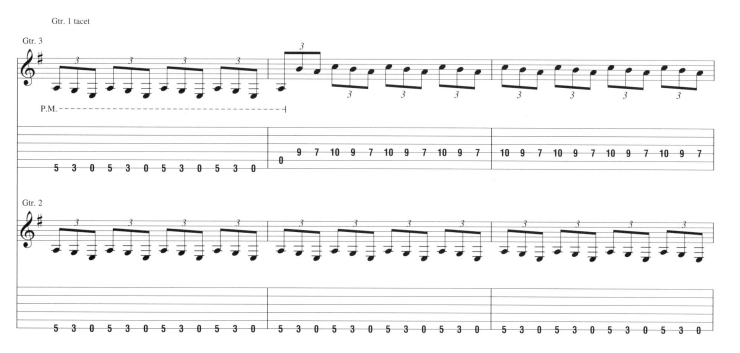

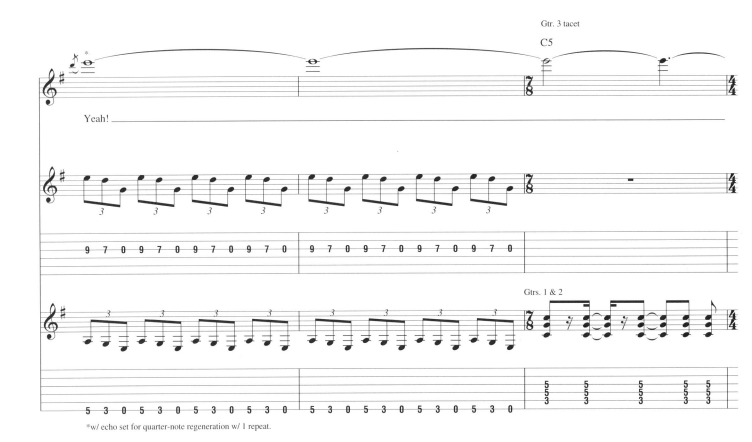

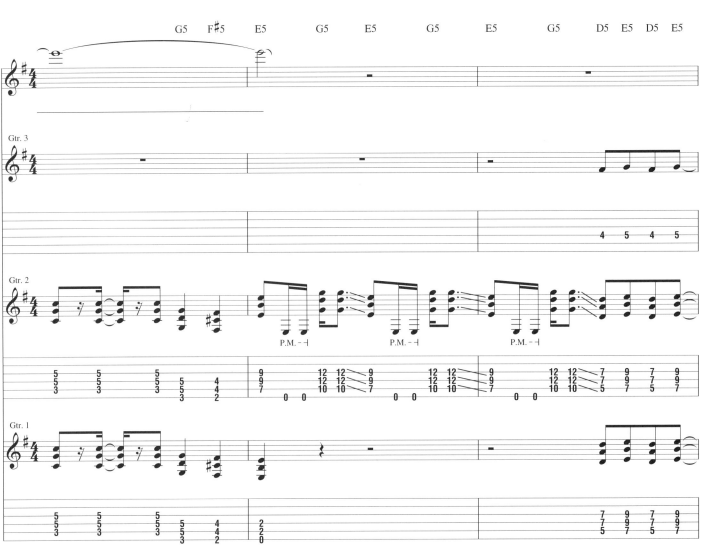

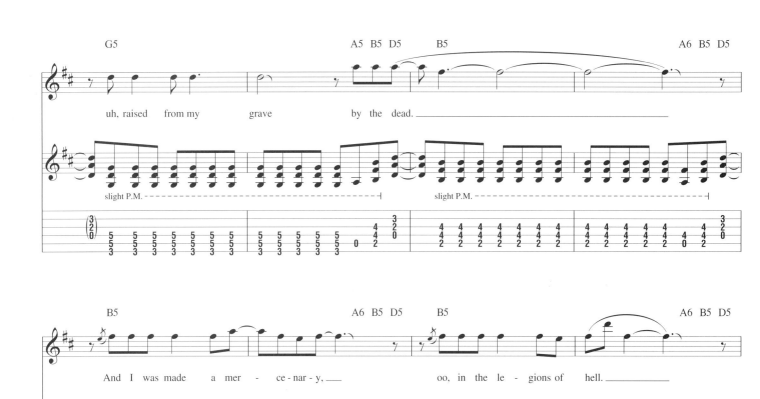

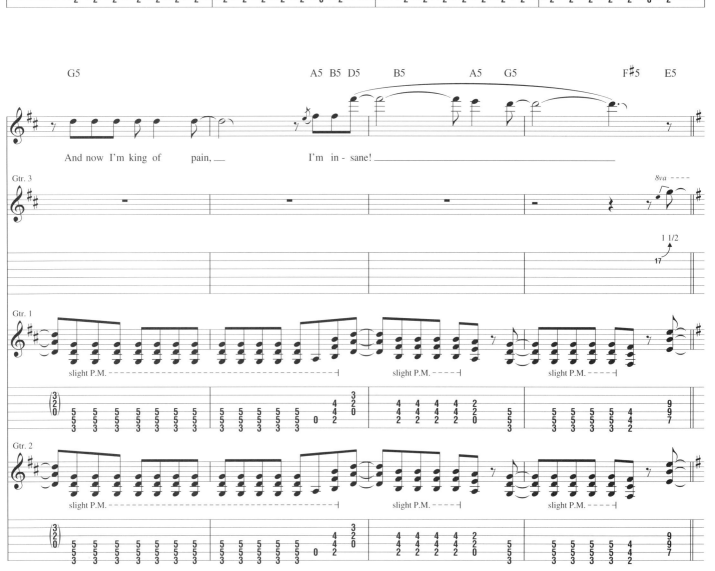

Guitar Solo

Pre-Chorus

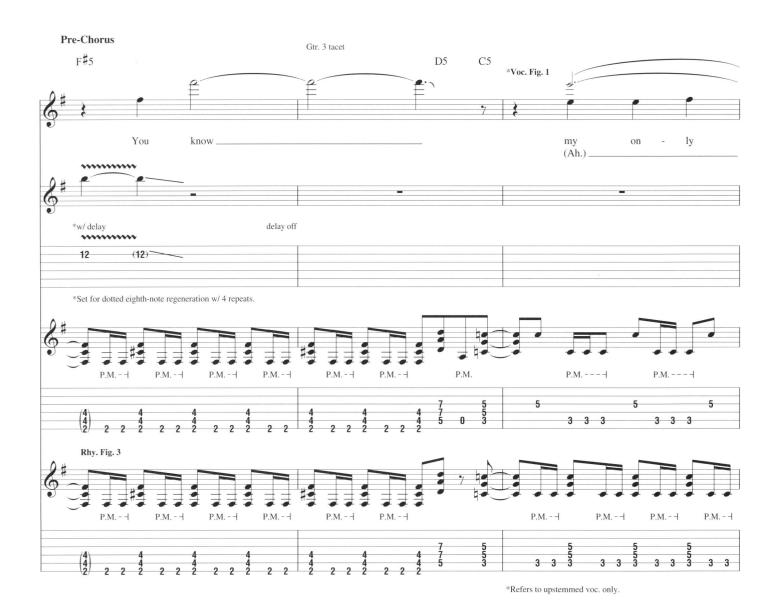

*Refers to upstemmed voc. only.

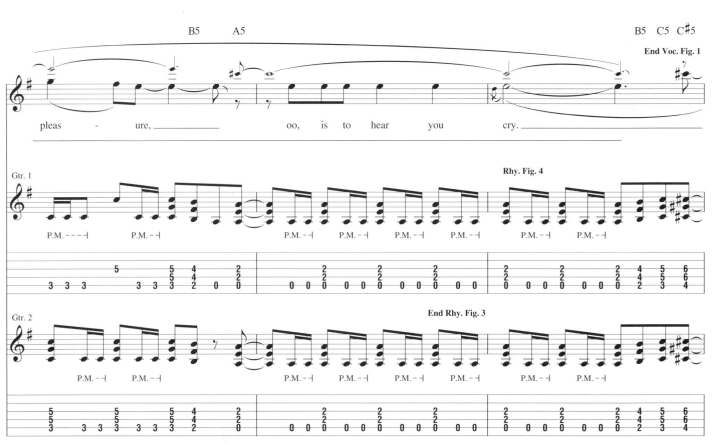

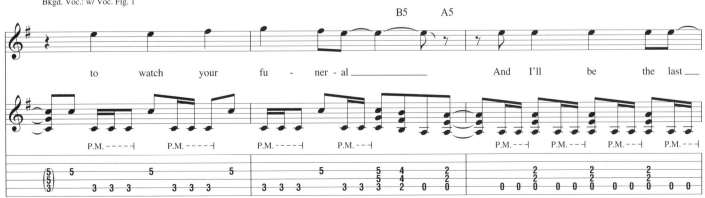

Gtrs. 1 & 2: w/ Rhy. Fig. 4

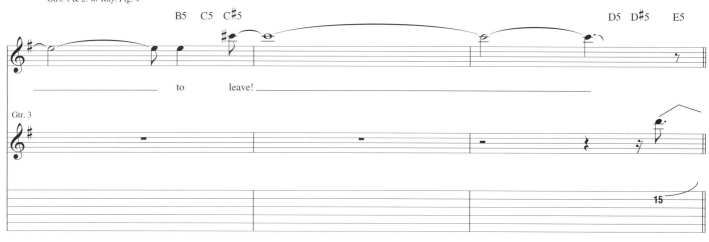

B5 C5 C#5

to leave!

D5 D#5 E5

Gtr. 3

Chorus

Gtr. 1: w/ Rhy. Fig. 1 (3 times)
Gtr. 2: w/ Rhy. Fig. 2 (3 times)

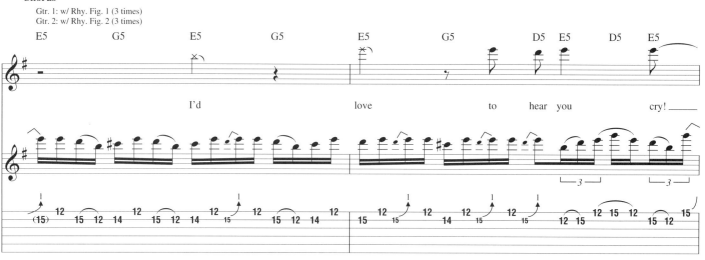

E5   G5   E5   G5   E5   G5   D5 E5   D5   E5

I'd   love   to   hear you   cry! _____

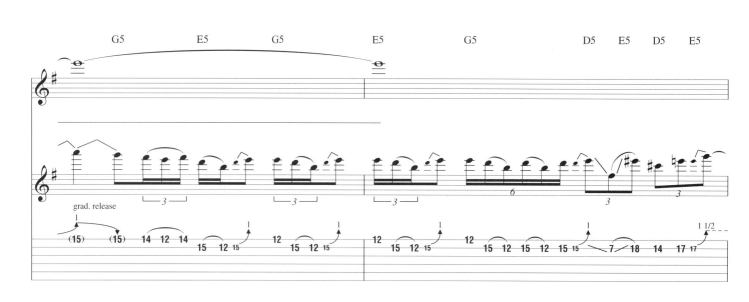

G5   E5   G5   E5   G5   D5   E5   D5   E5

grad. release

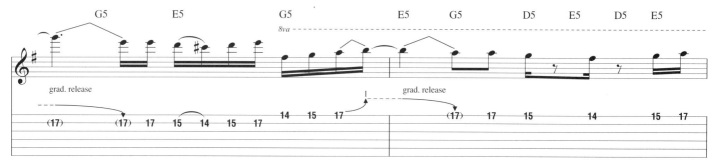

G5   E5   G5   E5   G5   D5   E5   D5   E5

grad. release   grad. release

Bridge

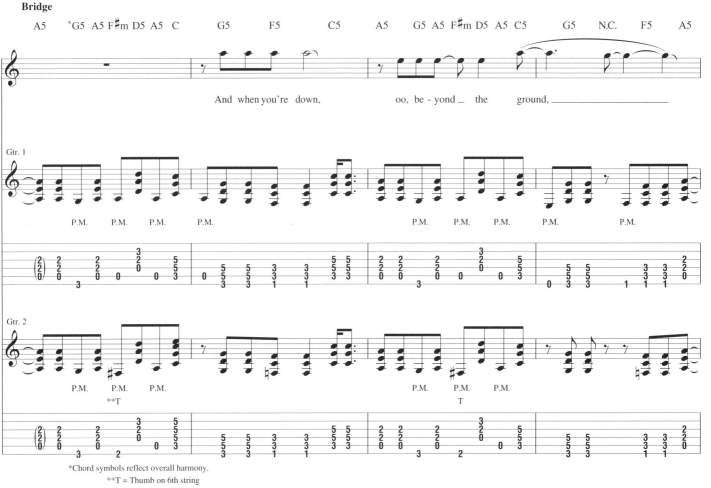

*Chord symbols reflect overall harmony.

**T = Thumb on 6th string

And when you're down, oo, be - yond __ the ground, _____

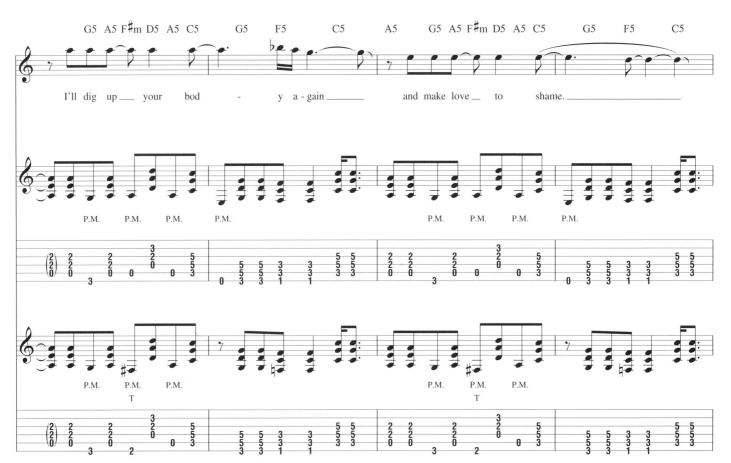

I'll dig up __ your bod - y a - gain _____ and make love __ to shame.

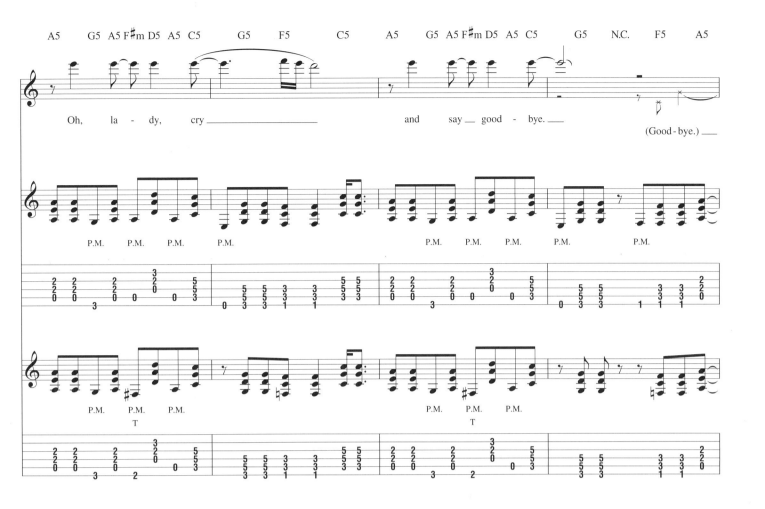

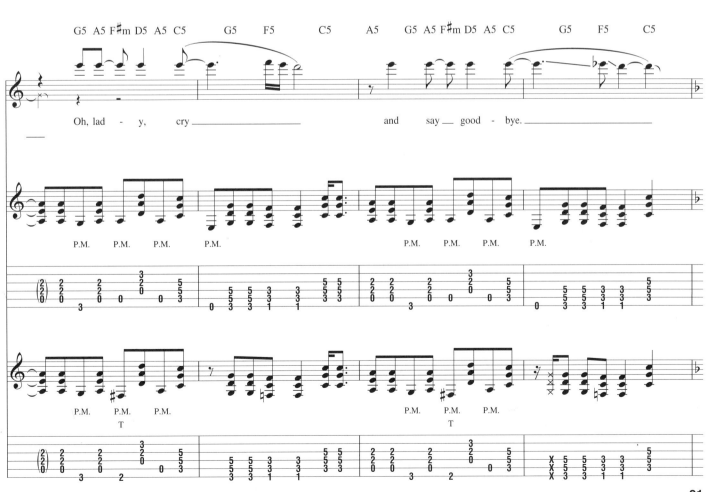

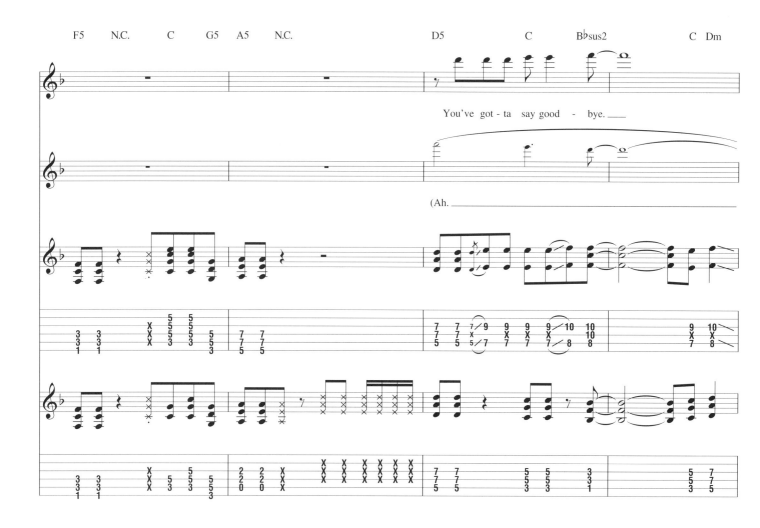

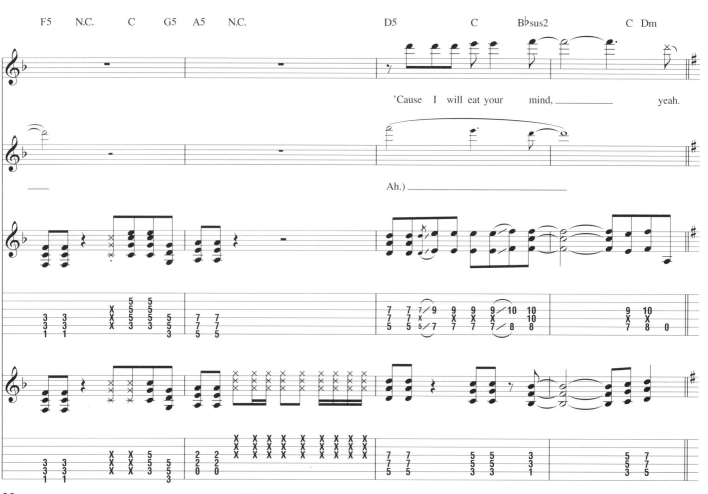

Guitar Solo

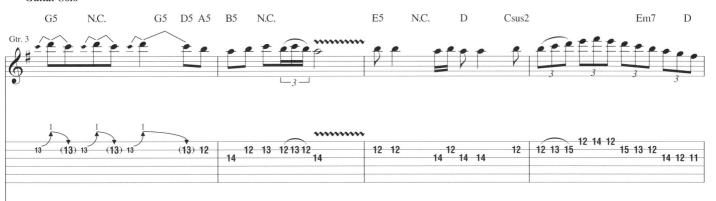

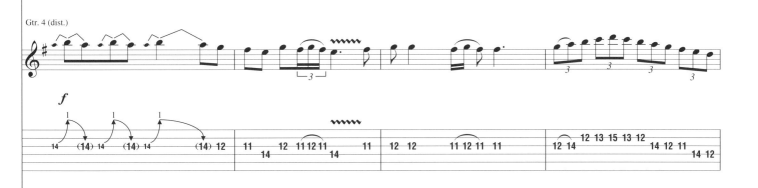

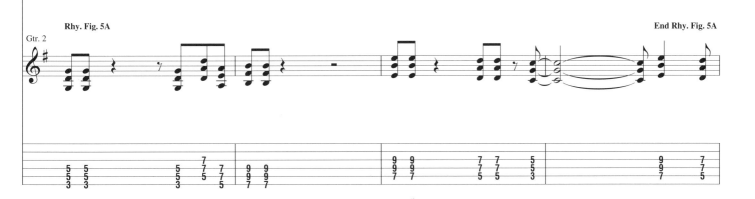

Gtrs. 1 & 2: w/ Rhy. Figs. 5 & 5A

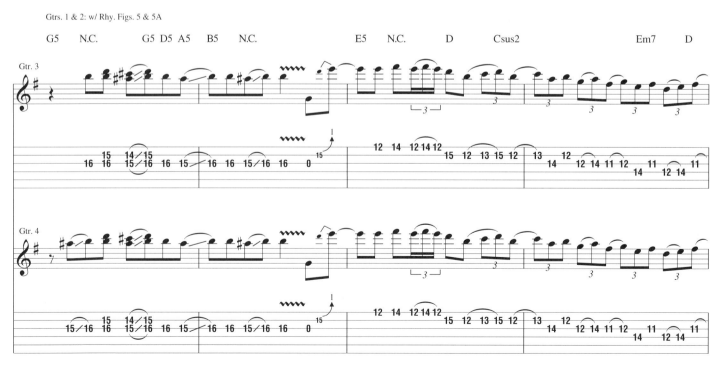

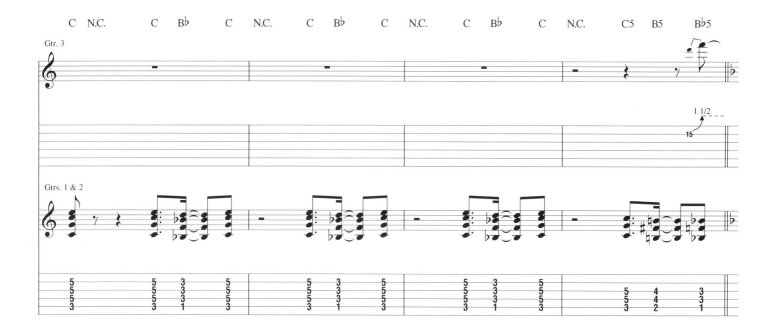

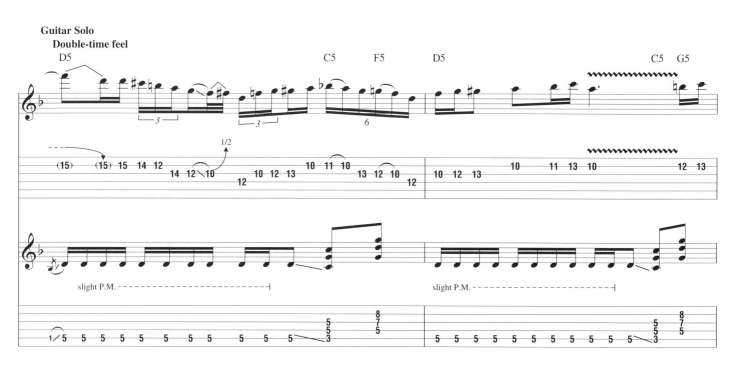

Guitar Solo

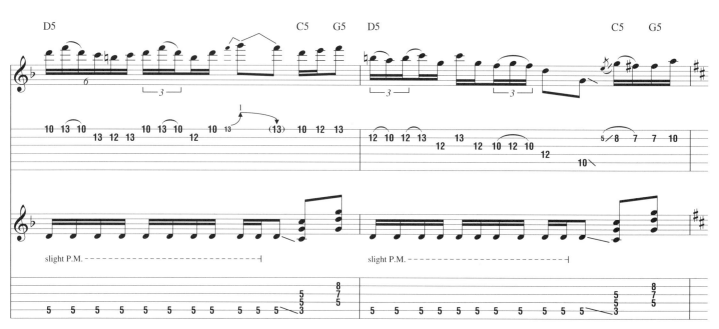

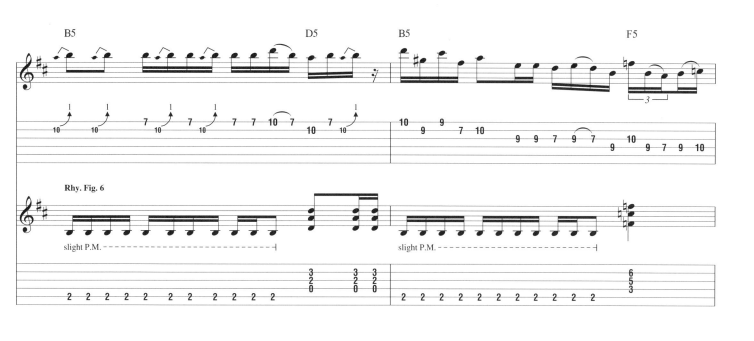

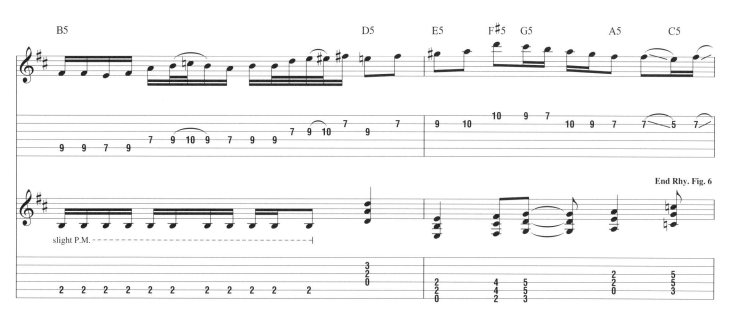

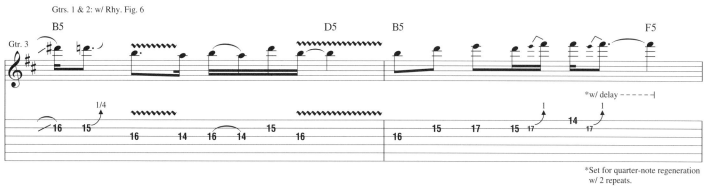

*Set for quarter-note regeneration
w/ 2 repeats.

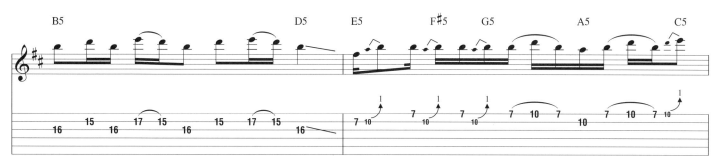

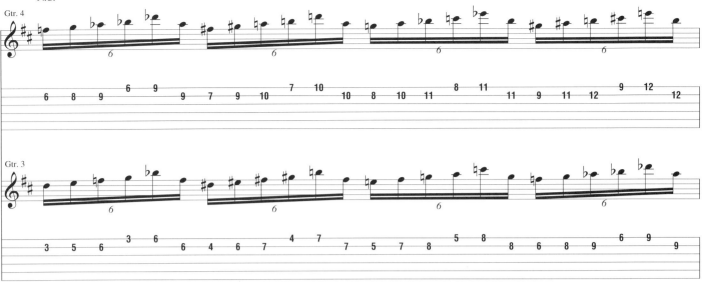

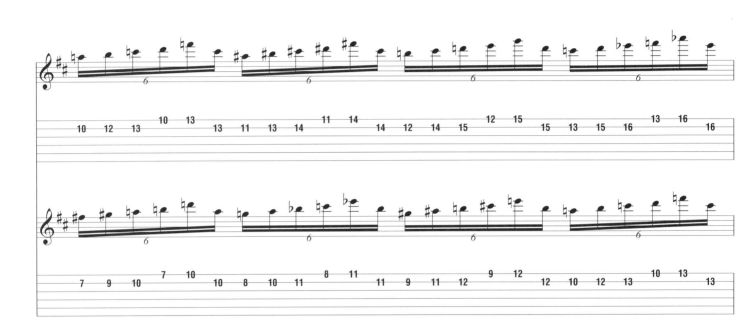

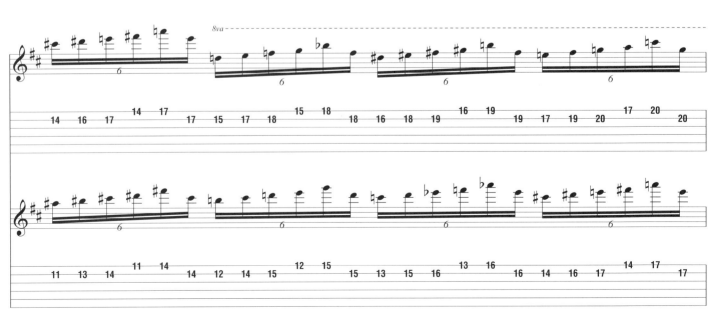

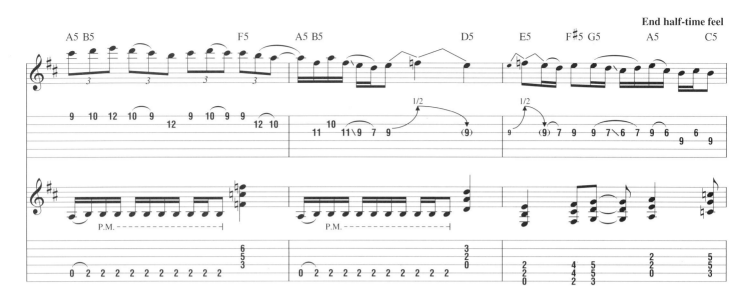

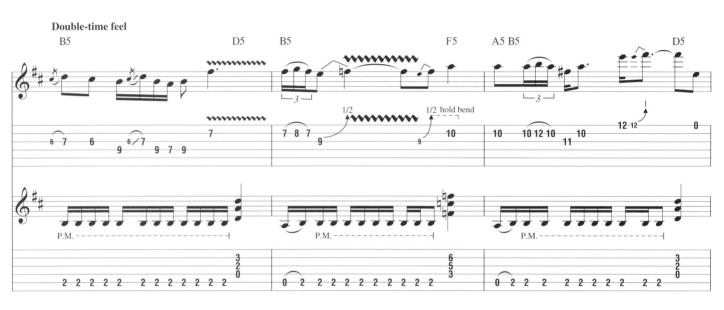

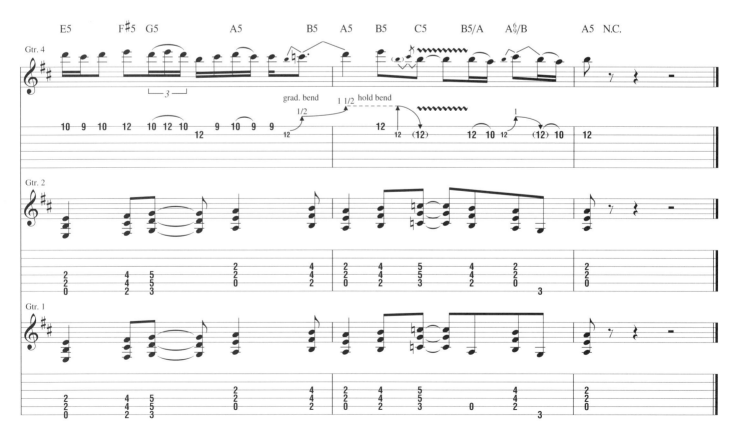

Freak on a Leash

Words and Music by Jonathan Davis, Reginald Arvizu, Brian Welch, James Schaffer and David Silveria

***Chord symbols reflect overall harmony.

†Delay set for dotted-eighth note regeneration w/ 3 repeats.

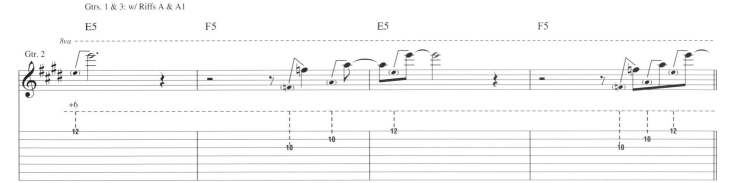

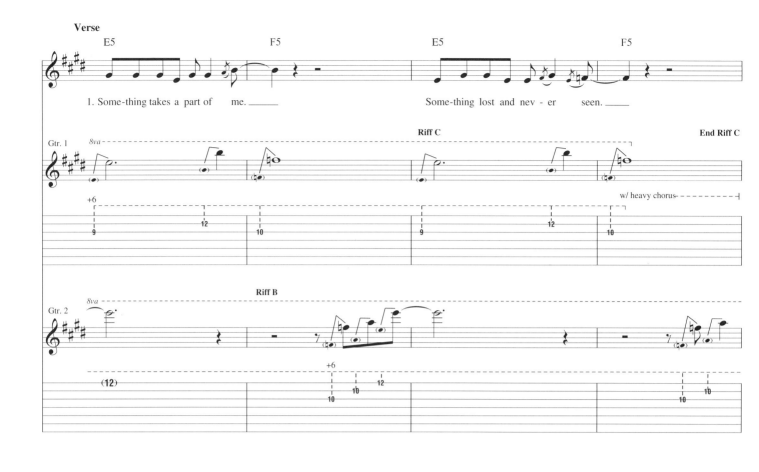

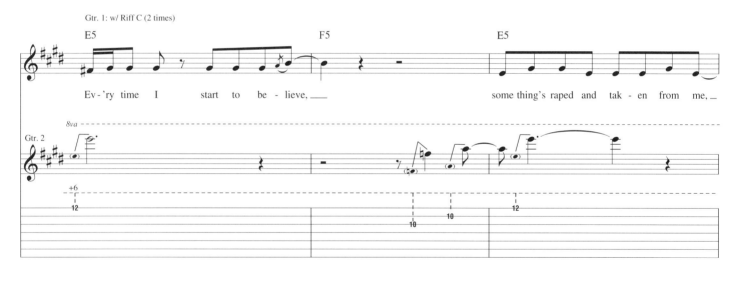

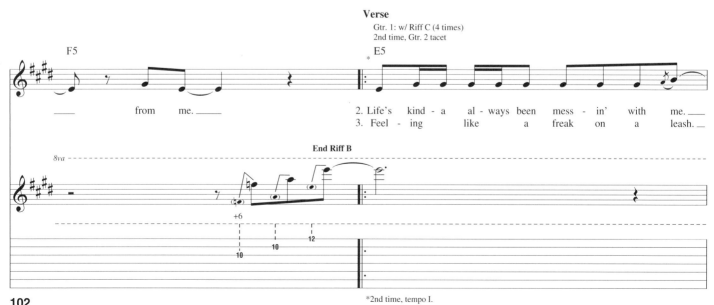

*2nd time, tempo I.

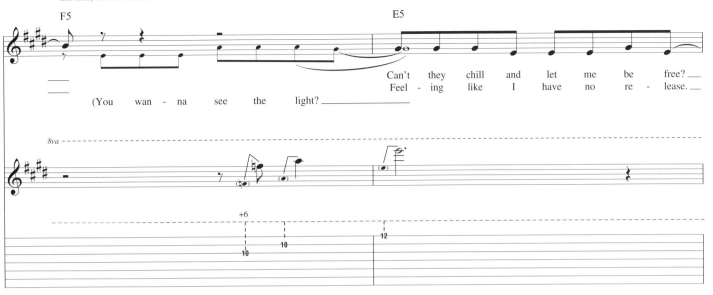

Can't they chill and let me be free? ___
Feel - ing like I have no re - lease. ___

(You wan - na see the light? ___

Can't I take a - way all this pain? ___
How man - y times have I felt dis - eased? ___

So do I. ___

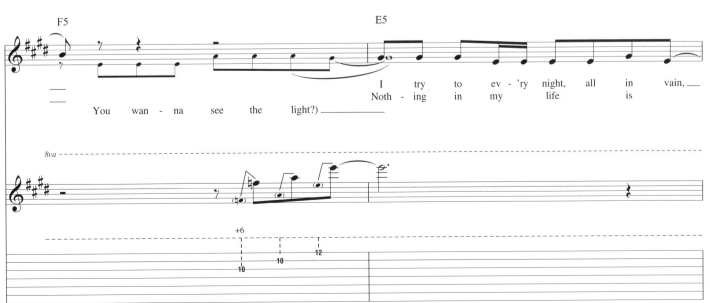

I try to ev - 'ry night, all in vain, ___
Noth - ing in my life is

You wan - na see the light?) ___

Pre-Chorus

Slightly faster ♩ = 108

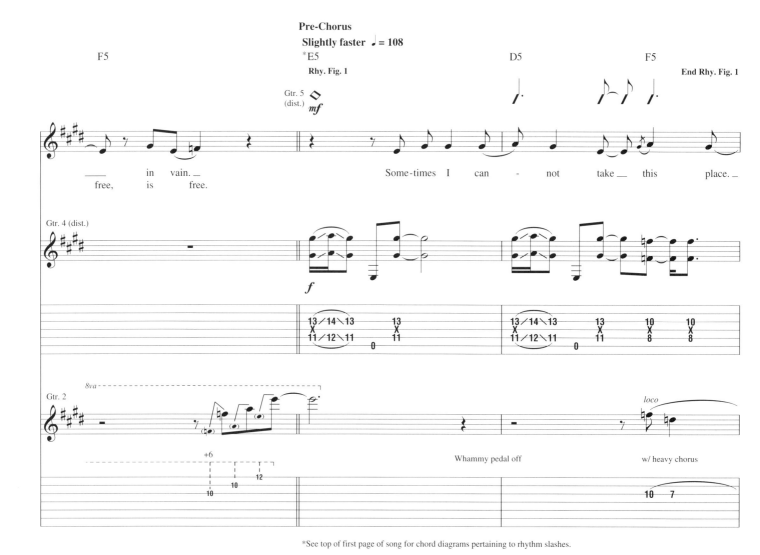

*See top of first page of song for chord diagrams pertaining to rhythm slashes.

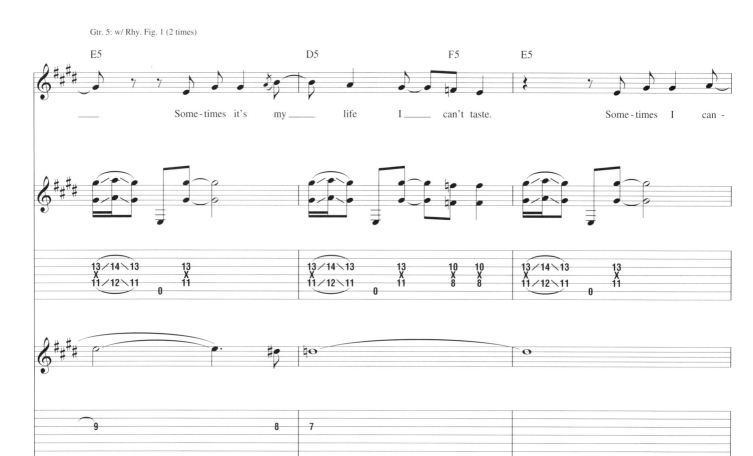

104

- not feel ___ my ___ face. ___ You'll nev - er ___ see ___ me fall ___ from grace.

Chorus

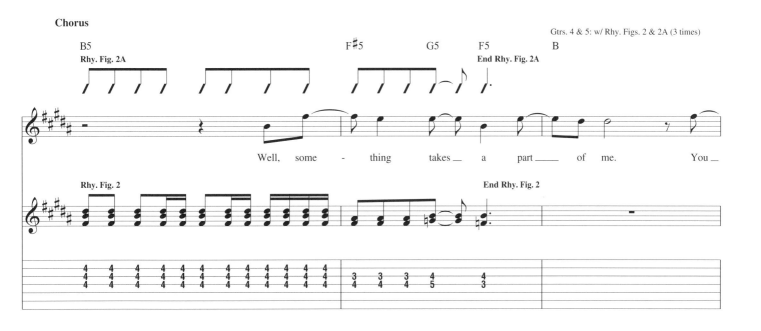

Well, some - thing takes ___ a part ___ of me. You ___

___ and I ___ were meant ___ to be. A ___ cheap fuck ___ for me ___

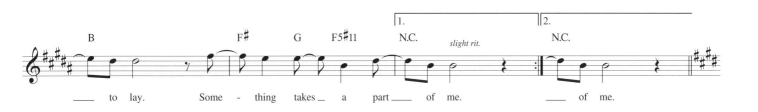

___ to lay. Some - thing takes ___ a part ___ of me. ___ of me.

Interlude

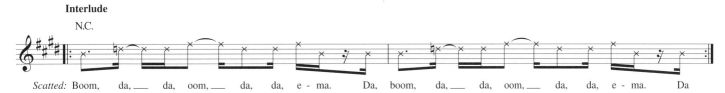

Scatted: Boom, da, ___ da, oom, ___ da, da, e - ma. Da, boom, da, ___ da, oom, ___ da, da, e - ma. Da

Chorus

Who, boy? Some things ain't, boy! Some, some, nin-ga, na, nin-ga. Boy, some things ain't, boy!

Boy, some, nin-ga, na, nin-ga. No, some things ain't, boy!

Boy, some, nin-ga, na, nin-ga. Boy, some things ain't, boy!

Some - thing takes a part of me. You and I were meant to be. A

cheap   fuck ___ for   me ___ to   lay.   Some - thing   takes ___ a   part ___

Gtr. 2: w/ Riff D (2 times)

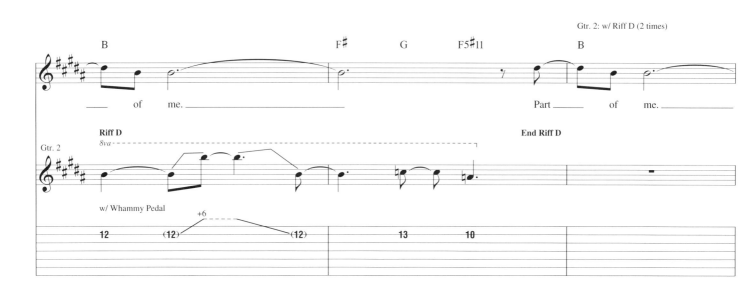

___   of   me. _____   Part ___ of   me. _____

Riff D

Gtr. 2

8va -   End Riff D

w/ Whammy Pedal

+6

| 12 | (12) | (12) | 13 | 10 | |

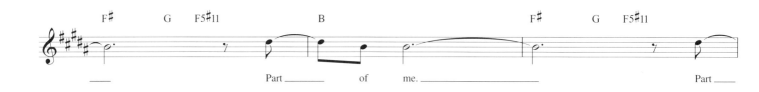

___   Part _____ of   me. _____   Part ___

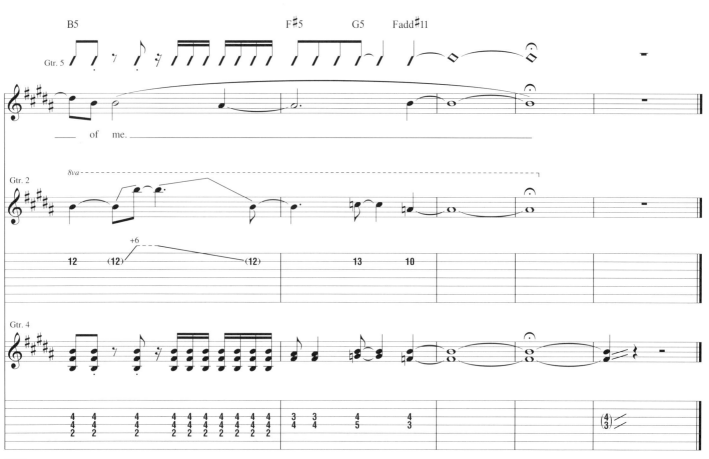

___   of   me. _____

Gtr. 2

8va -

+6

| 12 | (12) | (12) | 13 | 10 | |

Gtr. 4

4 4	4	4 4 4 4 4 4 4 4	3 3	4 4	4 3		
4 4	4	4 4 4 4 4 4 4 4	4 4	5	3		(4)
2 2	2	2 2 2 2 2 2 2 2					(3)

from Megadeth - *Rust in Peace*

Hangar 18

Words and Music by Dave Mustaine

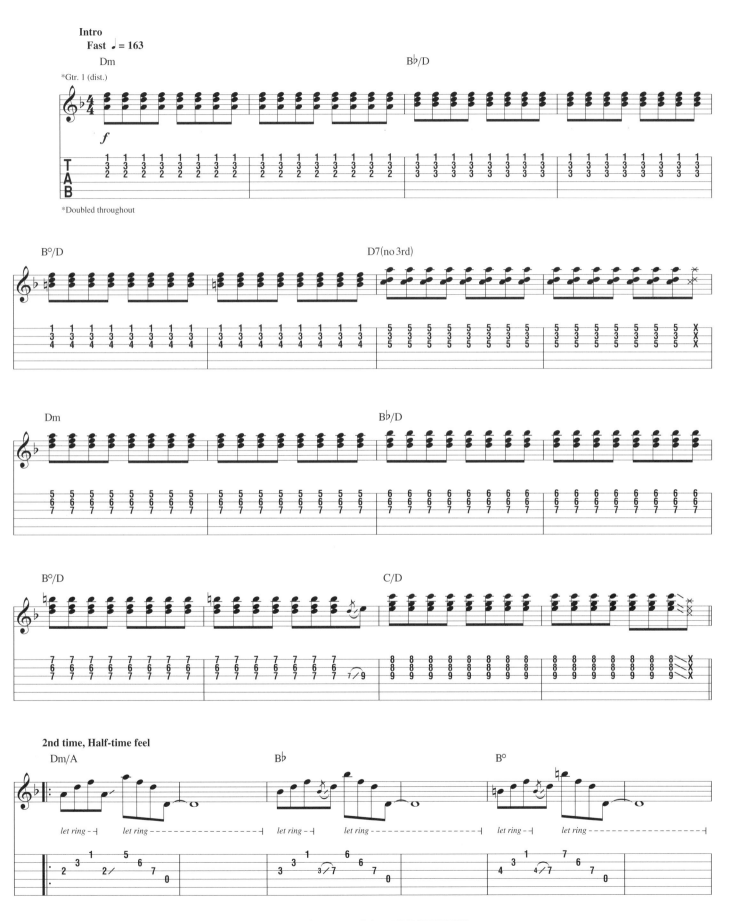

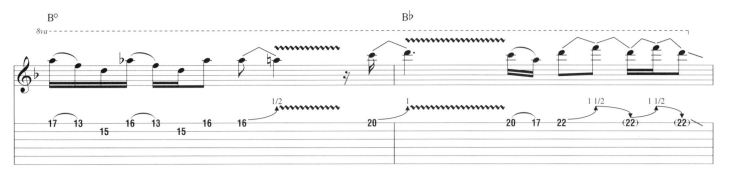

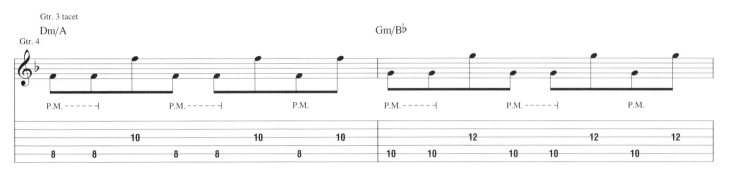

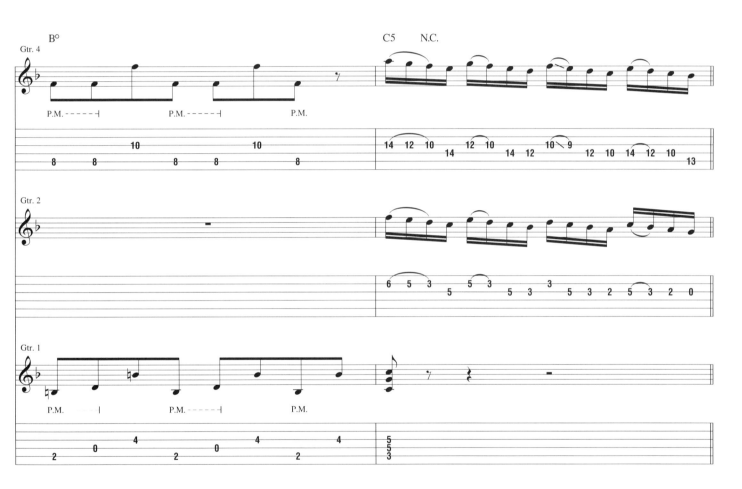

Interlude

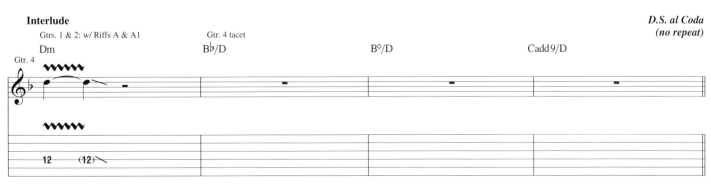

⊕ Coda

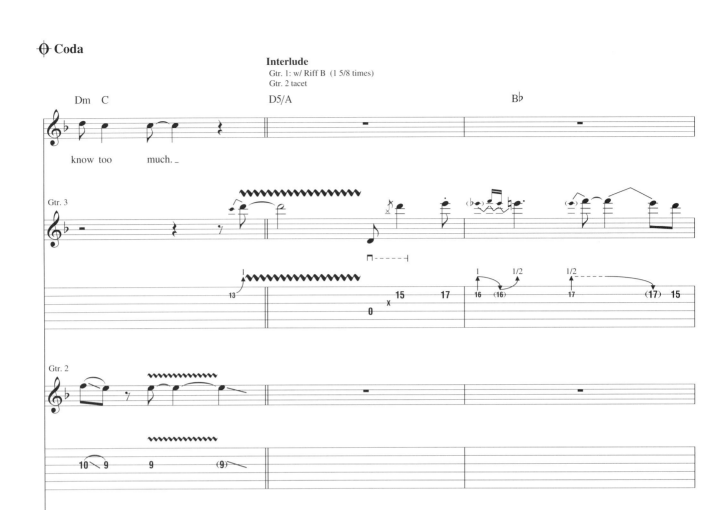

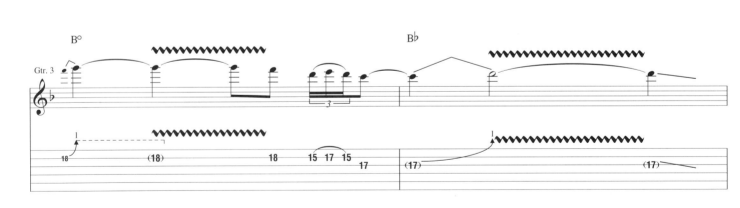

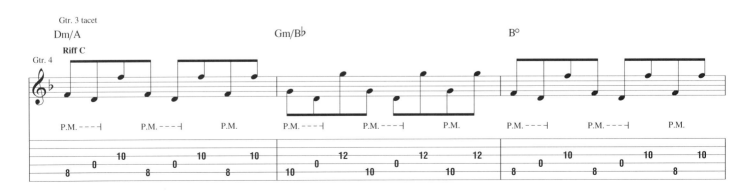

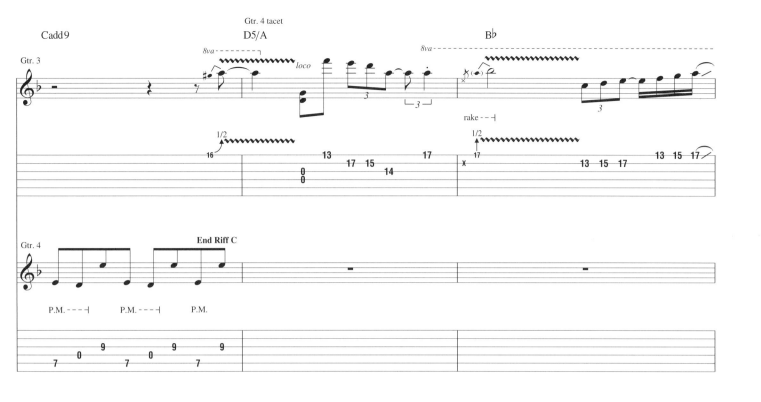

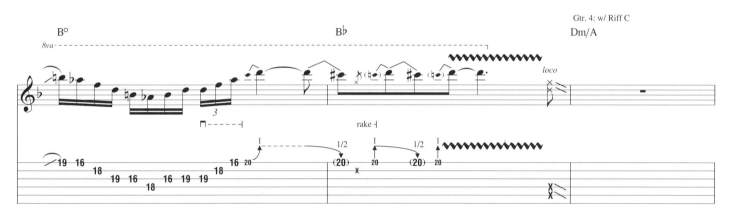

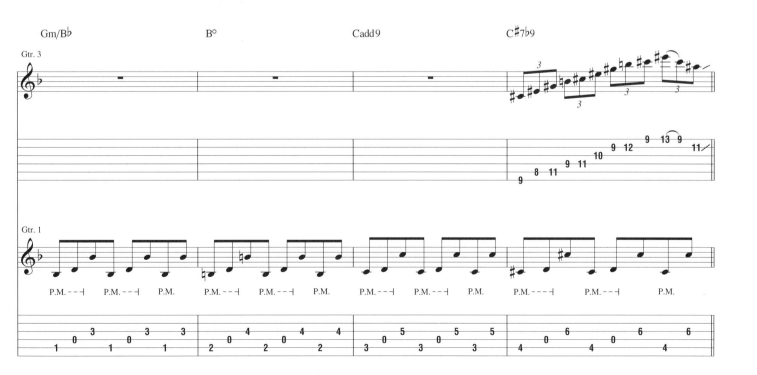

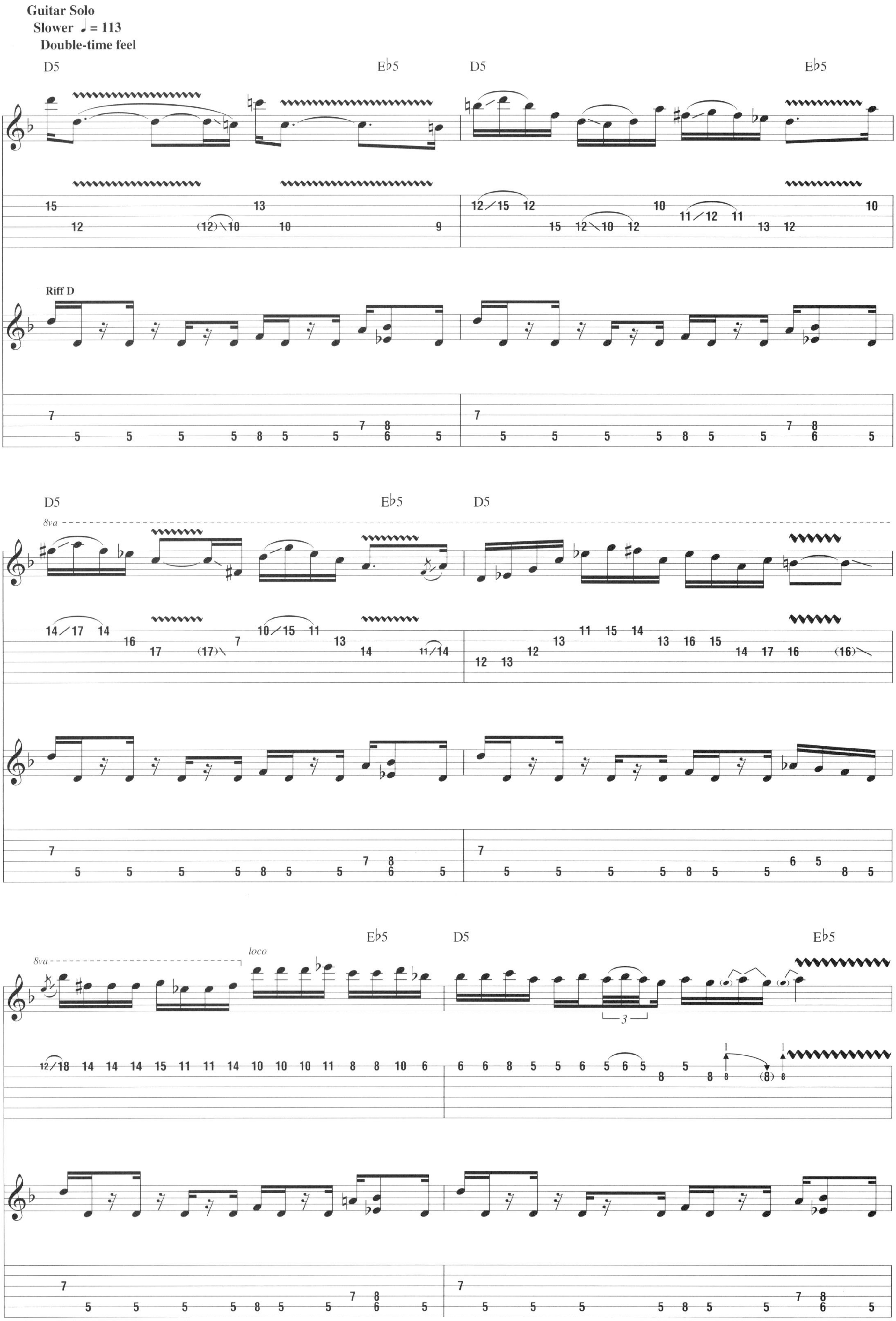
Guitar Solo
Slower ♩ = 113
Double-time feel
D5
E♭5
Riff D
8va
loco

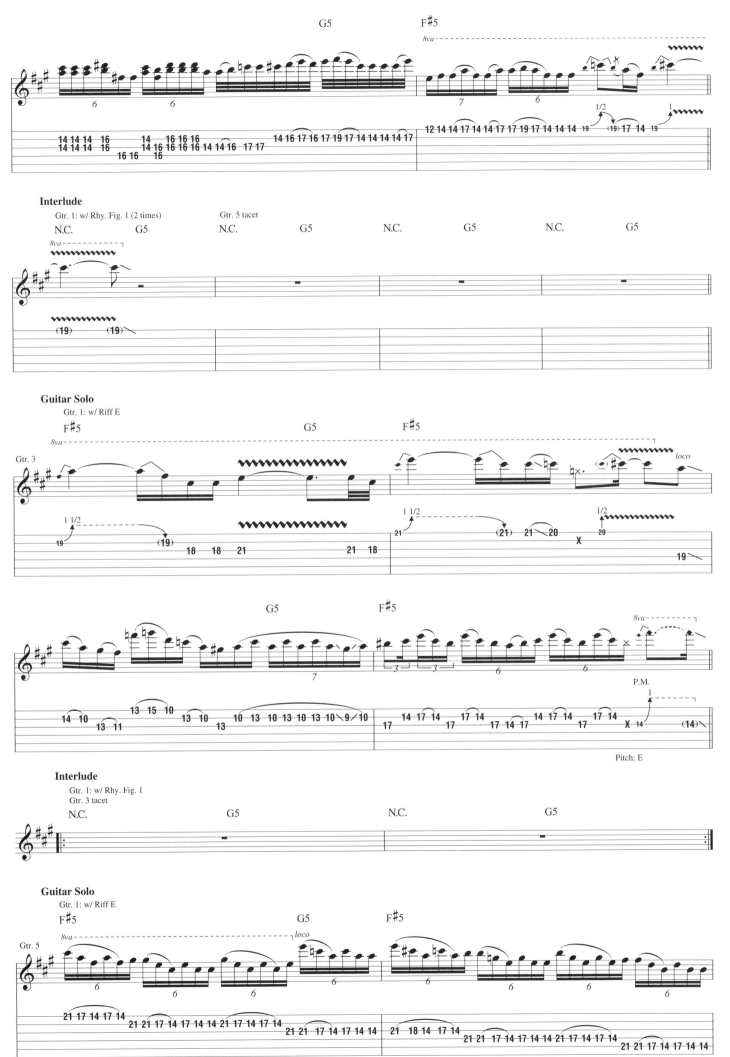

119

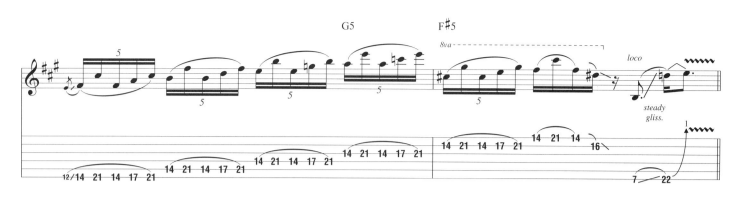

Interlude

Gtr. 1: w/ Rhy. Fig. 1

Gtr. 5 tacet

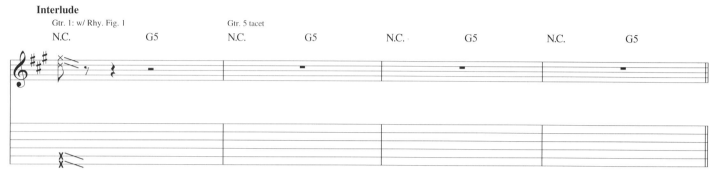

Guitar Solo

Slightly faster ♩ = 128

Gtr. 1: w/ Riff E

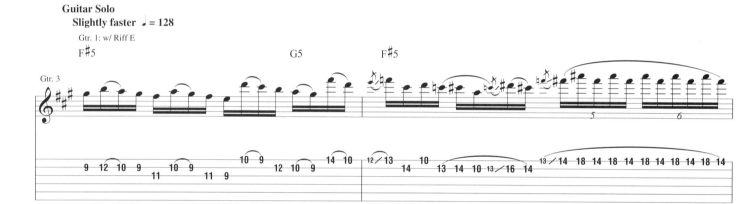

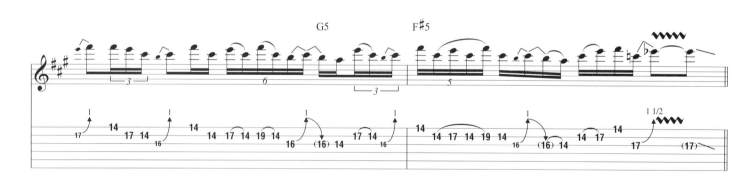

Interlude

Gtr. 1: w/ Rhy. Fig. 1 (2 times)
Gtr. 3 tacet

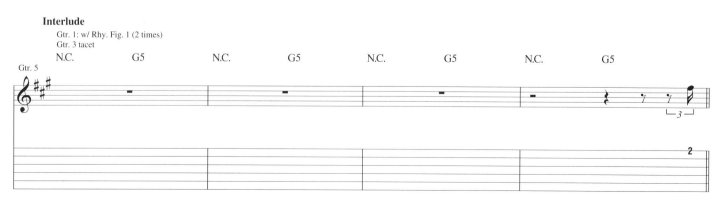

Guitar Solo

Gtr. 1: w/ Riff E (2 times)

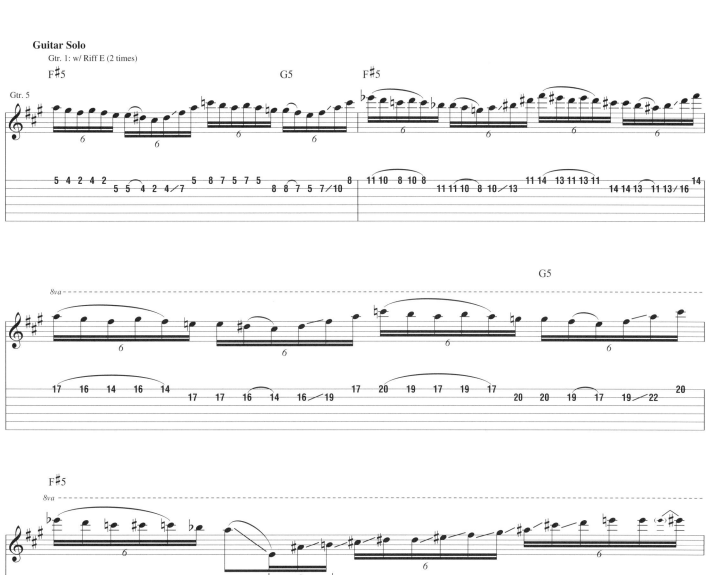

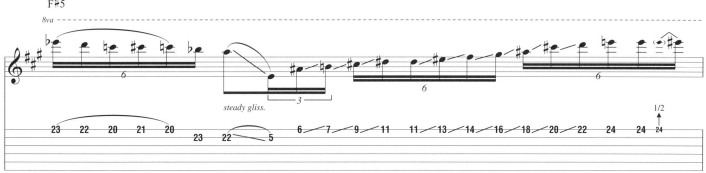

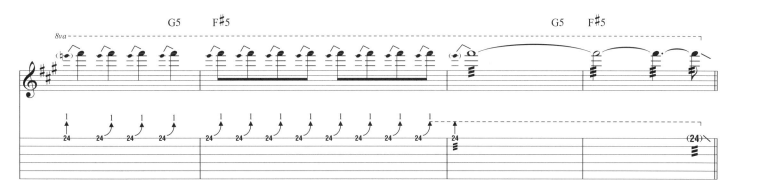

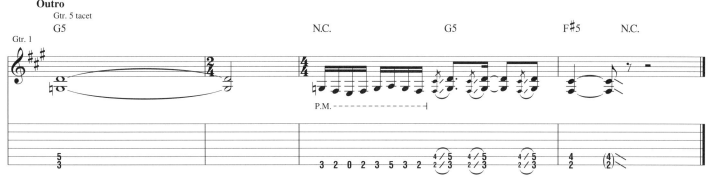

Outro

Gtr. 5 tacet

Iron Man

Words and Music by Frank Iommi, John Osbourne, William Ward and Terence Butler

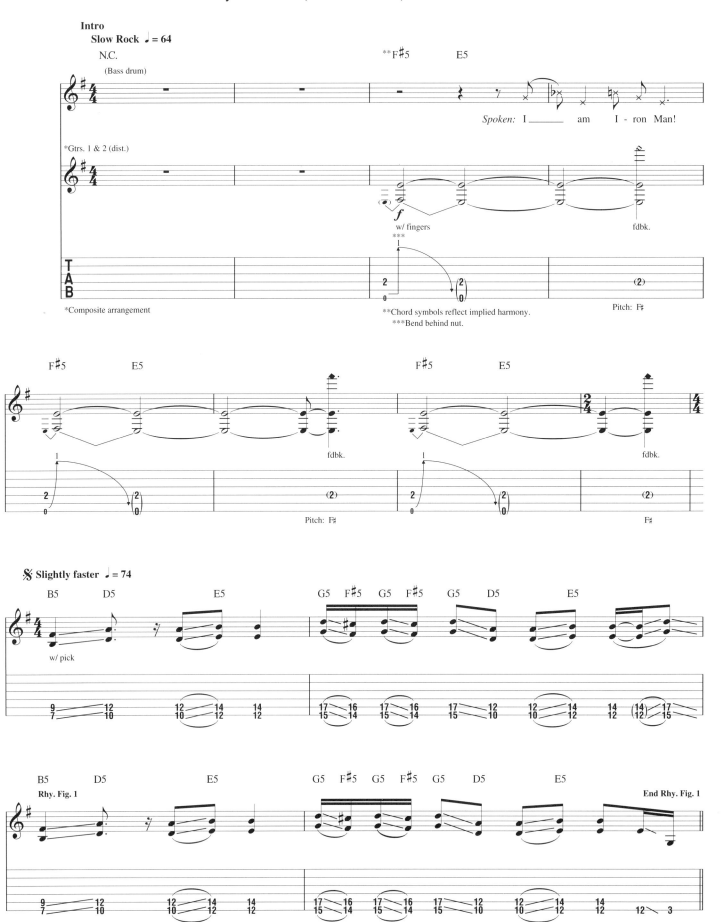

Guitar Solo
Gtr. 2 tacet

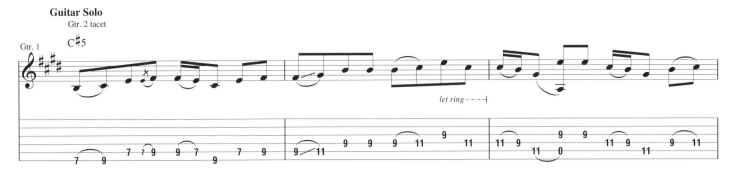

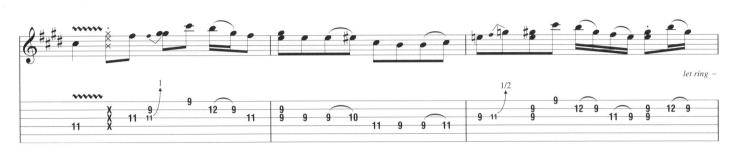

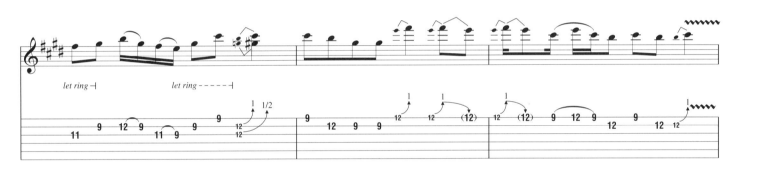

Interlude

Gtrs. 1 & 2: w/ Riff C

A tempo

Gtrs. 1 & 2: w/ Riff B (2 times)

Coda

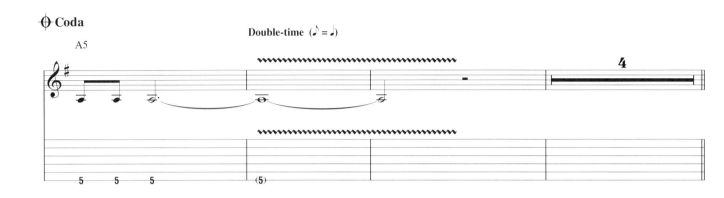

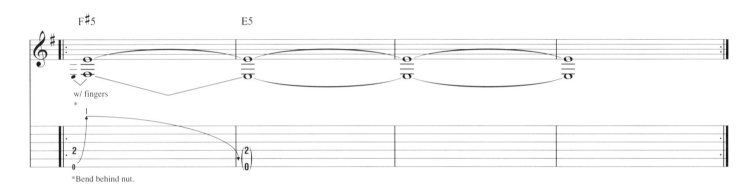

*Bend behind nut.

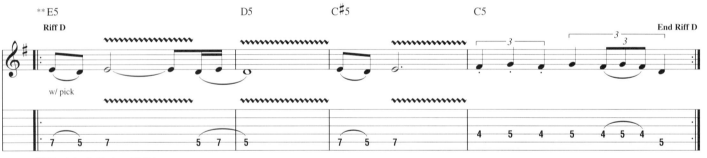

** Chords implied by bass, till Outro.

Guitar Solo

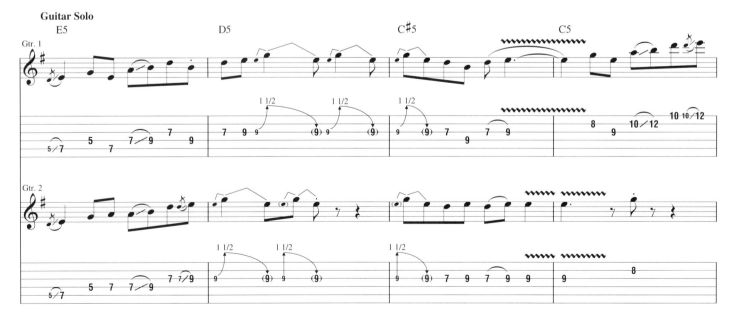

126

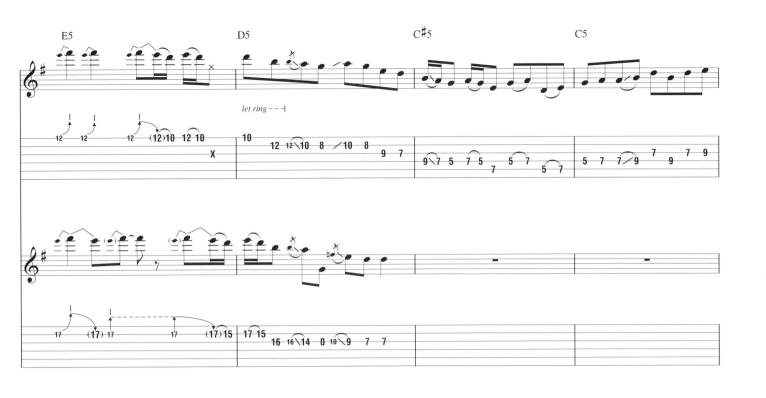

Outro
Gtrs. 1 & 2: w/ Riff D (3 times)

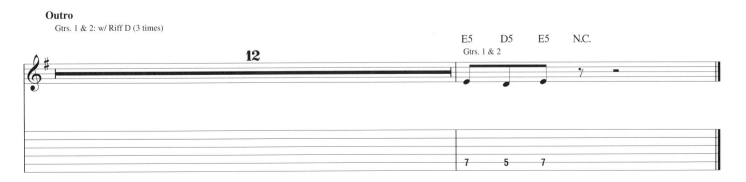

Laid to Rest

Words and Music by Chris Adler, David Blythe, John Campbell, Mark Morton and Will Adler

*Chord symbols reflect implied harmony.

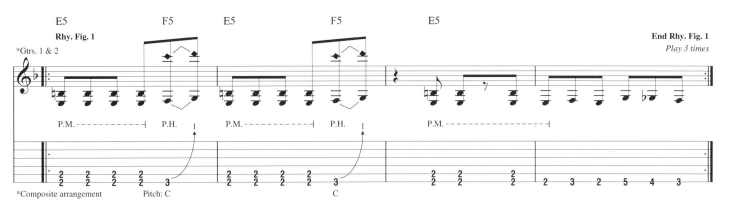

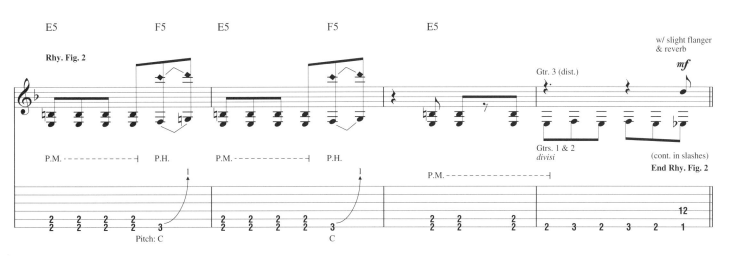

Verse
Half-time feel

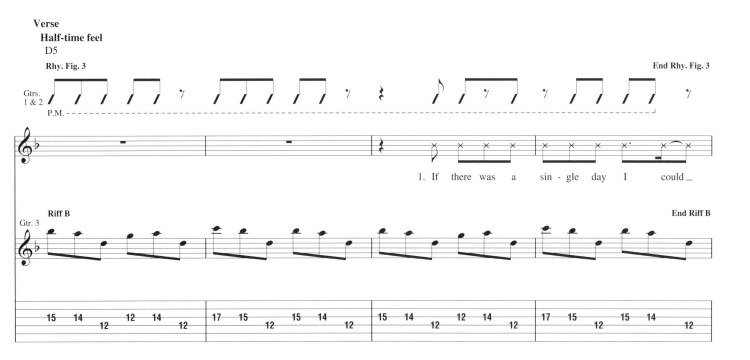

Gtrs. 1 & 2: w/ Rhy. Fig. 3 (3 times)
Gtr. 3: w/ Riff B (2 times)

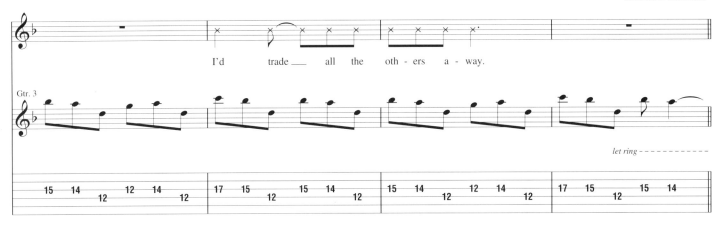

I'd trade ___ all the oth - ers a - way.

Interlude

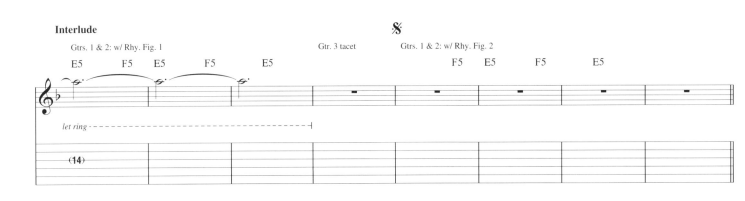

Gtrs. 1 & 2: w/ Rhy. Fig. 1

Gtr. 3 tacet   Gtrs. 1 & 2: w/ Rhy. Fig. 2

E5   F5   E5   F5   E5   F5   E5   F5   E5

let ring -

(14)

Verse

Gtr. 1: w/ Riff A (2 times)
Gtr. 2: w/ Riff A (4 times)

D5

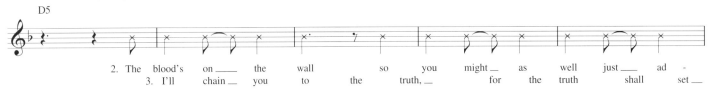

2. The blood's on ___ the wall   so   you   might ___ as   well   just ___ ad -
3. I'll chain ___ you   to   the   truth, ___   for   the   truth   shall   set ___

mit   it, ___   and   bleach   out ___ the   stains,   com -
___   you ___   free. ___   I'll   turn ___ the   screws   of   ven -

mit   to ___   for - get - ting ___   it.
- geance and   bur - y ___   you ___   with   hon - es - ty.

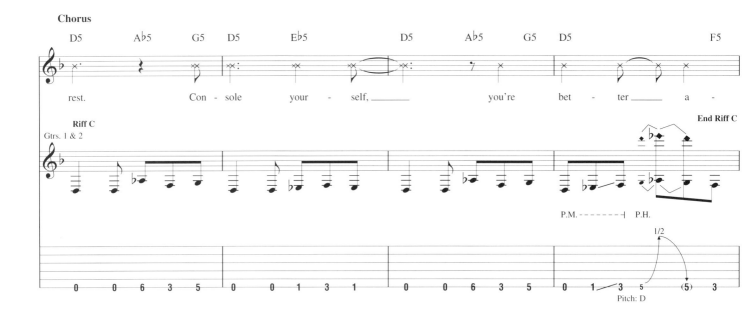

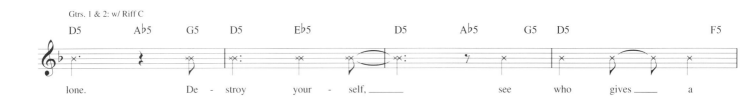

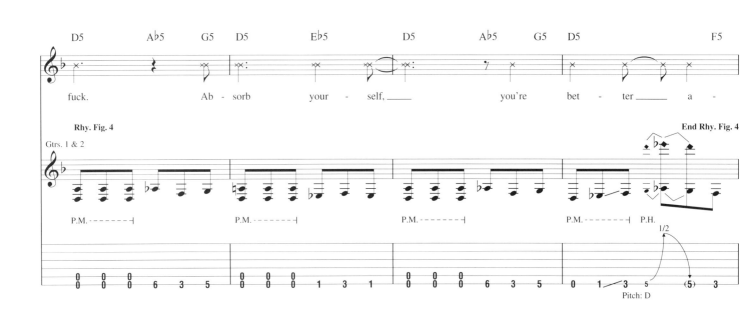

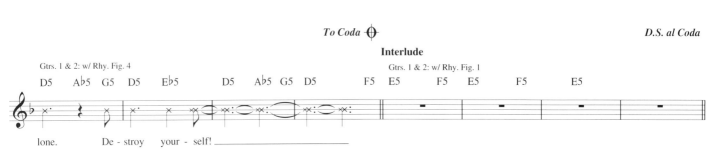

⬦ Coda

Bridge

E♭5

Gtrs. 1 & 2

N.C.

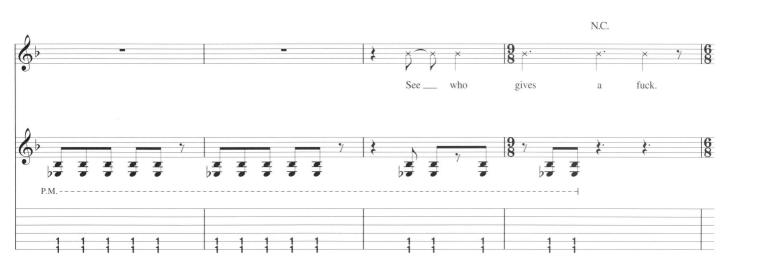

See __ who gives a fuck.

Half-time feel

Gtrs. 1 & 2: w/ Rhy. Fig. 3 (4 times)

D5

See __ who gives a

fuck.

See __ who gives a

Interlude

Gtr. 1: w/ Riff A (1st 4 meas.)
Gtr. 2: w/ Rhy. Fig. 3

Gtr. 1: w/ Riff A (1st 4 meas.)
Gtr. 2: w/ Rhy. Fig. 3

D5

fuck.

Gtr. 1: w/ Riff A (last 4 meas.)

Gtr. 2

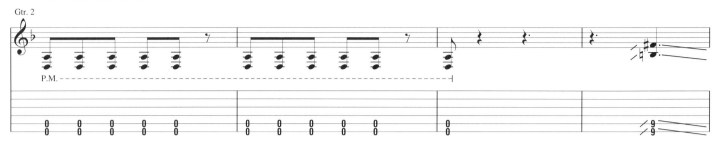

Gtrs. 1 & 2: w/ Riff C (2 times)

| D5 | A♭5 | G5 | D5 | E♭5 | D5 | A♭5 | G5 | D5 | F5 | D5 | A♭5 | G5 | D5 | E♭5 | D5 | A♭5 | G5 | D5 | F5 |

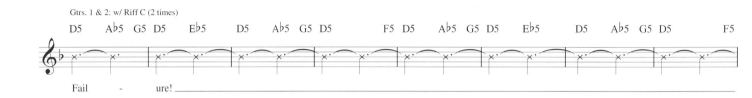

Fail - ure! _____

Gtrs. 1 & 2: w/ Rhy. Fig. 4 (2 times)

| D5 | A♭5 | G5 | D5 | E♭5 | D5 | A♭5 | G5 | D5 | F5 | D5 | A♭5 | G5 | D5 | E♭5 | D5 | A♭5 | G5 | D5 | F5 |

Verse

Gtr. 1 tacet

| D5 | | F5 | D5 | | F♯5 | D° |

4. If there was ___ a

Riff D

Gtr. 1   Gtr. 2   Gtrs. 1 & 2

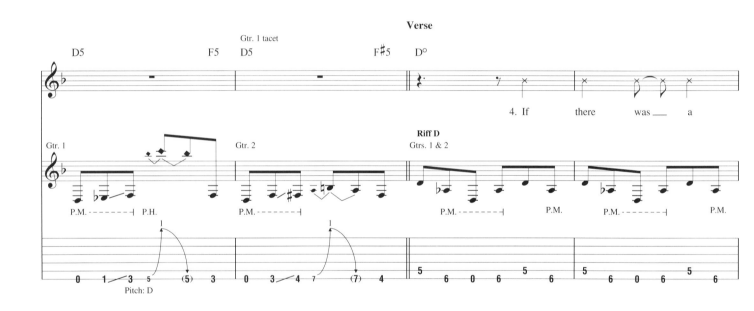

Pitch: D

| E♭ | | | Gm | |

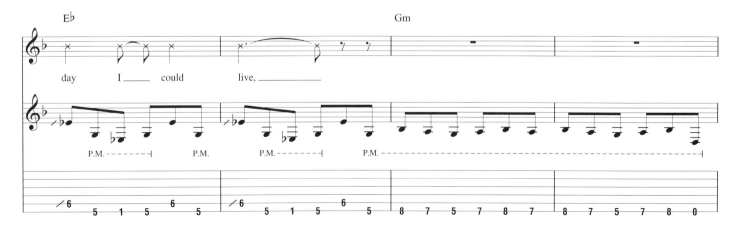

day I ___ could live, _____

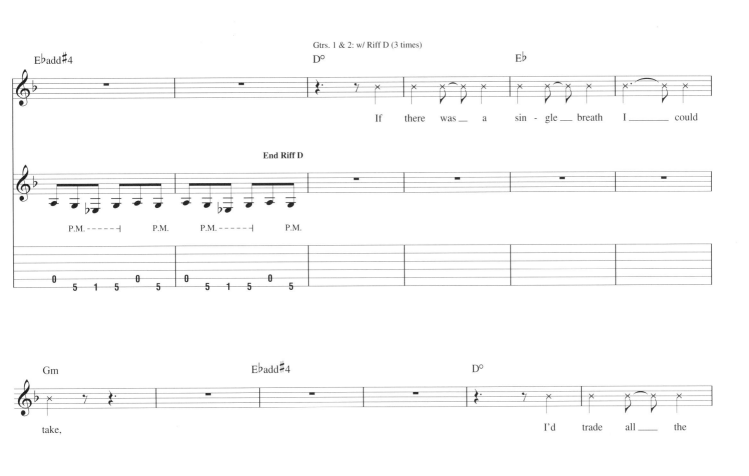

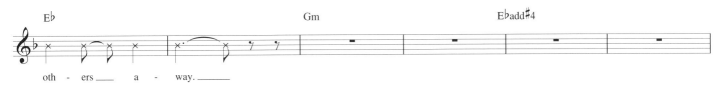

Outro

Half-time feel

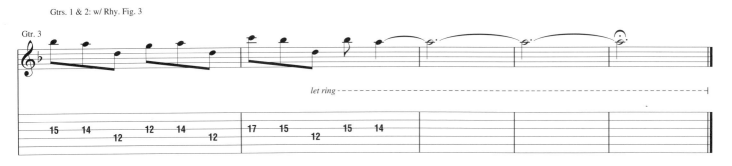

from Dio - *Last in Line*

The Last in Line

Words and Music by Ronnie James Dio, Jimmy Bain and Vivian Campbell

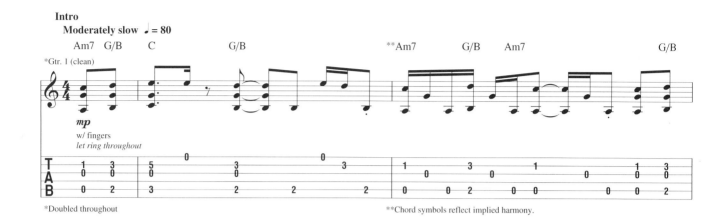

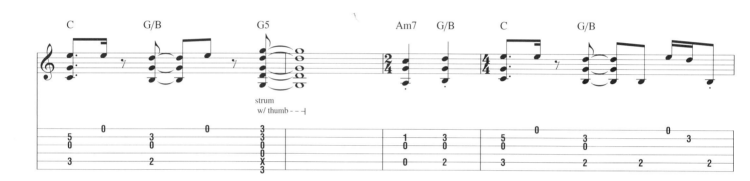

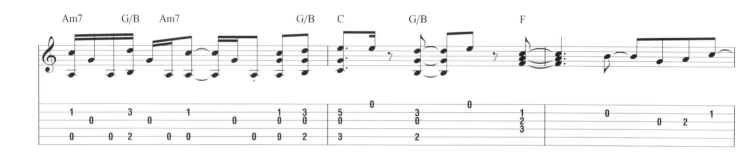

We're a ship with-out __ a storm, __ a cold __ with-out __ the warm, __

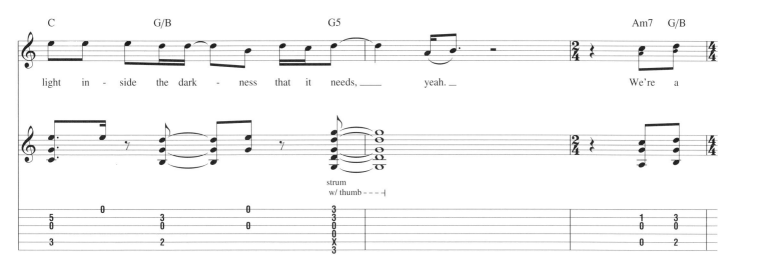

light in - side the dark - ness that it needs, ___ yeah. ___ We're a

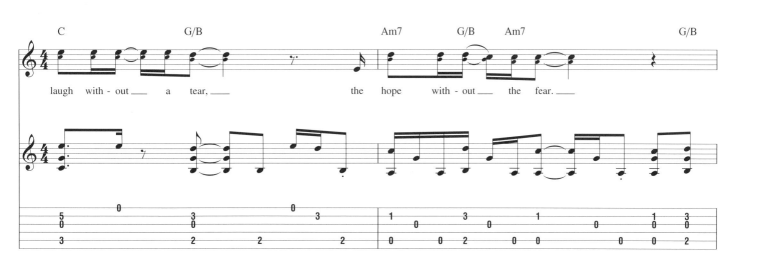

laugh with - out ___ a tear, ___ the hope with - out ___ the fear. ___

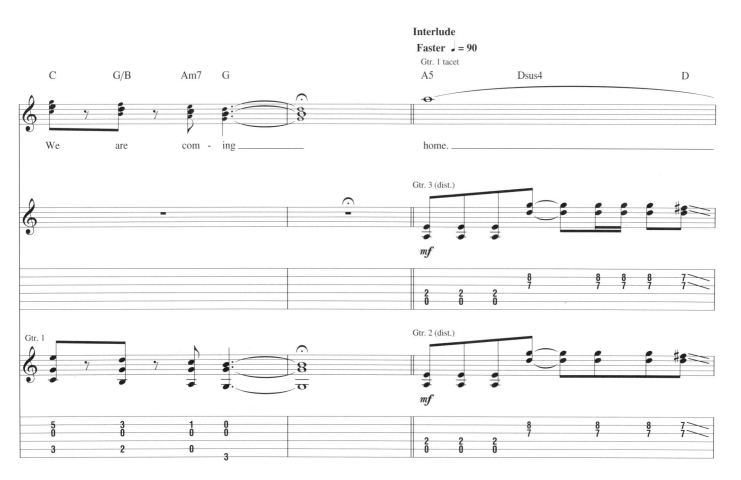

Interlude

Faster ♩ = 90

We are com - ing ___ home. _____

137

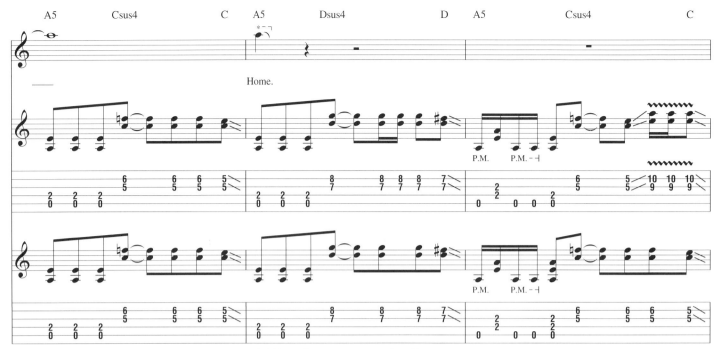

*w/ delay set for quarter-note regeneration w/ 3 repeats

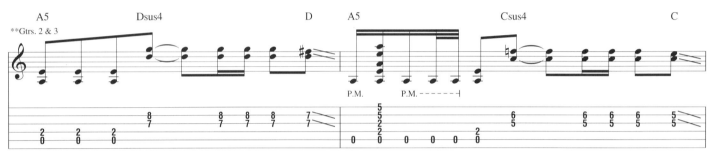

**Composite arrangement

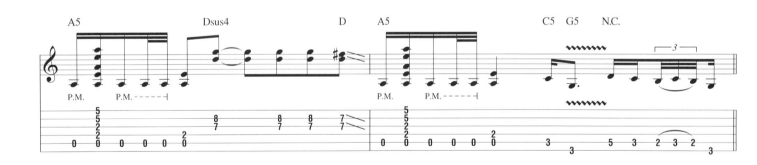

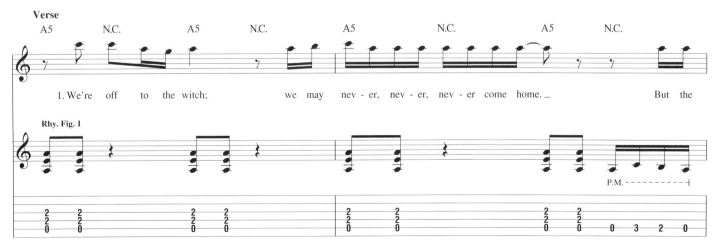

1. We're off to the witch; we may nev-er, nev-er, nev-er come home. But the

Rhy. Fig. 1

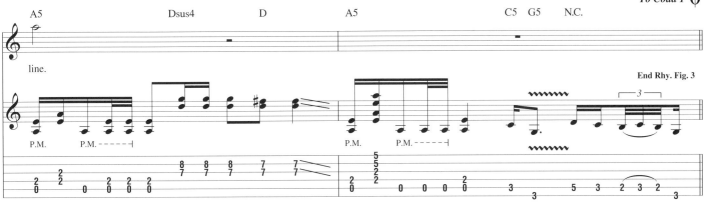

Verse

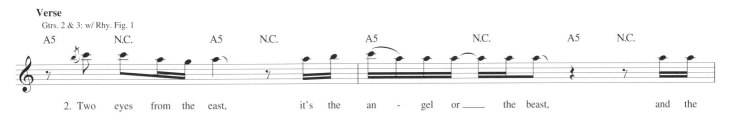

2. Two eyes from the east, it's the an - gel or ___ the beast, and the

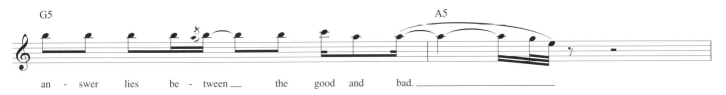

an - swer lies be - tween ___ the good and bad. ___

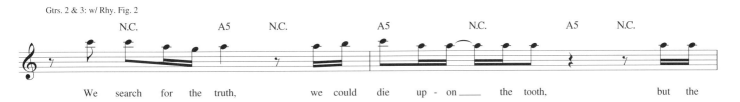

We search for the truth, we could die up - on ___ the tooth, but the

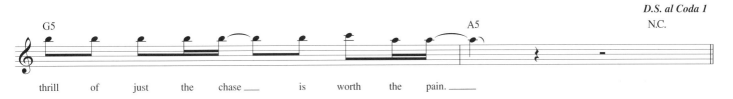

thrill of just the chase ___ is worth the pain. ___

 Coda 1

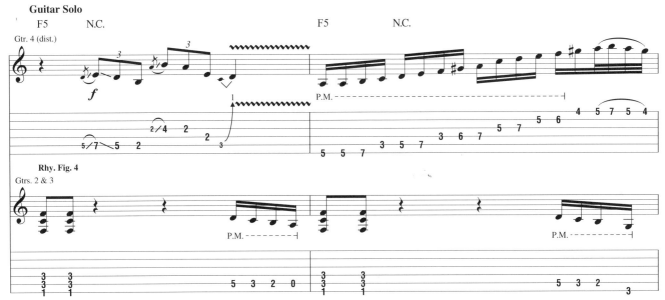

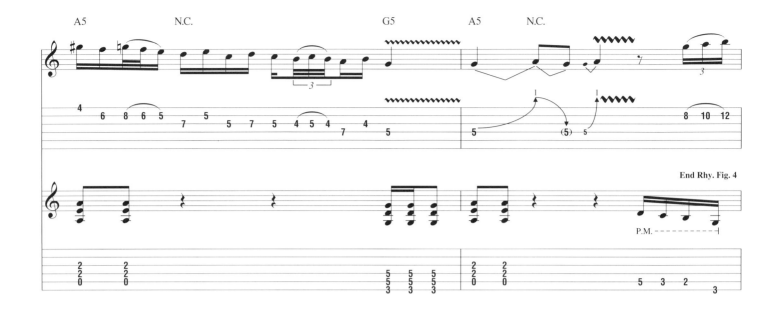

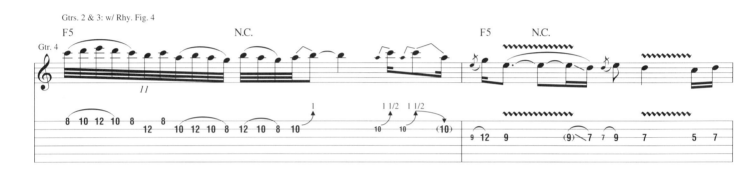

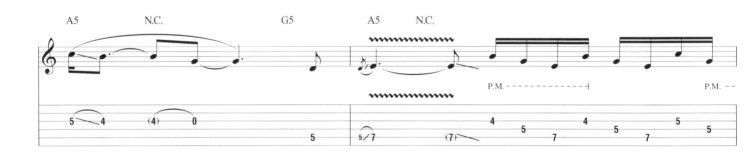

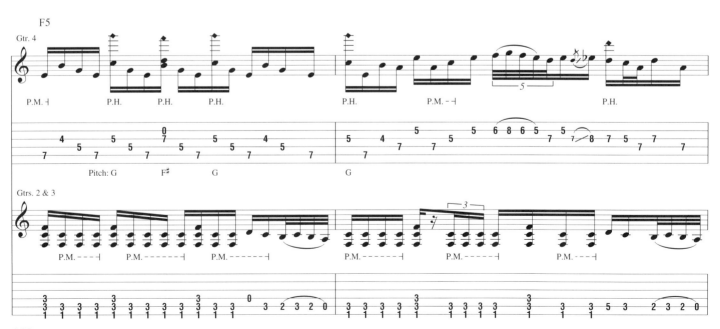

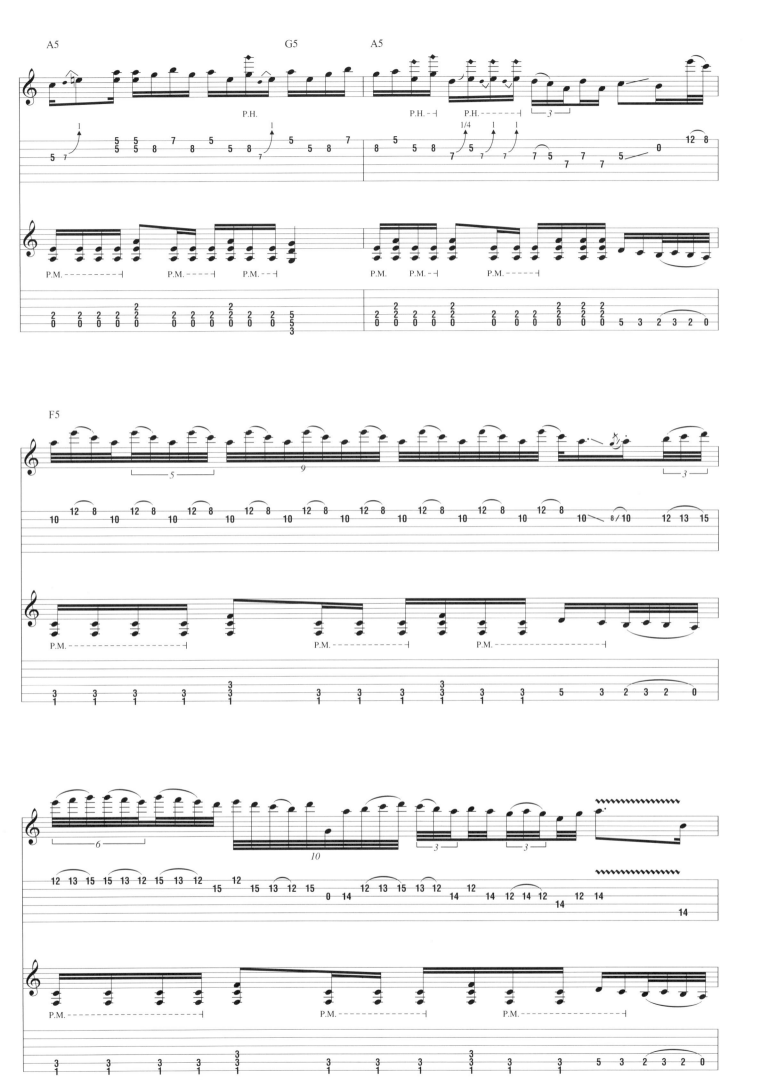

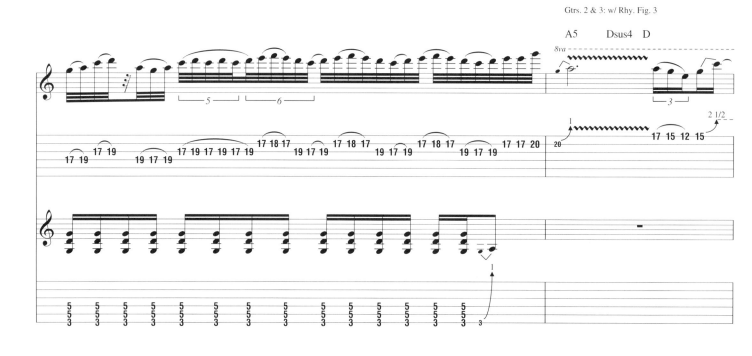

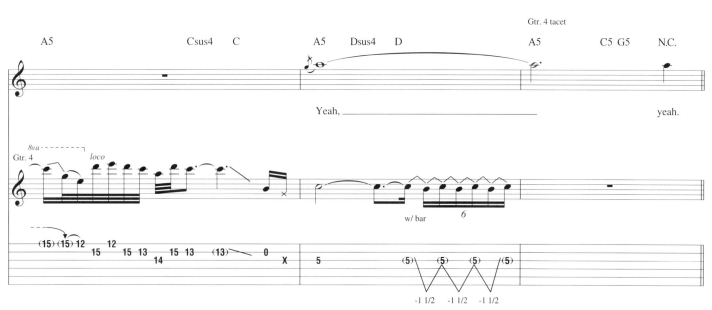

from Anthrax - *Spreading the Disease*

Madhouse

Words and Music by Joseph Bellardini, Frank Bello, Charlie Benante, Scott Rosenfeld and Daniel Spitz

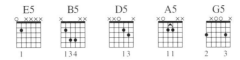

Spoken: It's time for your medication, Mister Brown. (Maniacal laughter:) Ooh, hoo, ha, ha, ha...

149

I'm in - sane.

Mad, mad - house.

(Mad!

Mad, mad, mad, mad - house.

Mad! Mad!)

from Ozzy Osbourne - *Blizzard of Ozz*

Mr. Crowley

Words and Music by Ozzy Osbourne, Randy Rhoads and Bob Daisley

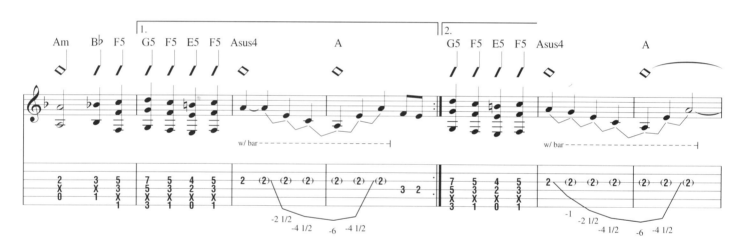

*Synth. arr. for gtr.

**See top of page for chord diagrams pertaining to rhythm slashes.

***Gtr. 3 (dist.)

***Two gtrs. arr. for one.

1. Mis - ter Crow - ley, what went on in your head?

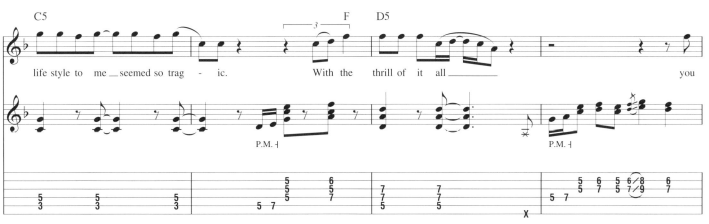

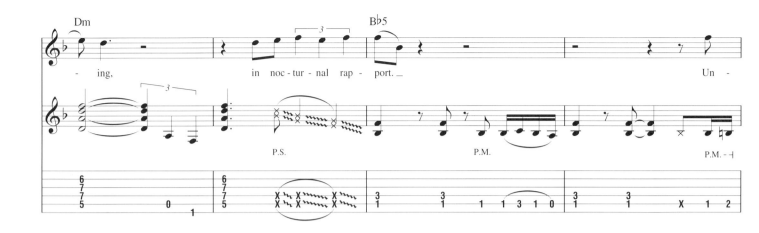

-ing, in noc-tur-nal rap-port. Un-

cov-er-ing things that were sa-cred, man-i-fest on this earth. Ah, con-

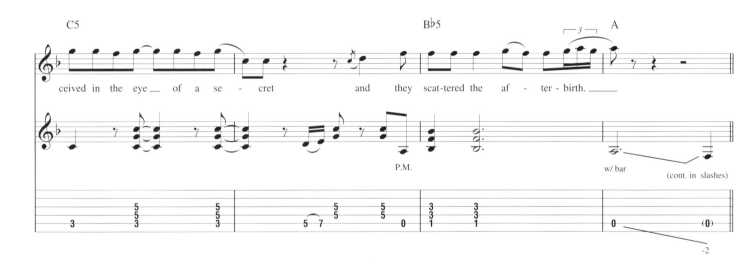

ceived in the eye of a se-cret and they scat-tered the af-ter-birth.

Guitar Solo

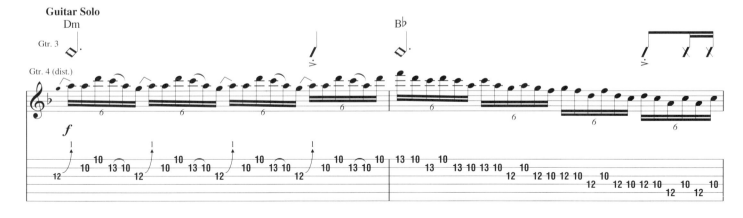

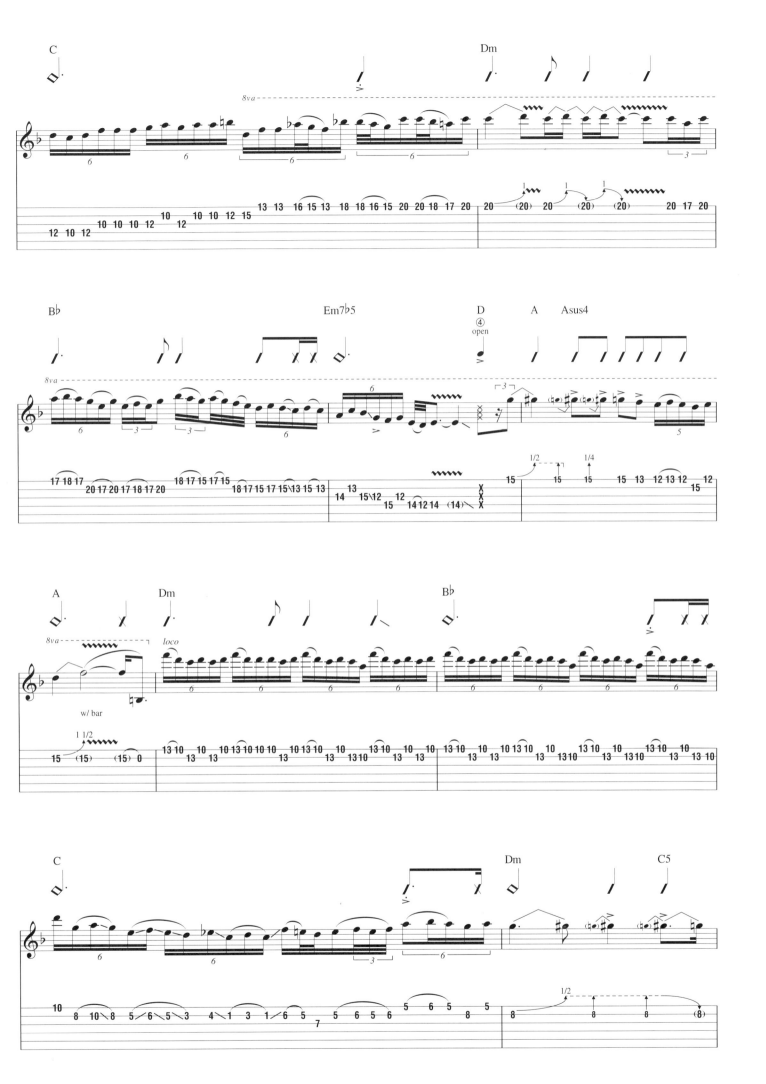

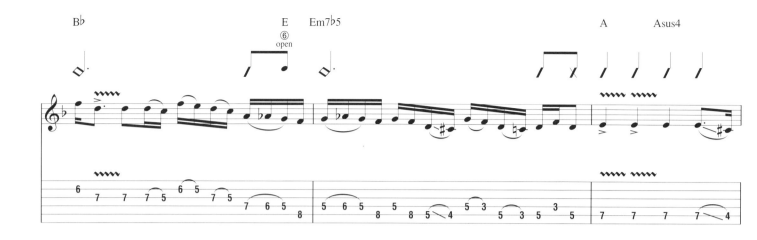

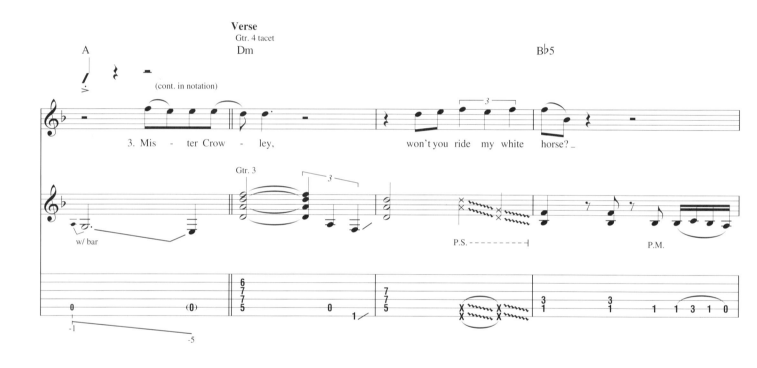

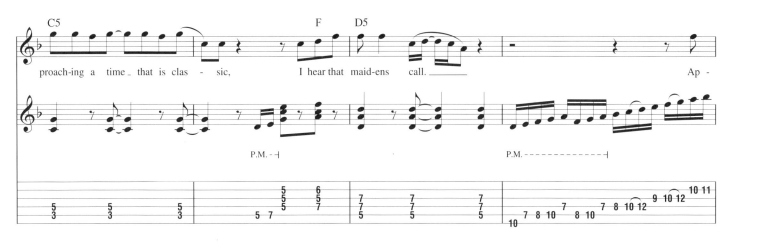

proach-ing a time that is clas - sic, I hear that maid-ens call. Ap -

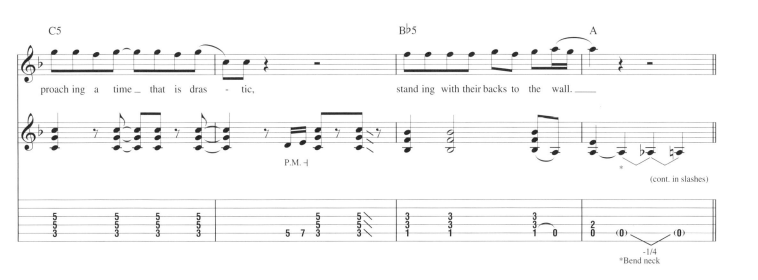

proach ing a time that is dras - tic, standing with their backs to the wall.

Interlude

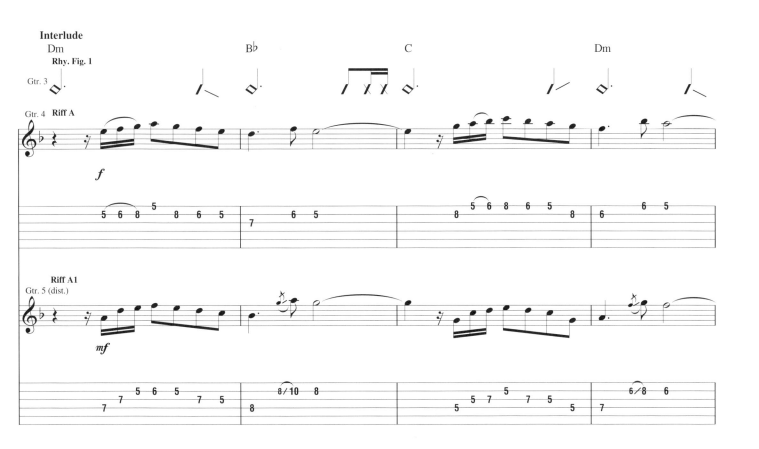

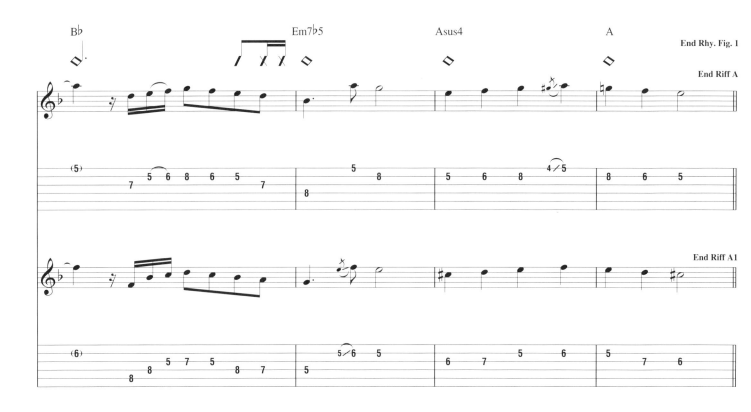

Bridge

Gtr. 3: w/ Rhy. Fig. 1
Gtrs. 4 & 5: w/ Riffs A & A1

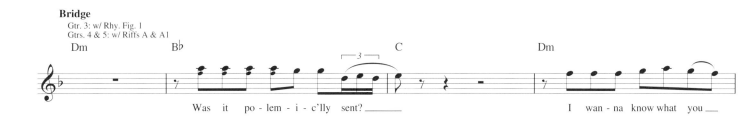

Was it po - lem - i - c'lly sent? _____ I wan - na know what you _____

meant. _____ I wan - na know, I wan - na know what you meant. _____ Yeah.

Outro - Guitar Solo

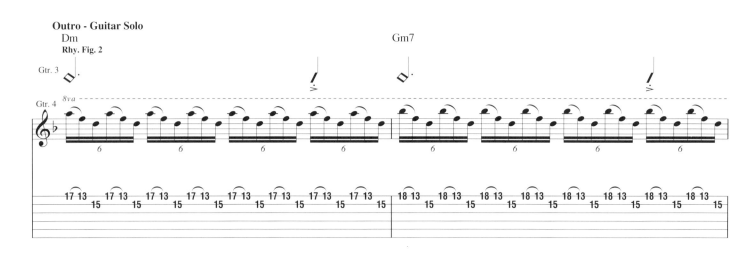

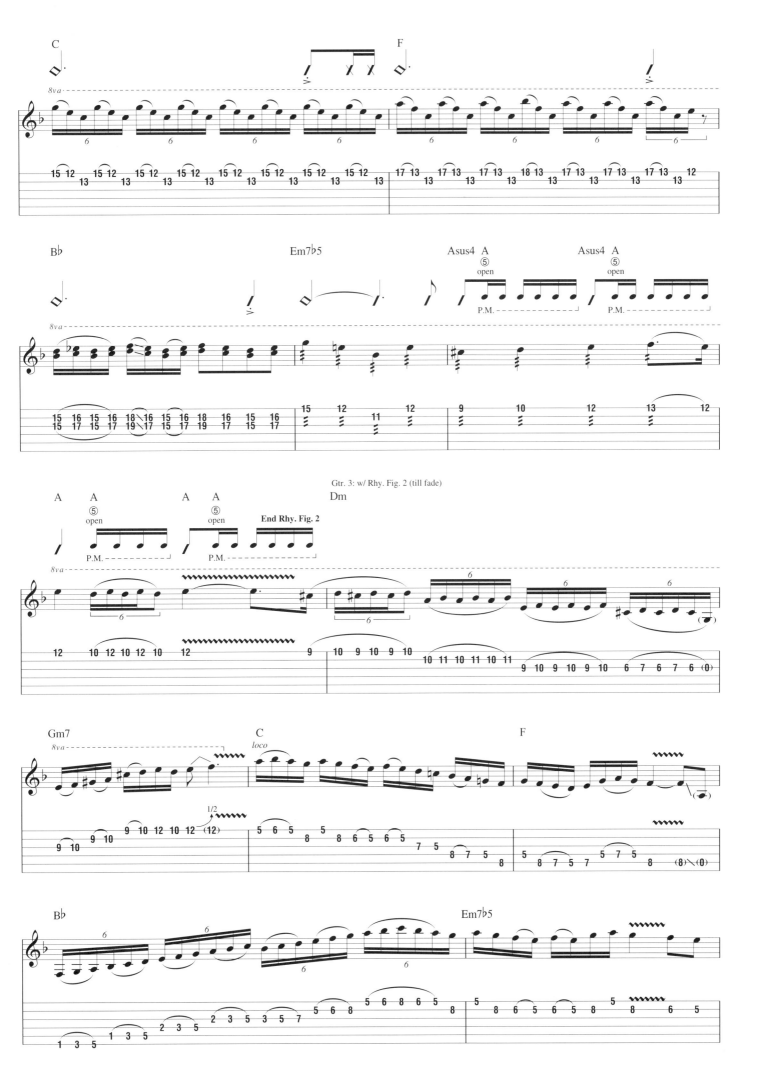

Psychosocial

Words and Music by M. Shawn Crahan, Paul Gray, Nathan Jordison, Corey Taylor, Chris Fehn, Mic Thomson, Sid Wilson, James Root and Craig Jones

Drop D tuning, down 2 1/2 steps:
(low to high) A-E-A-D-F♯-B

Intro
Moderately fast ♩ = 135

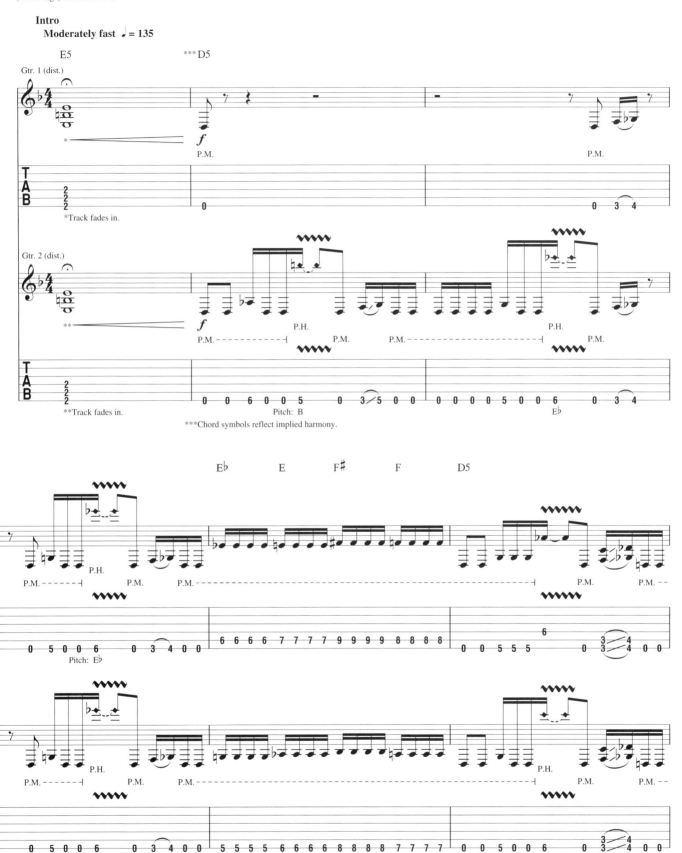

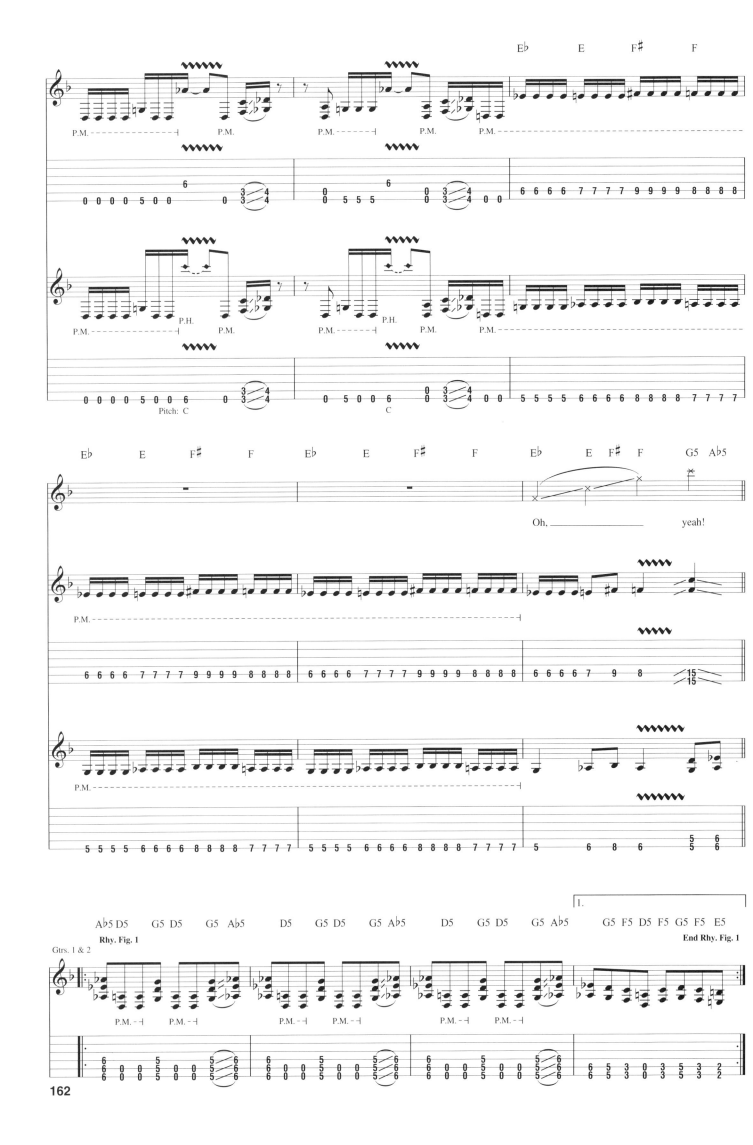

Guitar Solo

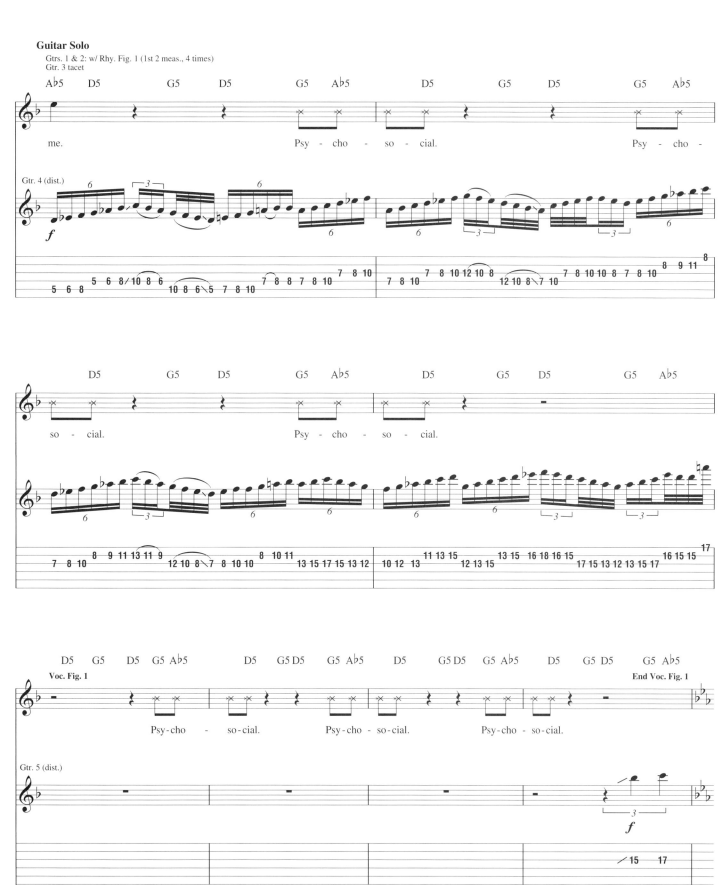

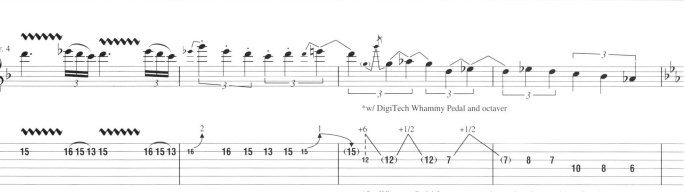

*Set Whammy Pedal for one octave above when depressed (toe down).
Set octaver for one octave above.

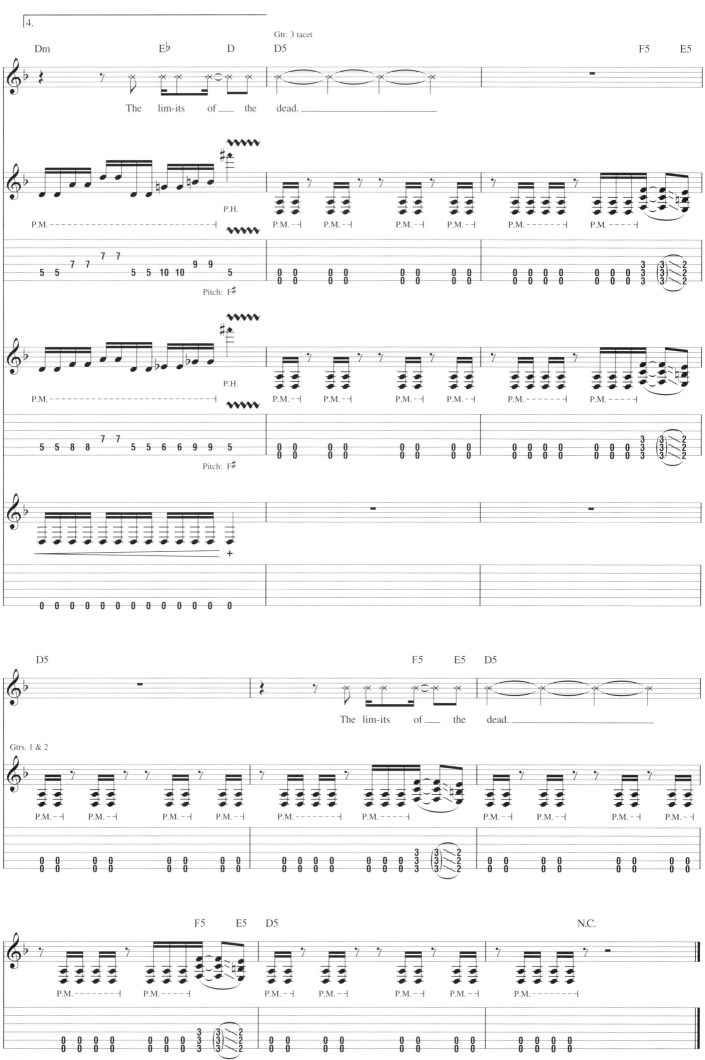

from Dream Theater - *Images and Words*

Pull Me Under

Words and Music by James LaBrie, Kevin Moore, John Myung, John Petrucci and Michael Portnoy

*Gtr. 1 (elec.) w/ clean tone
Gtr. 2 (acous.)
**Chord symbols reflect implied harmony.
***Applies to Gtr. 1 only, throughout.

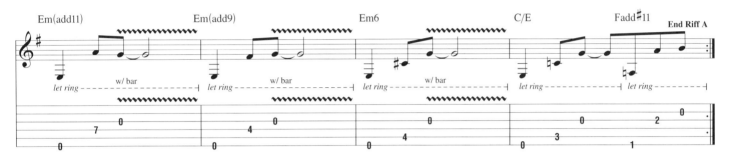

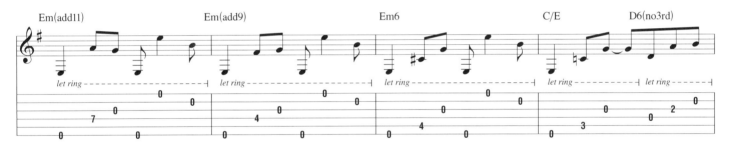

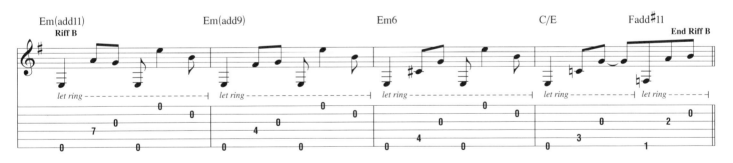

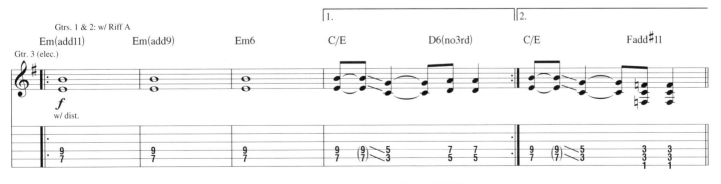

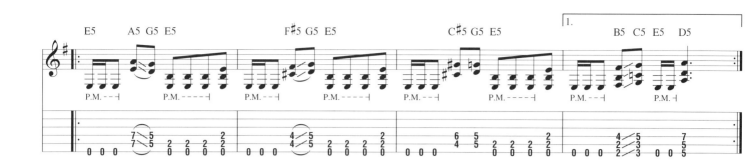

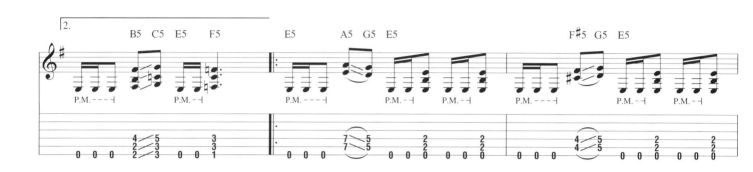

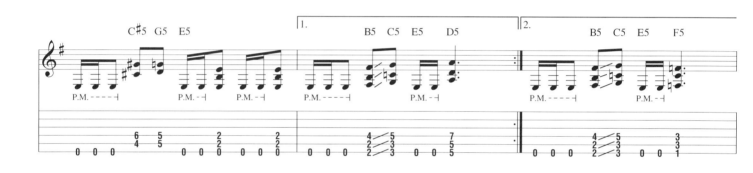

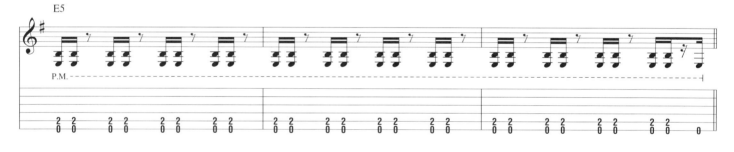

Verse

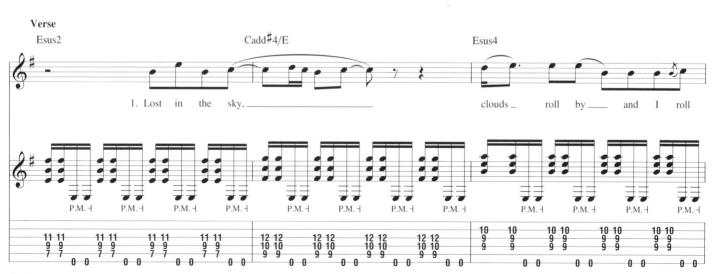

1. Lost in the sky, _____ clouds _ roll by ____ and I roll

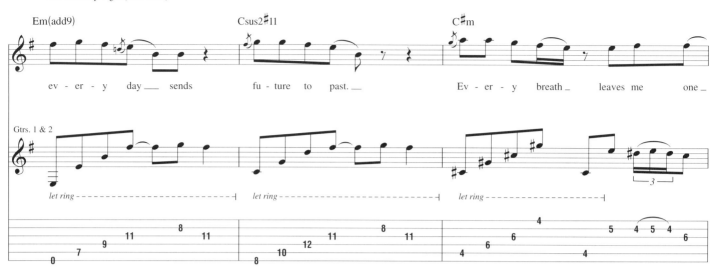

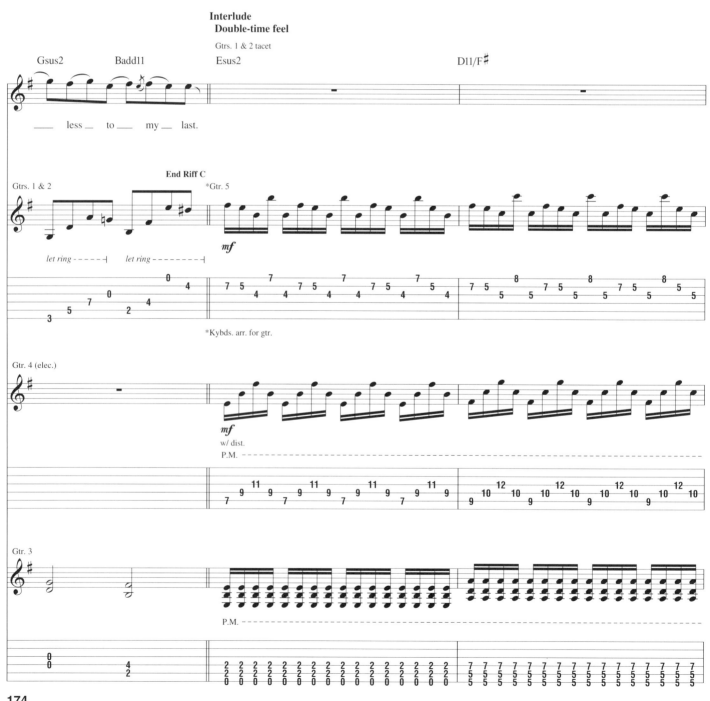

174

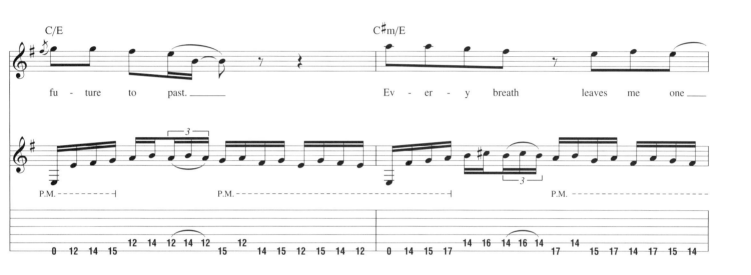

Interlude

End quadruple-time feel

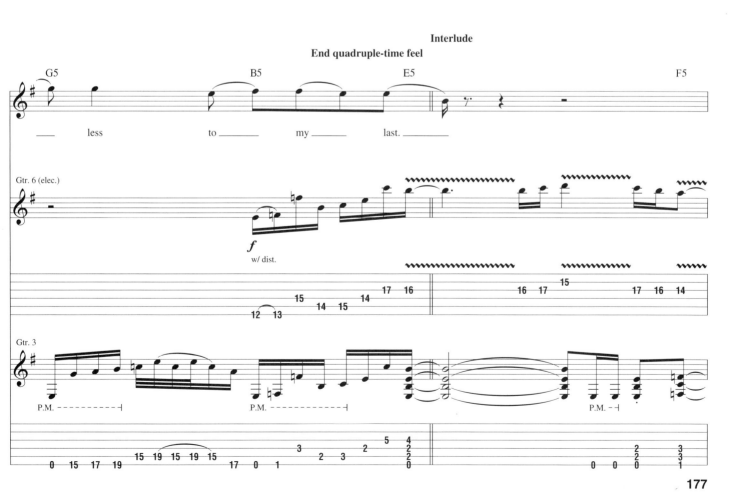

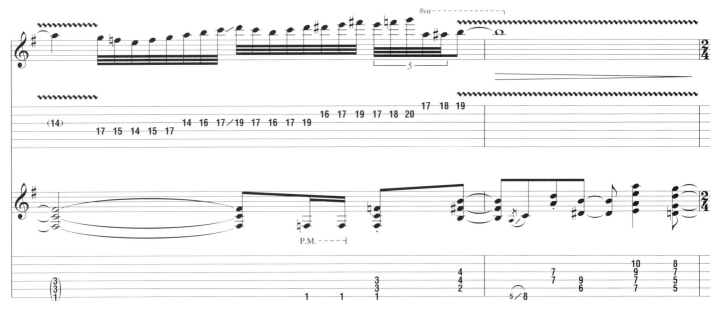

Gtr. 6 tacet

Gtr. 3   Csus2   N.C.

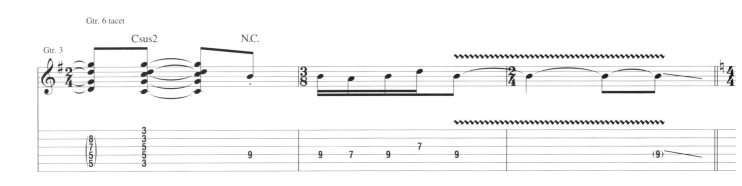

Chorus

Am(add11)   Am9   Am6

Pull   me   un-   der,   pull   me   un-   der.   Pull   me   un-   der,   I'm   not

Rhy. Fig. 2

Gtrs. 1 & 2

let ring   w/ bar   let ring   w/ bar   let ring   w/ bar

Rhy. Fig. 2A

Gtr. 3

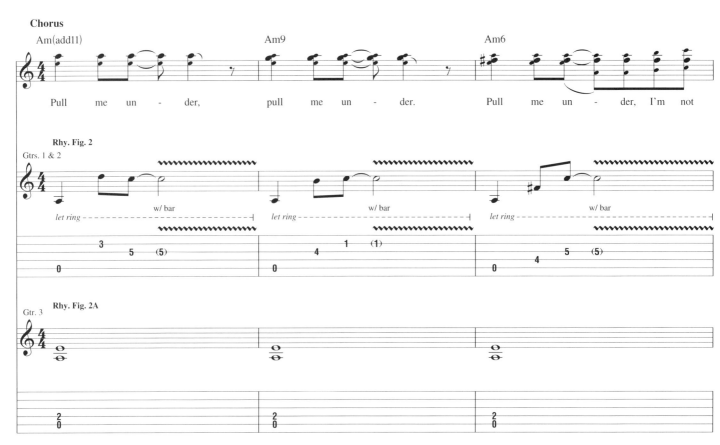

A5 Fsus2/C Gsus2/D Am(add11) G/B Cmaj7(no3rd)
a - fraid. All that I feel is hon - or and spite.
End Rhy. Fig. 2
let ring
w/ bar
End Rhy. Fig. 2A
let ring
Interlude
Gtrs. 1 & 2 tacet
D7 E5 F5 Fsus2 B♭sus2 D5 E5
All I can do is to set it right.
let ring
P.M.
Gtr. 3
D5 E5 D5 E5 D5 E5
P.M.
P.M.
P.M.

Verse

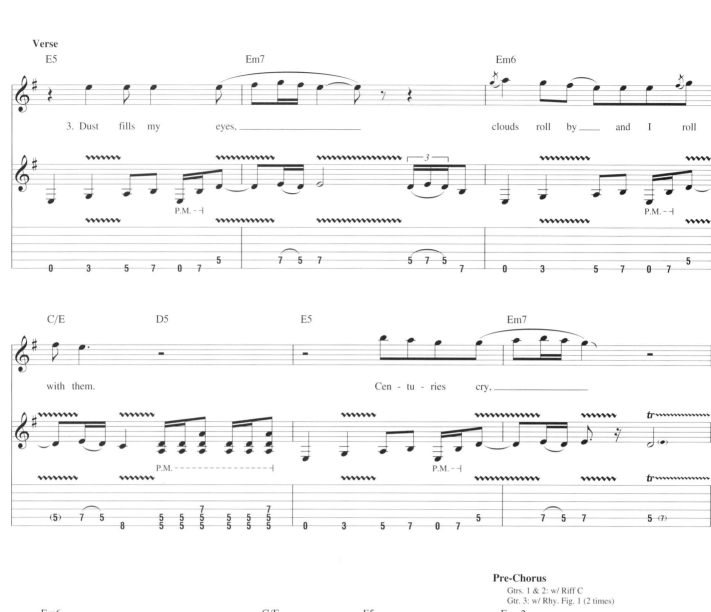

3. Dust fills my eyes, _____ clouds roll by ___ and I roll with them.

Cen-tu-ries cry, _____

Pre-Chorus

Gtrs. 1 & 2: w/ Riff C
Gtr. 3: w/ Rhy. Fig. 1 (2 times)

or-ders fly ___ and I fall a-gain. This world _ is

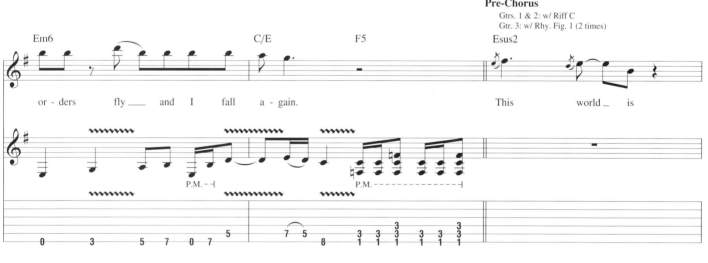

spin-ning in-side ___ me. The whole _ world _ is spin-ning in-side of me.

Ev-er-y day ___ sends fu-ture to past. _ Ev-er-y step brings me clos - er ___ to _ my _ last.

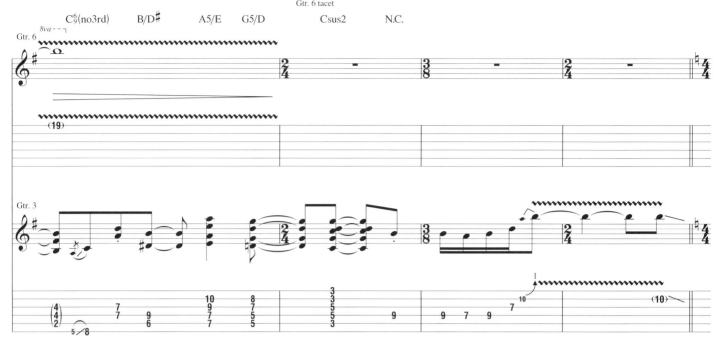

Chorus

Gtrs. 1 & 2: w/ Rhy. Fig. 2
Gtr. 3: w/ Rhy. Fig. 2A

Pull me un - der, pull me un - der. Pull me un - der, I'm not a - fraid.

Liv - ing my life __ too much in the sun __ on - ly un - til __ your will is done. __

Keyboard Solo

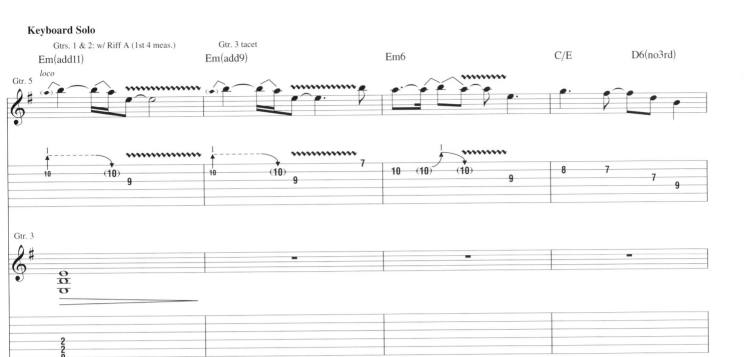

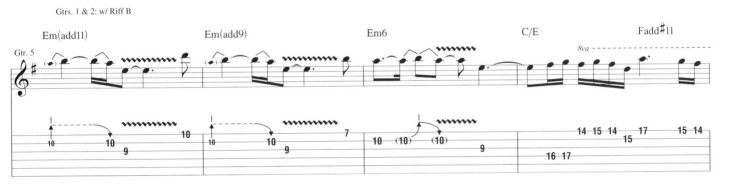

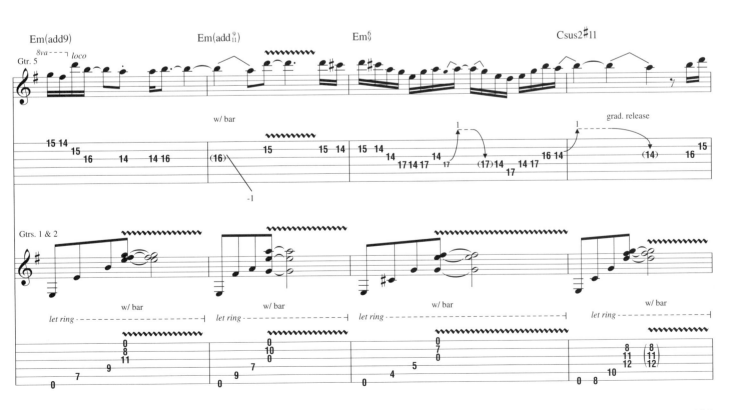

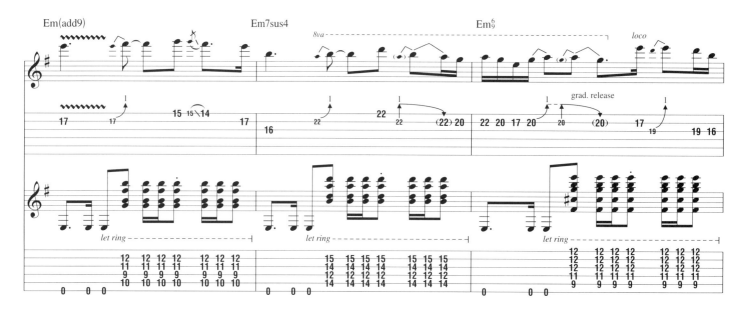

Guitar Solo

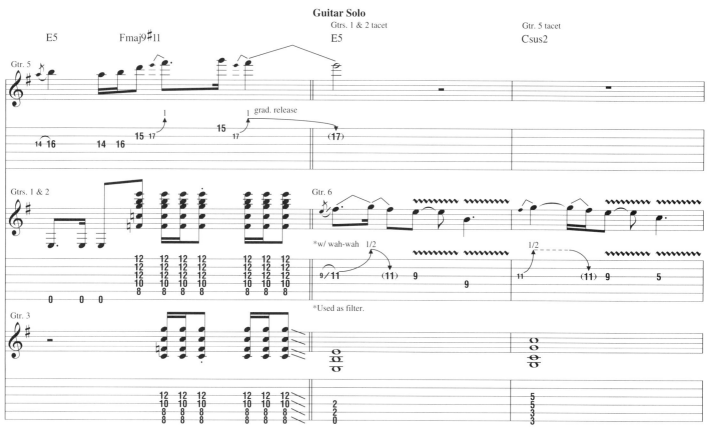

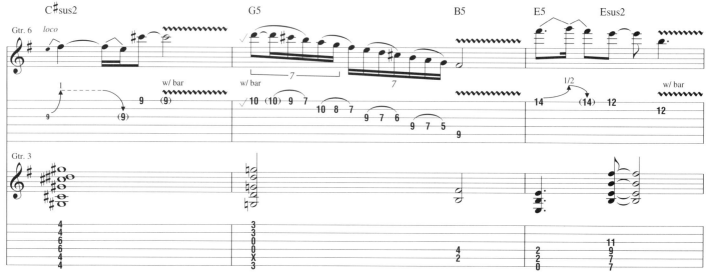

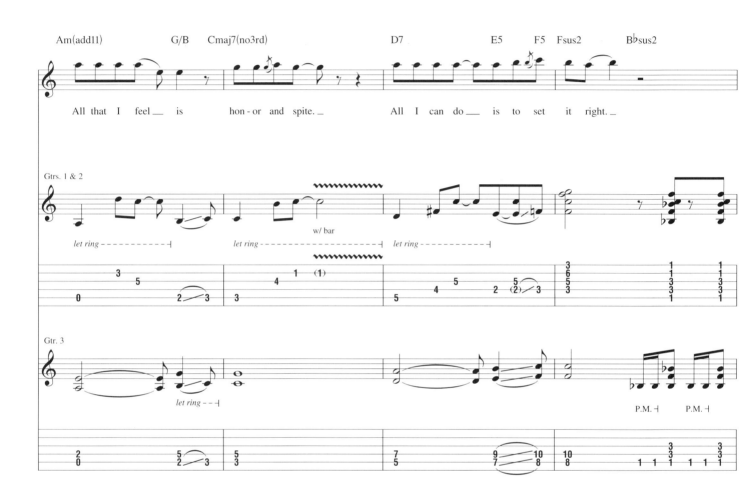

from Slayer - *Reign in Blood*

Raining Blood

Words and Music by Jeff Hanneman and Kerry King

Tune down 1/2 step:
(low to high) E♭-A♭-D♭-G♭-B♭-E♭

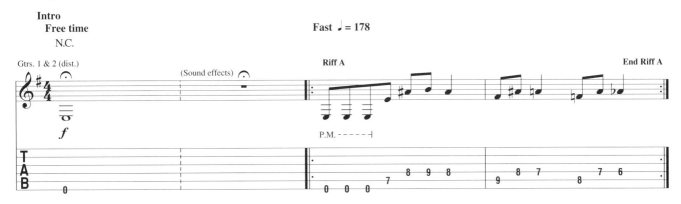

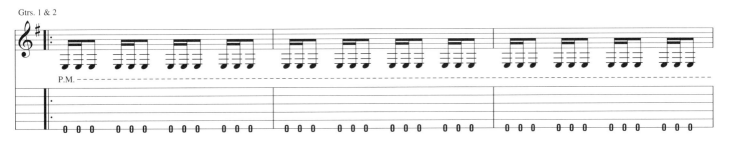

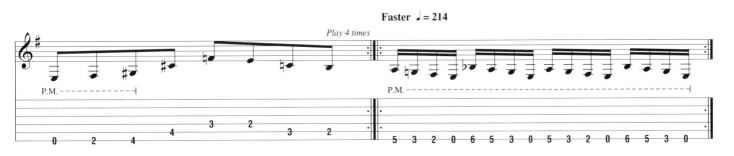

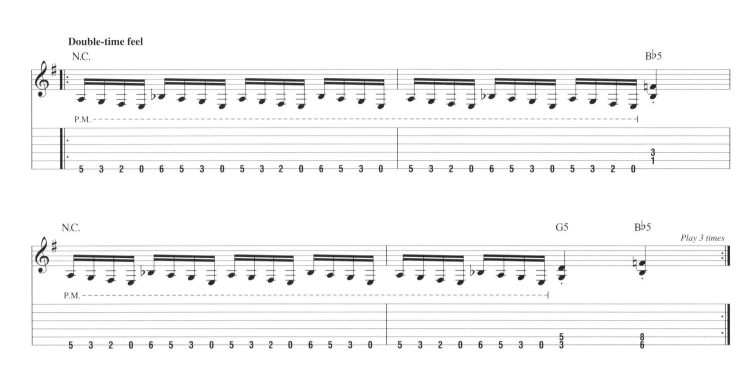

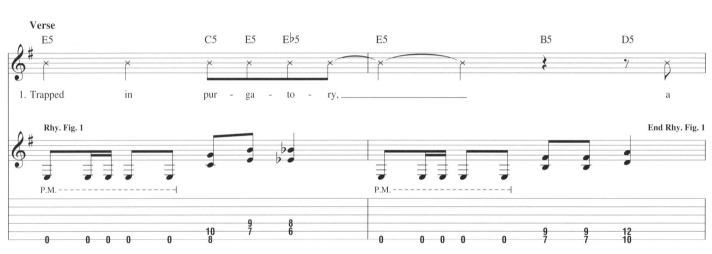

Verse

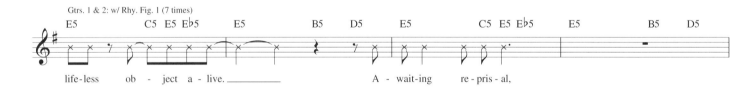

1. Trapped in pur - ga - to - ry, _____ a life-less ob - ject a - live. _____ A - wait-ing re - pris - al,

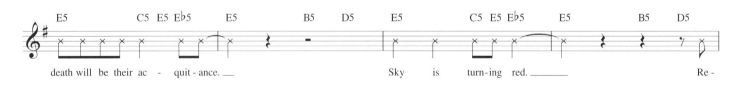

death will be their ac - quit - ance. ___ Sky is turn-ing red. ___ Re -

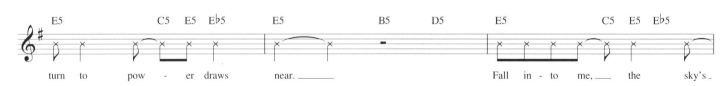

turn to pow - er draws near. ___ Fall in - to me, ___ the sky's _

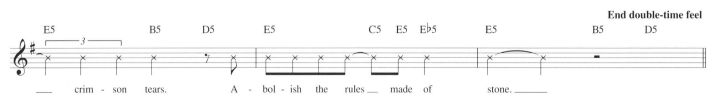

___ crim - son tears. A - bol - ish the rules _ made of stone. ___

Interlude
Slower ♩ = 188

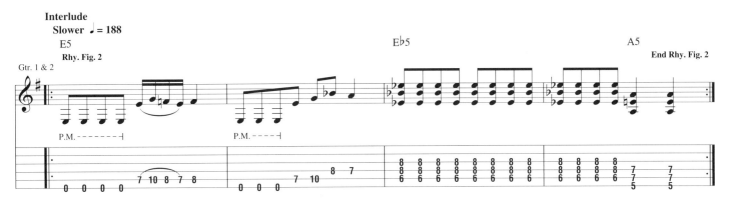

Verse

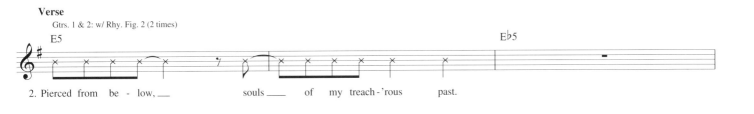

2. Pierced from be - low, ___ souls ___ of my treach - 'rous past.

Be - trayed by man - y now, or - na - ments drip - ping a - bove. __

Bridge
Gtrs. 1 & 2: w/ Riff A (2 times)

Half-time feel
Gtr. 1: w/ Riff A (2 times)

A - wait - ing the hour of re - pris - al, your time _____

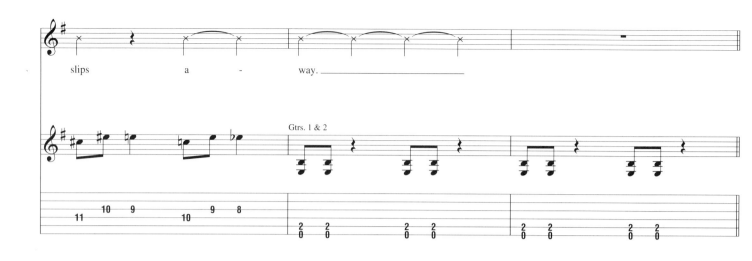

slips a - way.

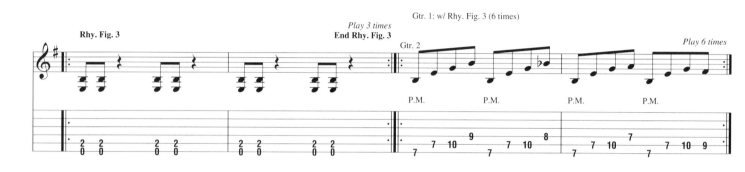

Chorus

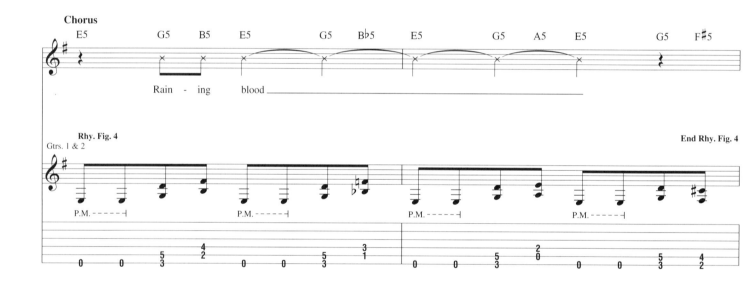

Rain - ing blood

from a lac - er - at - ed sky.

Bleed - ing its hor - ror.

Cre - at - ing my struc - ture, now I shall reign in

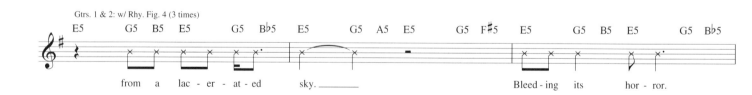

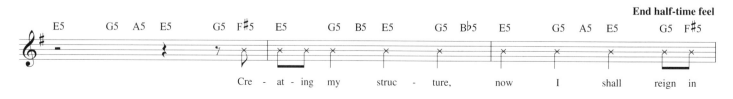

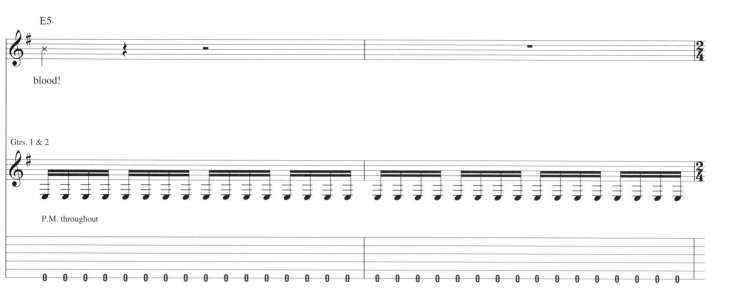

blood!

Gtrs. 1 & 2

P.M. throughout

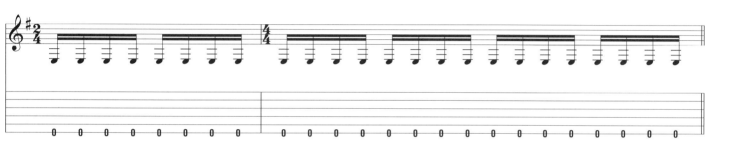

Outro
Faster ♩ = 247
Double-time feel

*Gtrs. 3 & 4 (dist.): w/ misc. whammy bar effects

Gtr. 2

Play 4 times

Gtr. 1

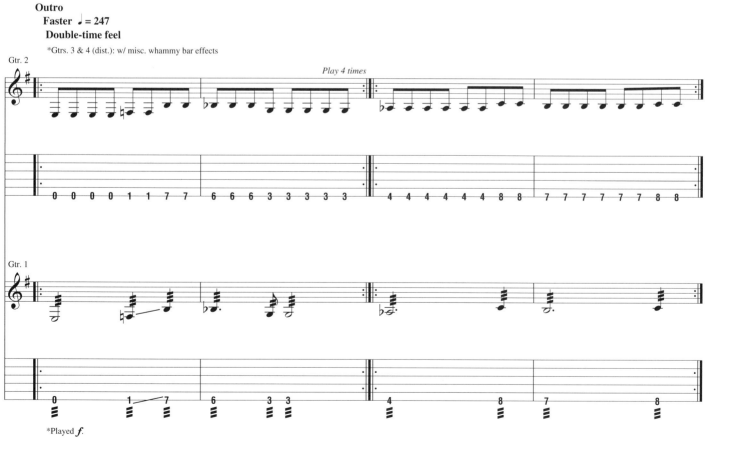

*Played *f*.

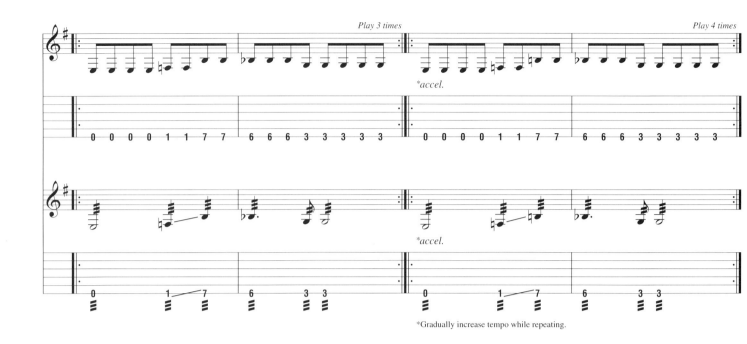

*accel.

*accel.

*Gradually increase tempo while repeating.

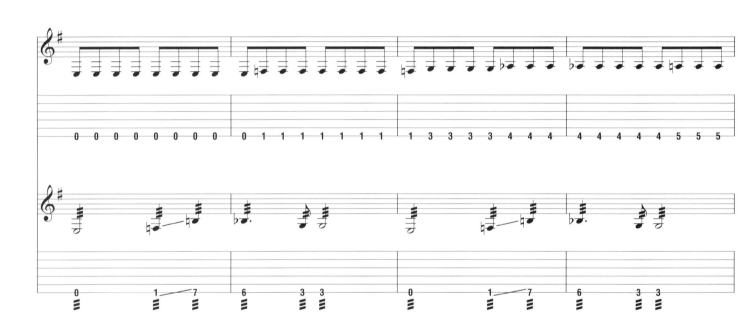

Gtrs. 1-4 tacet
w/ misc. sound effects

from Sepultura - *Roots*

Roots Bloody Roots

Words and Music by Andreas R. Kisser, Igor Cavalera, Paulo Xisto Pinto Jr. and Max Cavalera

Tune down 2 1/2 steps:
(low to high) B-E-A-D-F♯-B

Intro
Moderately ♩ = 124

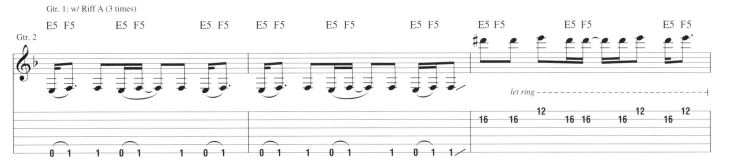

*Chord symbols reflect implied harmony.

Gtr. 1: w/ Riff A (3 times)

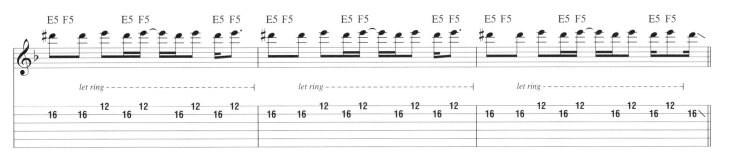

Chorus

Gtrs. 1 & 2: w/ Rhy. Fig. 1 (3 times)

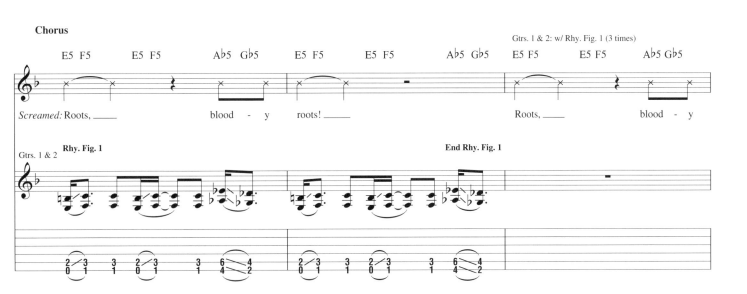

Screamed: Roots,____ blood - y roots!____ Roots,____ blood - y

roots! _____ Roots, _____ blood - y roots! _____

Interlude
Gtrs. 1 & 2: w/ Riff A (2 times)

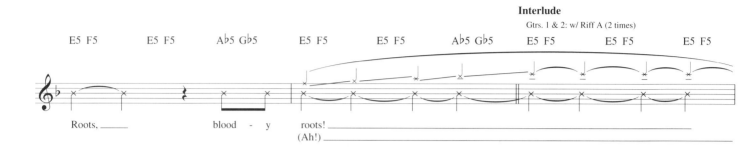

Roots, _____ blood - y roots! _____
(Ah!) _____

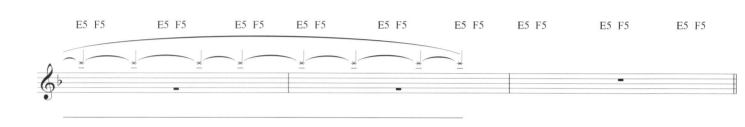

𝄋 Verse
Gtrs. 1 & 2: w/ Riff A (1 1/2 times)

1. I be - lieve in our fate. We don't need to fake. It's all we wan - na
4. Pray we don't need to change our ways to be saved. That's all we wan - na

be. Watch me freak! _____
be. Watch us freak! _____

Why ___ can't_ you see? Can't you feel this is real? Ah! ___

Interlude

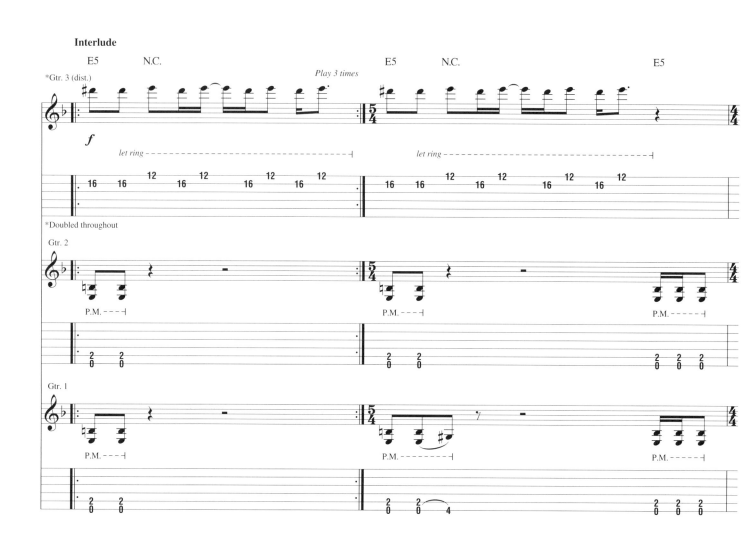

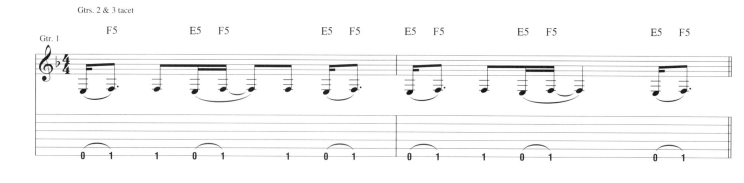

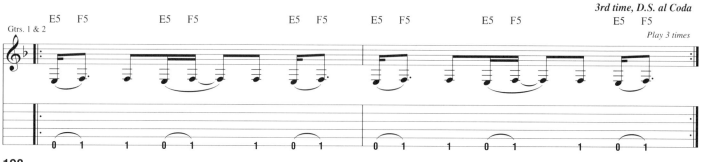

⊕ Coda

Guitar Solo

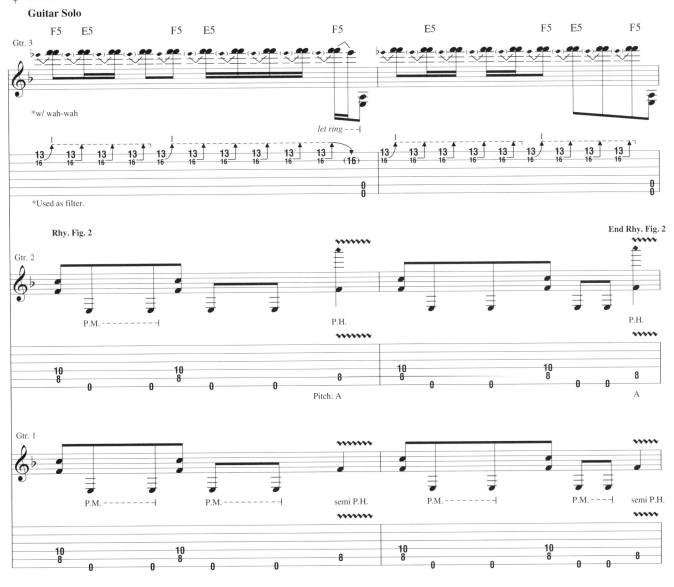

*w/ wah-wah

*Used as filter.

199

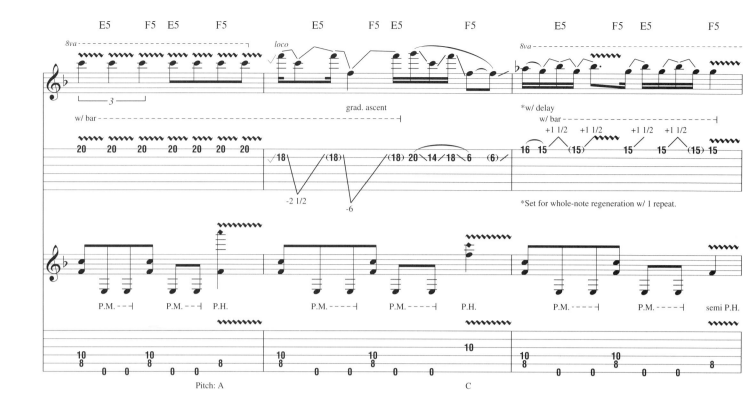

Interlude
Half-time feel

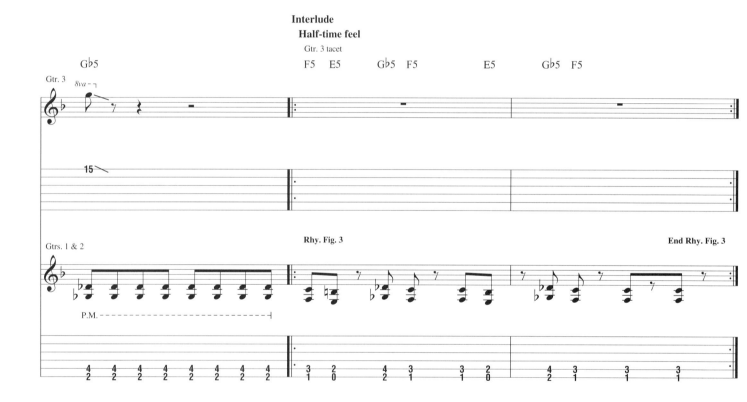

End half-time feel

from Tool - *Undertow*

Sober

Words and Music by Maynard James Keenan, Adam Jones, Daniel Carey and Paul D'Amour

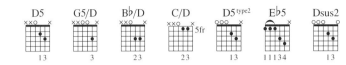

Drop D tuning:
(low to high) D-A-D-G-B-E

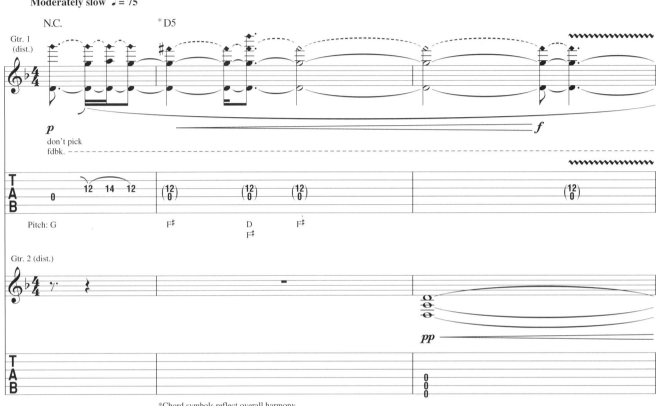

*Chord symbols reflect overall harmony.

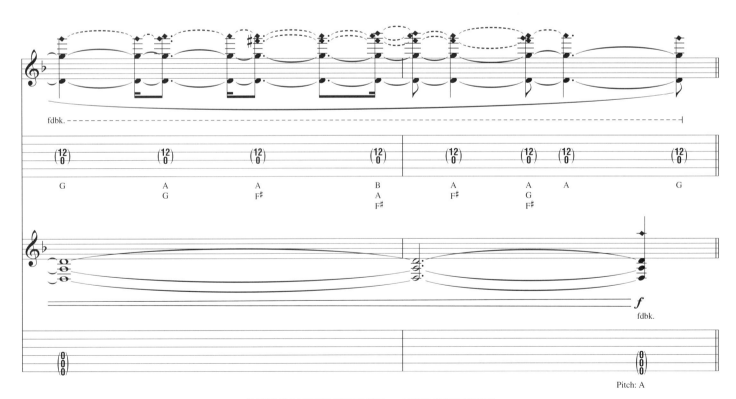

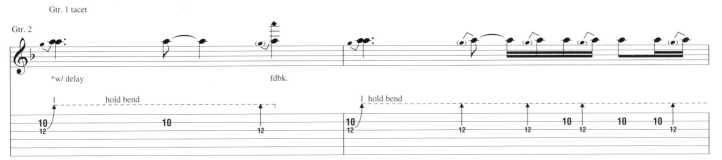

Gtr. 1 tacet

Gtr. 2

*w/ delay   fdbk.

*Set for eighth-note regeneration w/ 4 repeats.

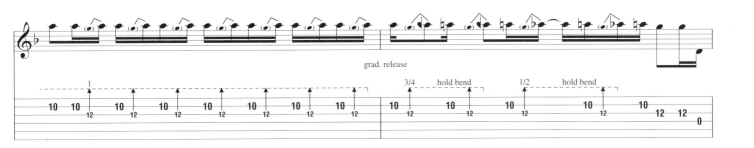

grad. release

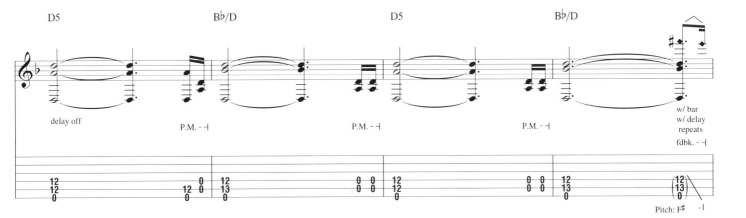

delay off   w/ bar
                                                  w/ delay
                        P.M. -| P.M. -| P.M. -| repeats
                                                                          fdbk. -|

                                                          Pitch: F#

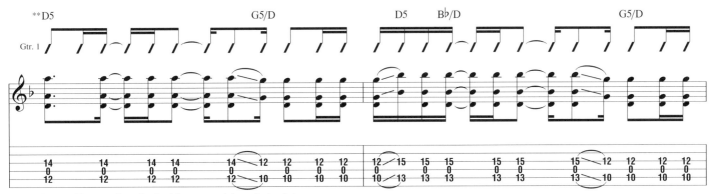

**D5   G5/D   D5   Bb/D   G5/D

Gtr. 1

**See top of first page of song for chord diagrams pertaining to rhythm slashes.

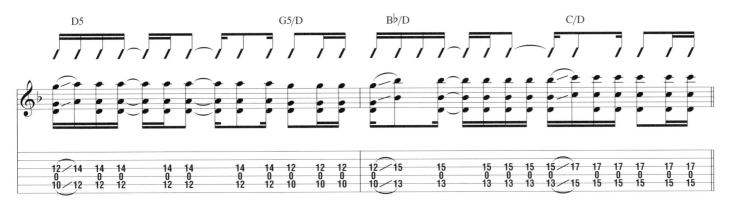

D5   G5/D   Bb/D   C/D

203

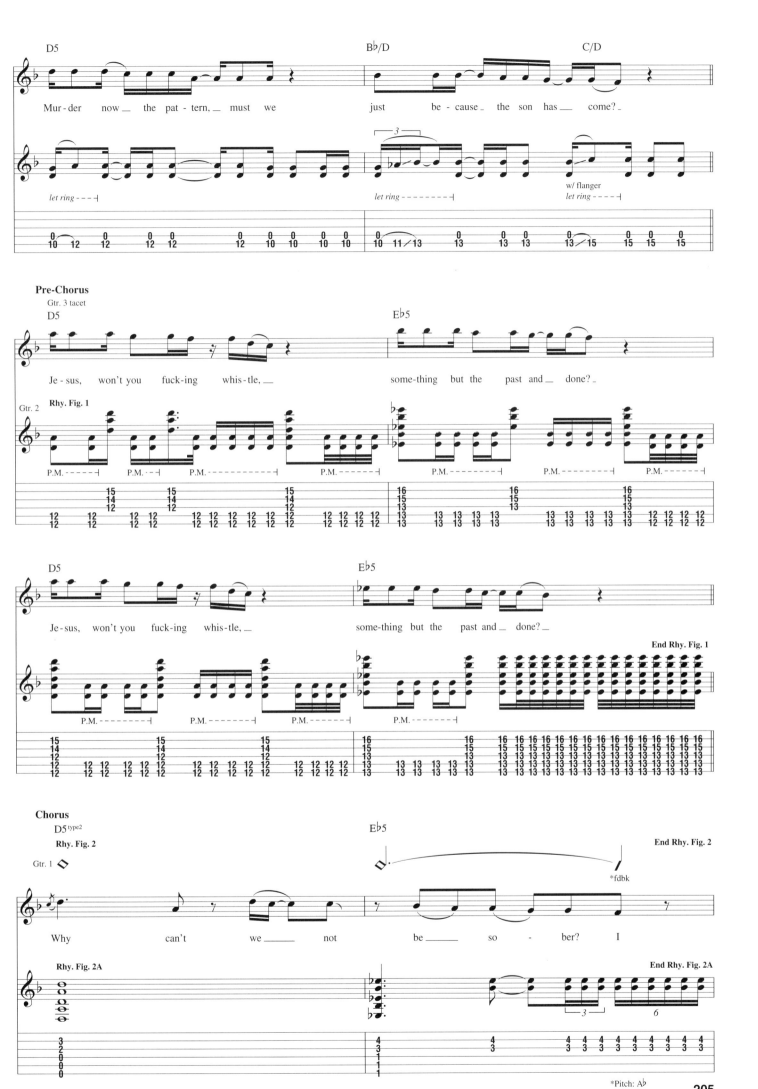

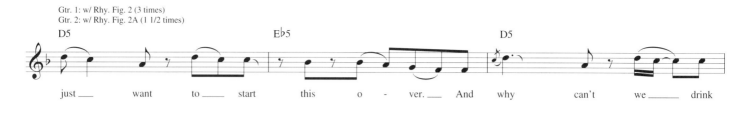

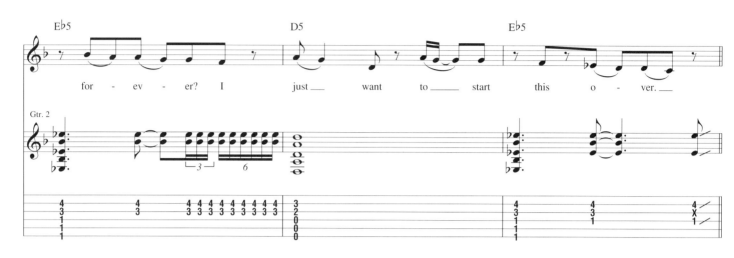

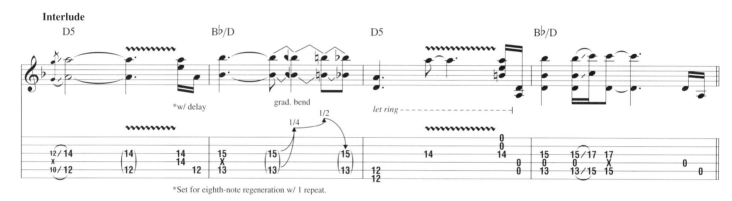

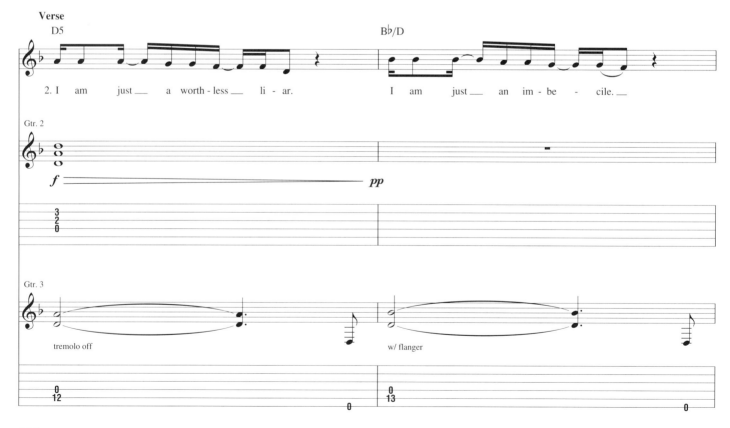

206

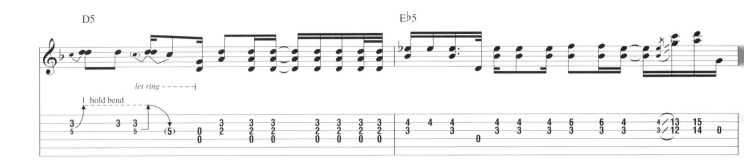

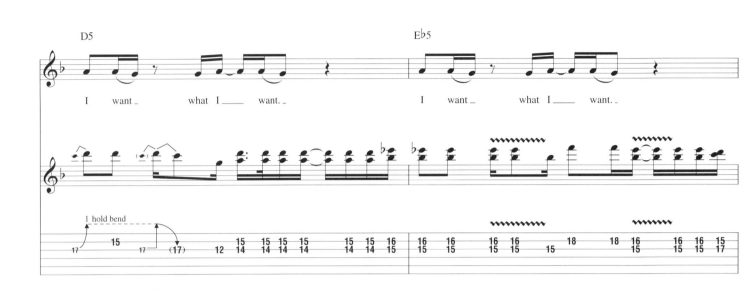

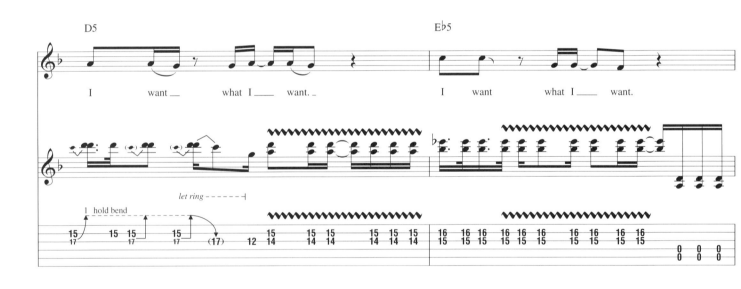

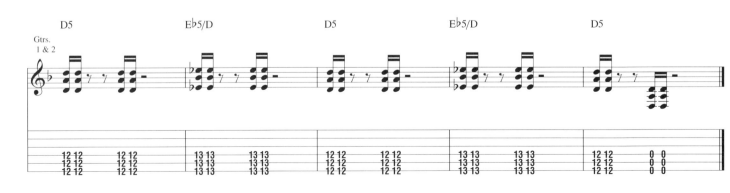

Tears Don't Fall

Words and Music by Matthew Tuck, Jason James, Michael Paget and Michael Thomas

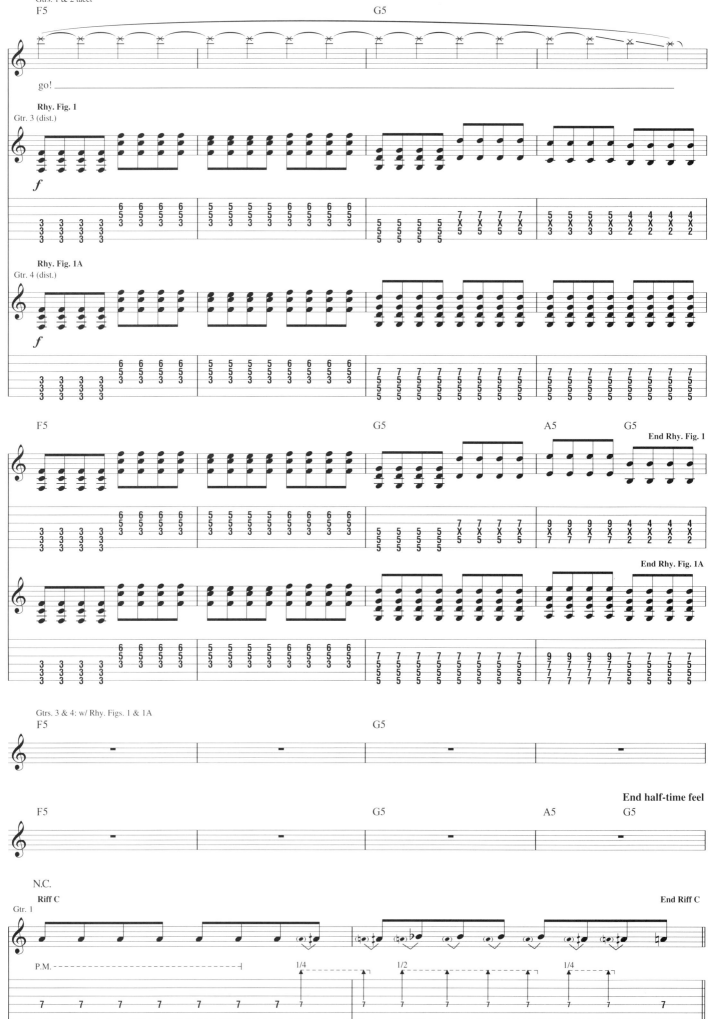

213

Pre-Chorus

Screamed: There's al - ways some - thin' dif - f'rent go - in' wrong. _____

The path I walk's in the wrong di - rec - tion.

There's al - ways some - one f**k - in' hang - in' on. _____

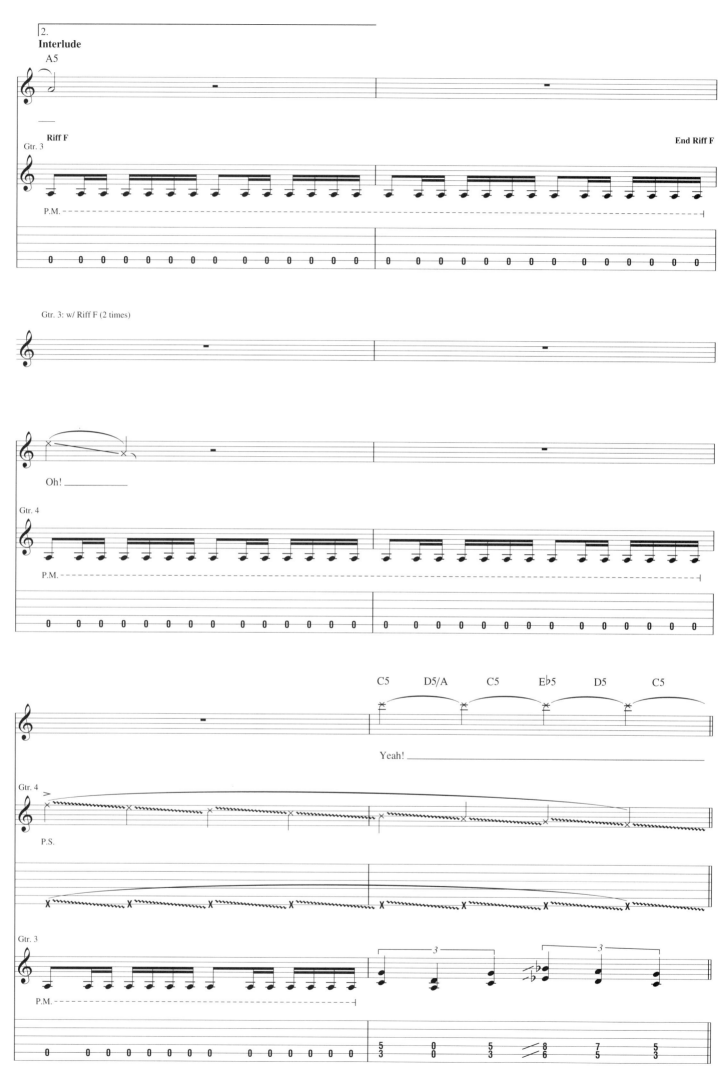

Bridge

This bat-tered room ___ I've seen ___ be - fore. ___

The bro - ken bones, ___ they heal ___ no more, ___ no more. ___

With my ___ last breath, ___ I'm chok - in'. ___ Will this ev - er end? ___

Gtrs. 3 & 4

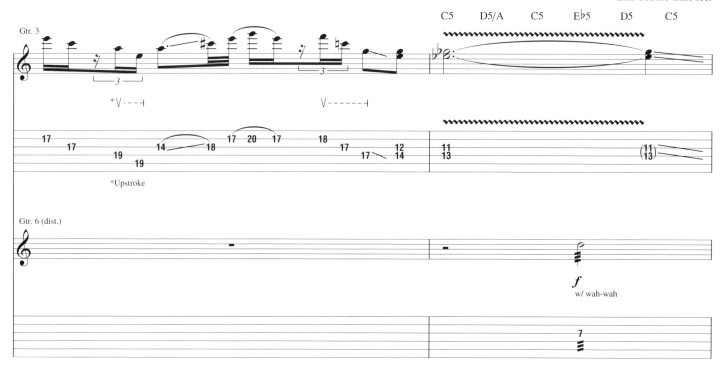

*Upstroke

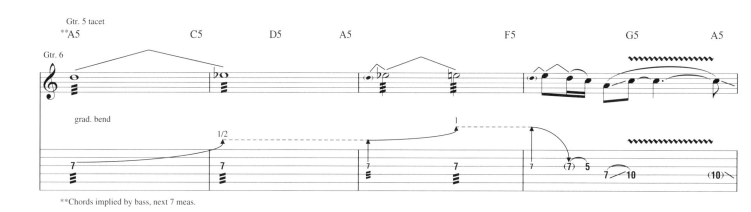

**Chords implied by bass, next 7 meas.

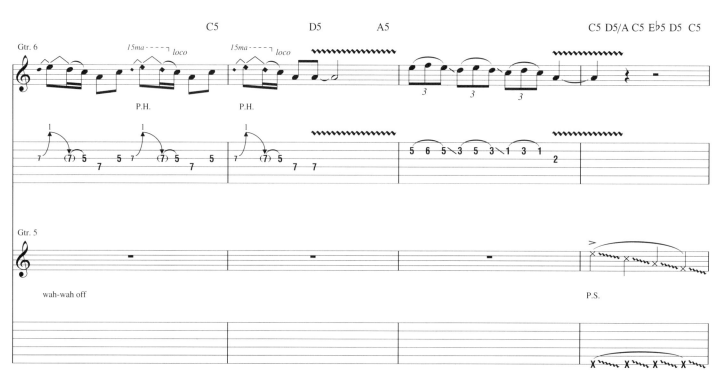

Thunder Kiss '65

Words and Music by Rob Zombie, Sean Reynolds, Ivan de Prume and Jay Yuenger

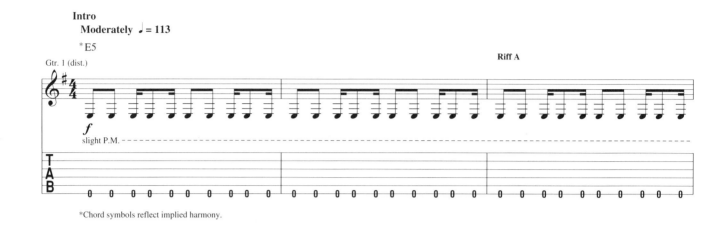

*Chord symbols reflect implied harmony.

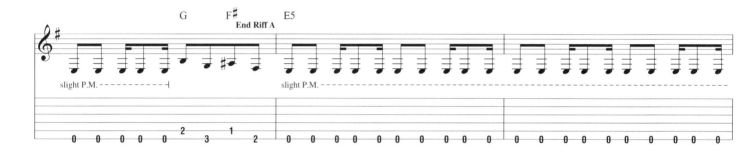

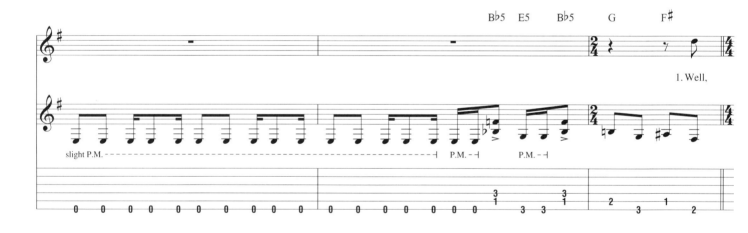

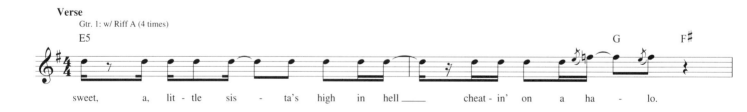

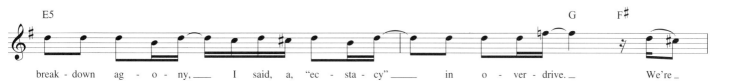

break - down ag - o - ny,___ I said, a, "ec - sta - cy"___ in o - ver - drive.__ We're _

rid - in' on the world __ thun - der kiss - in' _____ nine - teen six - ty -

Chorus

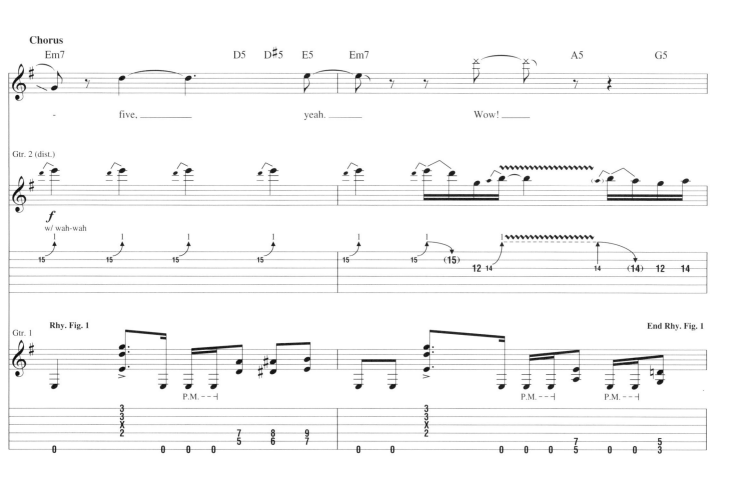

\- five, _____ yeah. _____ Wow! ____

Gtr. 2 (dist.)

Gtr. 1

Gtr. 1: w/ Rhy. Fig. 1 (3 times)

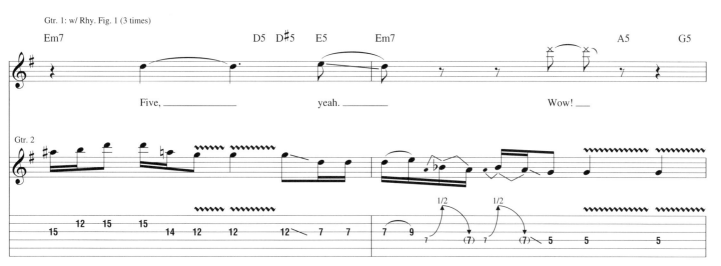

Five, _____ yeah. _____ Wow! __

Gtr. 2

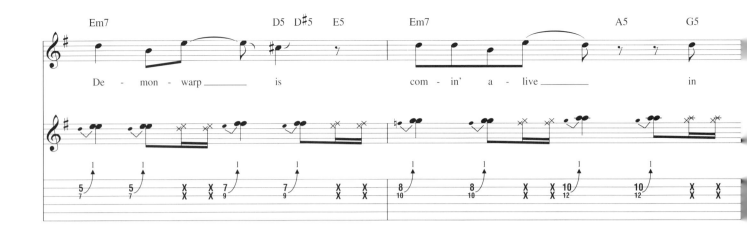

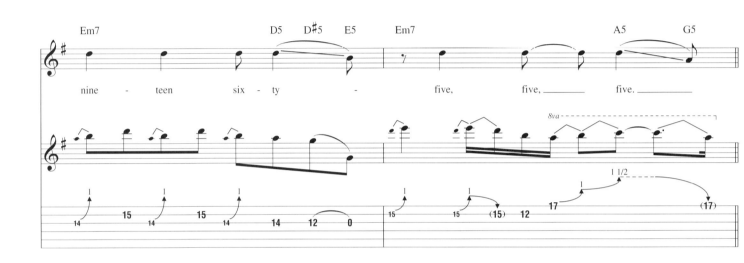

Verse
Gtr. 1: w/ Riff A (4 times)
Gtr. 2 tacet

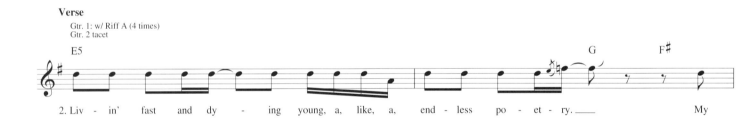

2. Liv - in' fast and dy - ing young, a, like, a, end - less po - et - ry. _____ My

mo - tor - psy - cho night - mare freak _____ out _____ in - side of me. _____ My

soul sal - va - tion lib - er - a - tion on the drive. _____ The

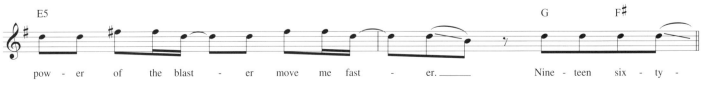

pow - er of the blast - er move me fast - er. _____ Nine - teen six - ty -

Chorus

Bridge

rollin' like a su - per - son - ic, an - oth - er fool that gets ___ down on ___ it.

Pig sweat a mil - lion miles. ___ I got a heart a - tom - ic style.

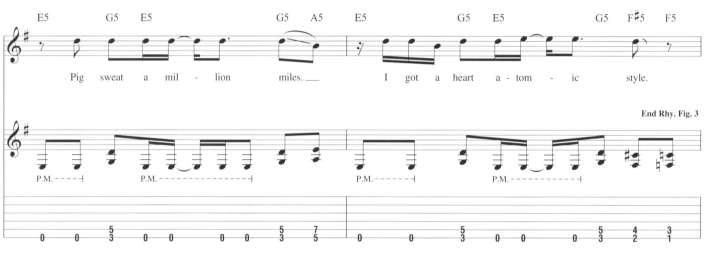

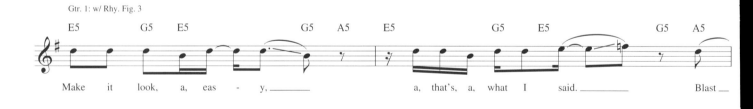

Make it look, a, eas - y, ___ a, that's, a, what I said. ___ Blast ___

Guitar Solo

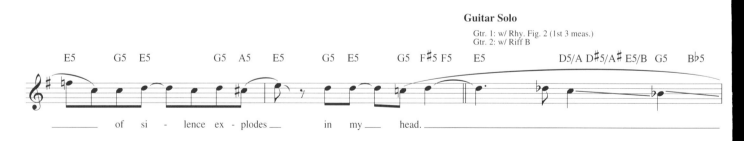

___ of si - lence ex - plodes ___ in my ___ head. ___

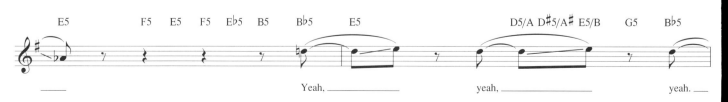

___ Yeah, ___ yeah, ___ yeah.

new, pus - sy - cat? ___ Can you dig ___ the sat - is - fac - tion? Well,

you can't take it with ___ you, but you can ___ in o - ver - drive. ___ Yeah,

some like it hot, ___ yeah, twist - in', nine - teen six - ty -

Chorus
Gtr. 1: w/ Rhy. Fig. 1 (4 times)

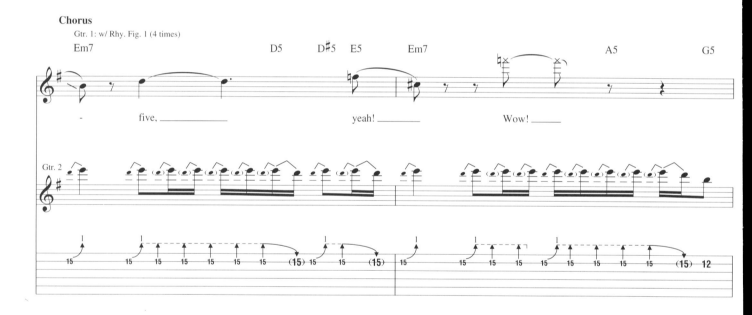

- five, ___ yeah! ___ Wow! ___

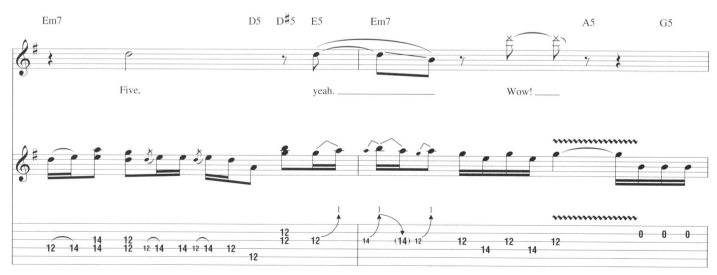

Five, yeah. ___ Wow! ___

232

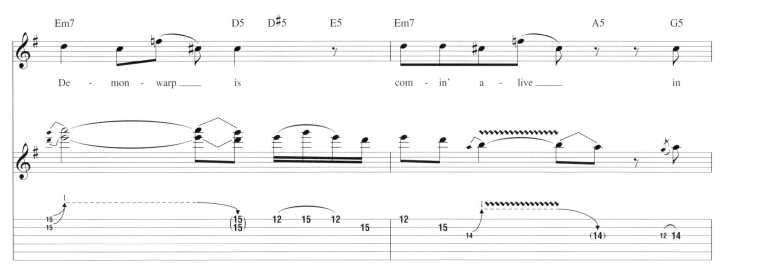

De - mon - warp ___ is com - in' a - live ___ in

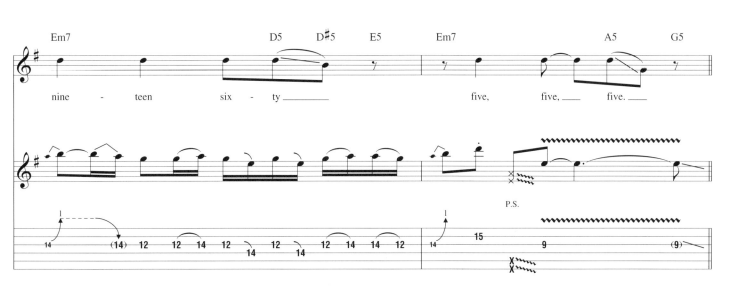

nine - teen six - ty ___ five, five, ___ five. ___

Outro

Gtr. 1: w/ Rhy. Fig. 4 (2 times)

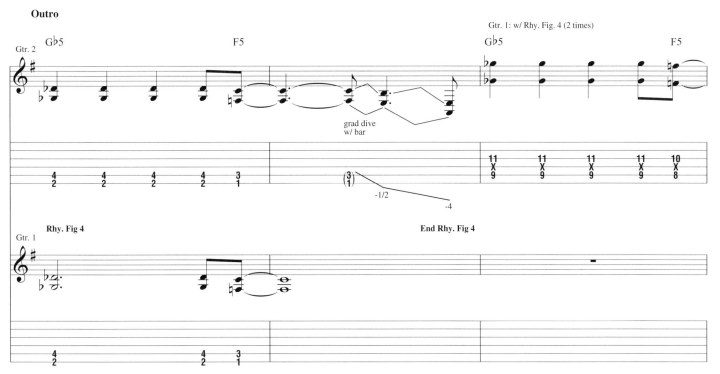

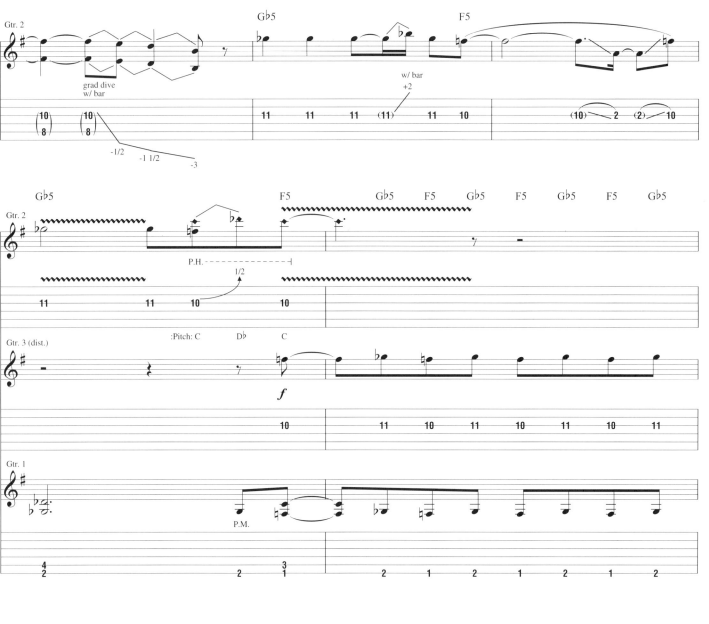

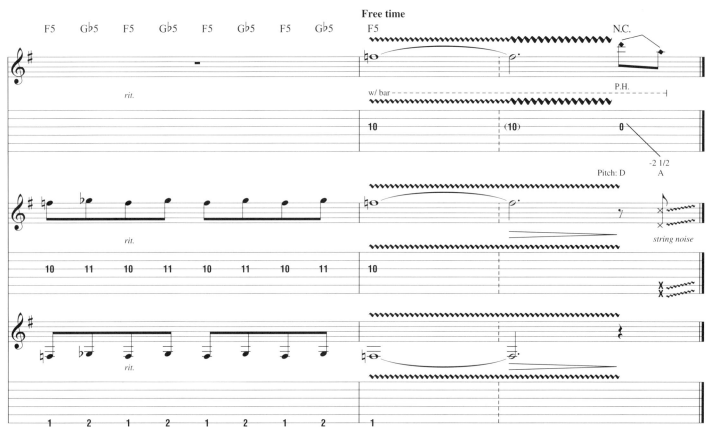

The Trooper

Words and Music by Steven Harris

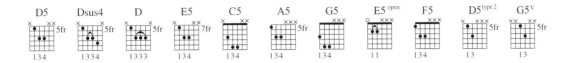

*Chord symbols reflect overall harmony.

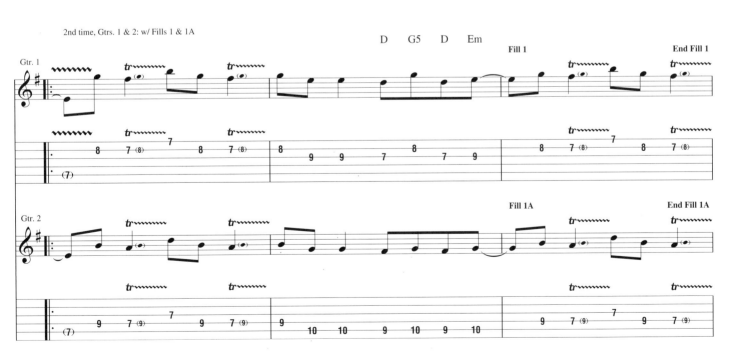

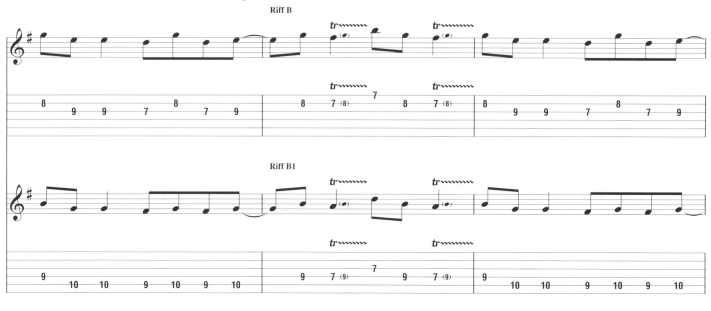

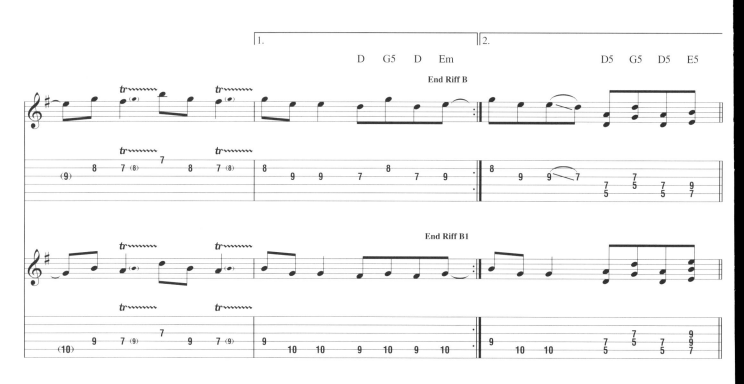

% Verse

2nd & 3rd times, Gtrs. 1 & 2: w/ Rhy. Fig. 1 (1 1/3 times)

1. You'll take my life   but I'll take yours   too. ____   You'll fire your mus - ket but I'll
2. The horse, he sweats with fear; we break to run. ____   The might - y roar of the
3. We got so close, near e - nough to fight. ____   When a Rus - sian gets me

Gtrs. 1 & 2

as I plunge on in - to cer - tain death.
We won't live ___ to fight an - oth - er day.
with - out a tear I draw my part - ing ___ groan. ___

Oh. ___

P.M.

(Gtr. 2, cont. in slashes)

*w/ slow flanger,
next 7 meas.

Chorus

2nd & 3rd times, Gtr. 2: w/ Rhy. Fill 1

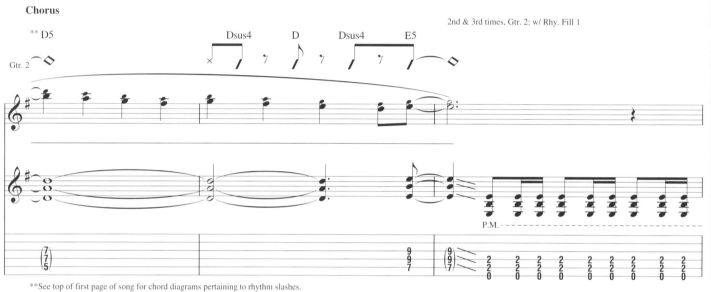

**See top of first page of song for chord diagrams pertaining to rhythm slashes.

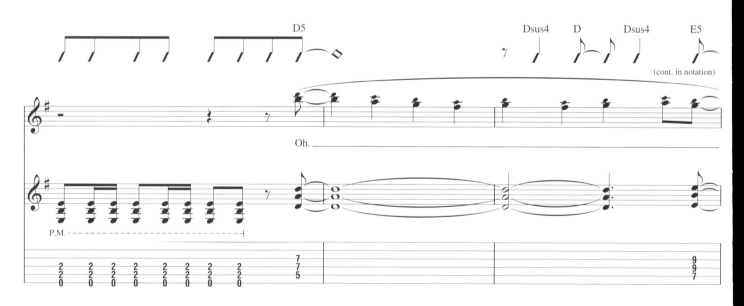

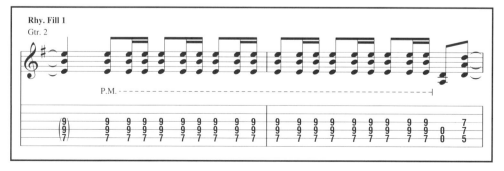

Guitar Solo

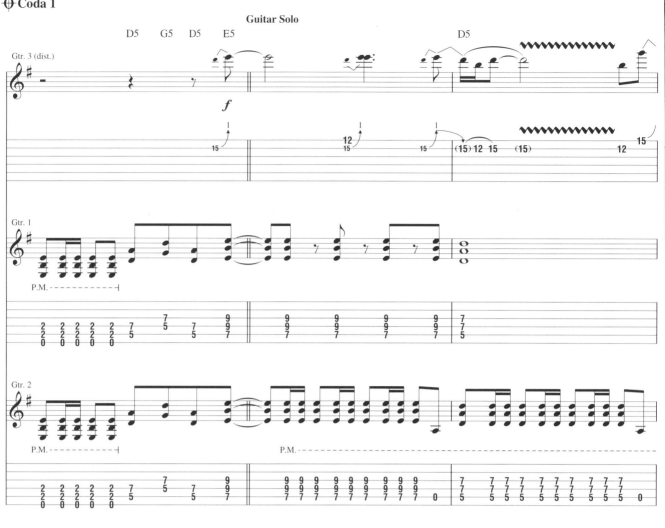

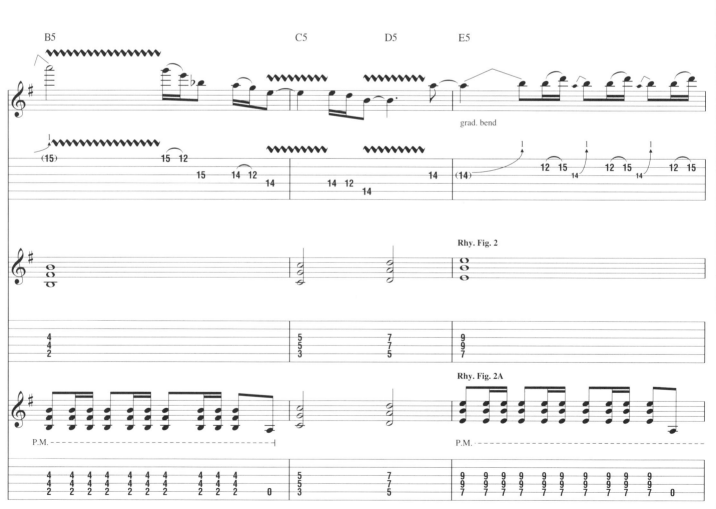

Unsung

Words and Music by Page Hamilton

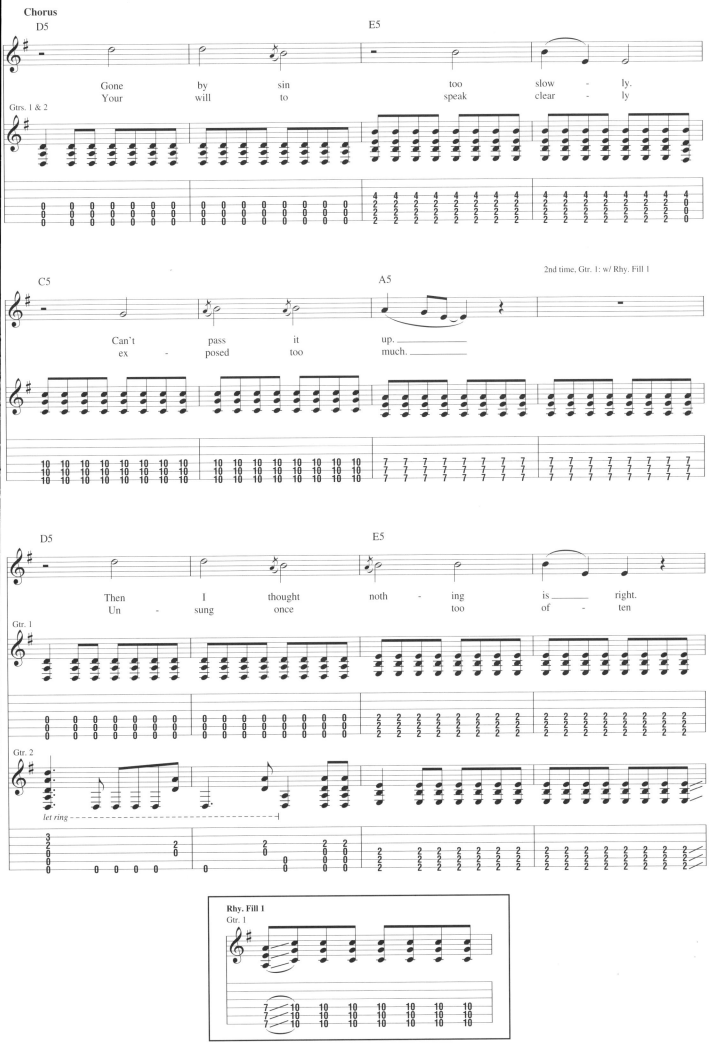

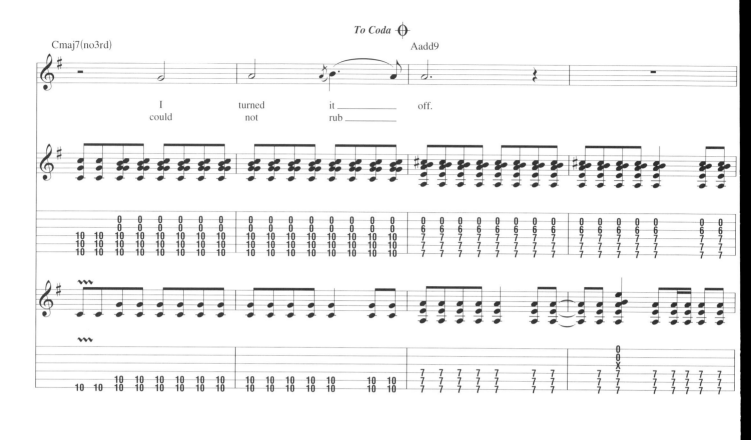

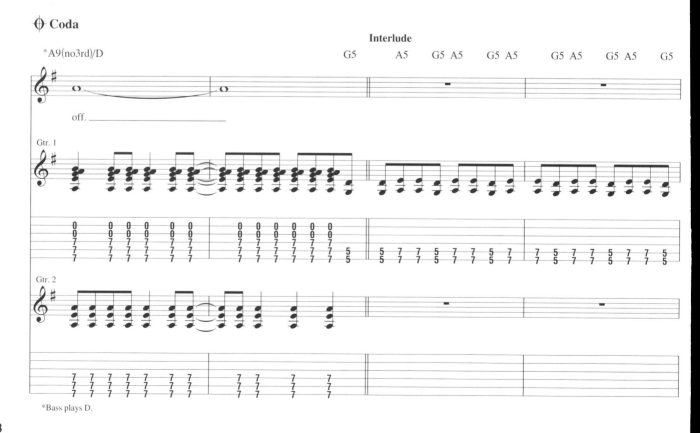

*Bass plays D.

248

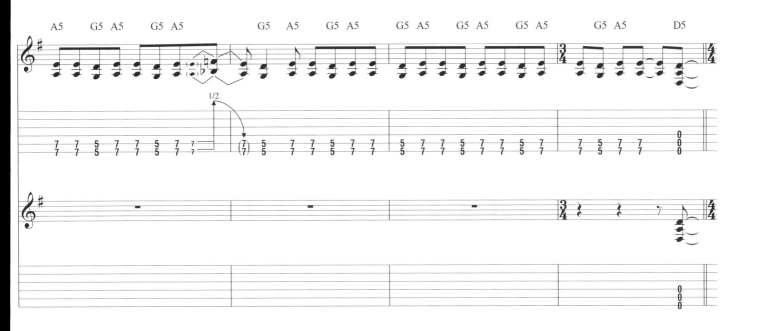

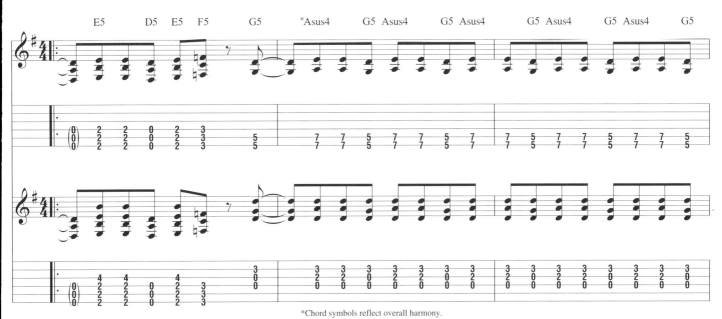

*Chord symbols reflect overall harmony.

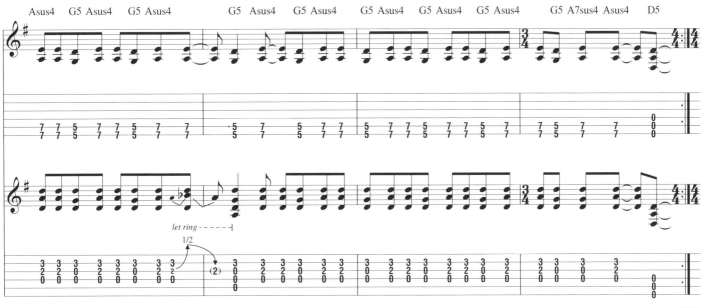

Outro

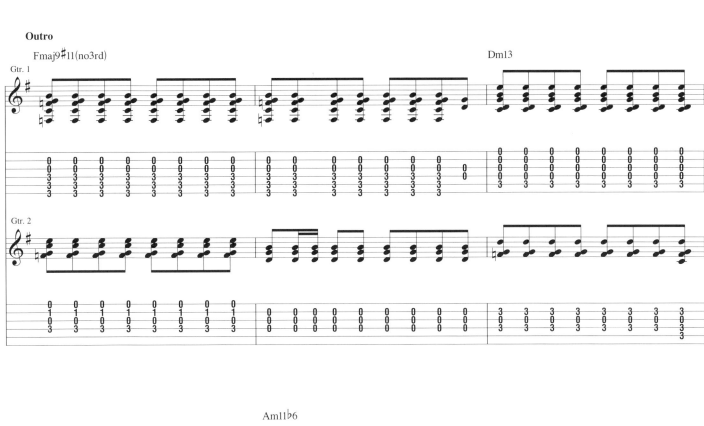

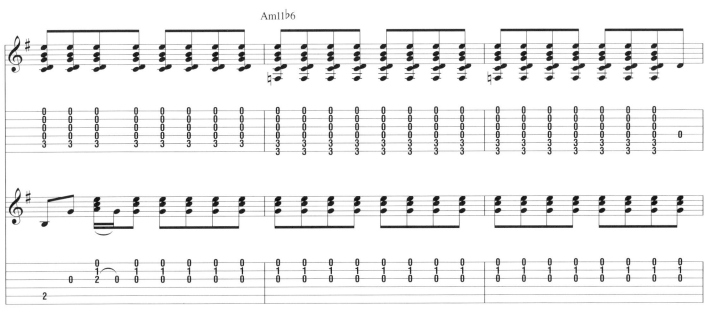

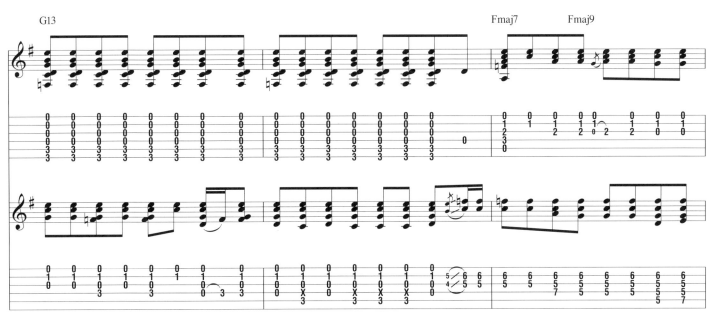

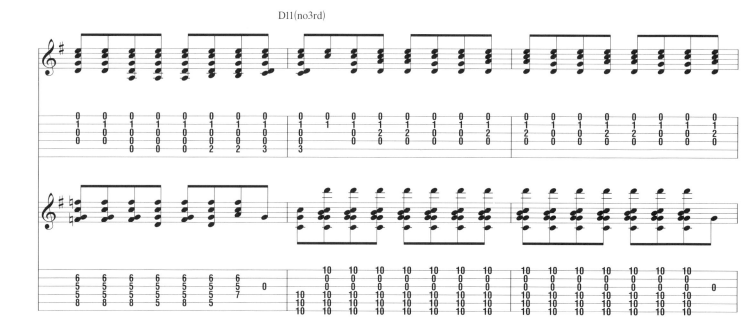

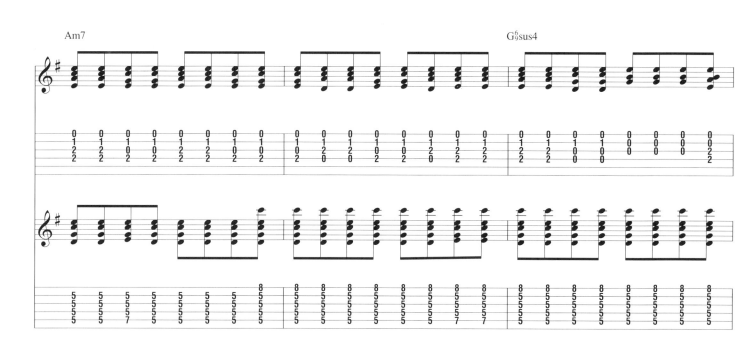

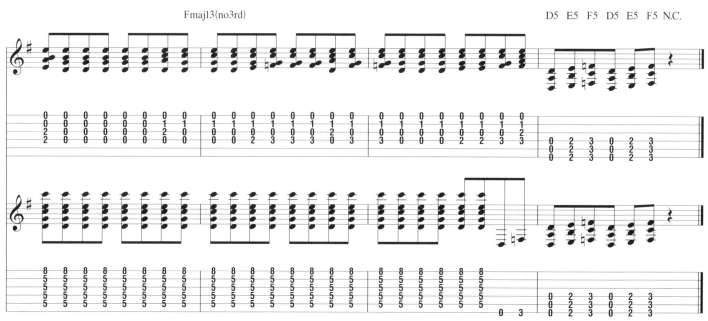

GUITAR NOTATION LEGEND

Guitar music can be notated three different ways: on a *musical staff*, in *tablature*, and in *rhythm slashes*.

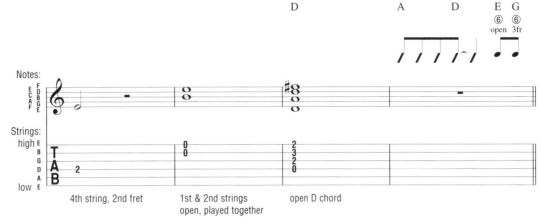

RHYTHM SLASHES are written above the staff. Strum chords in the rhythm indicated. Use the chord diagrams found at the top of the first page of the transcription for the appropriate chord voicings. Round noteheads indicate single notes.

THE MUSICAL STAFF shows pitches and rhythms and is divided by bar lines into measures. Pitches are named after the first seven letters of the alphabet.

TABLATURE graphically represents the guitar fingerboard. Each horizontal line represents a string, and each number represents a fret.

4th string, 2nd fret

1st & 2nd strings open, played together

open D chord

Definitions for Special Guitar Notation

HALF-STEP BEND: Strike the note and bend up 1/2 step.

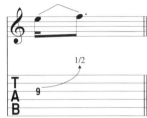

WHOLE-STEP BEND: Strike the note and bend up one step.

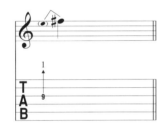

GRACE NOTE BEND: Strike the note and immediately bend up as indicated.

SLIGHT (MICROTONE) BEND: Strike the note and bend up 1/4 step.

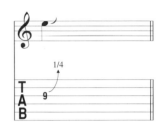

BEND AND RELEASE: Strike the note and bend up as indicated, then release back to the original note. Only the first note is struck.

PRE-BEND: Bend the note as indicated, then strike it.

PRE-BEND AND RELEASE: Bend the note as indicated. Strike it and release the bend back to the original note.

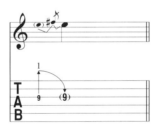

UNISON BEND: Strike the two notes simultaneously and bend the lower note up to the pitch of the higher.

VIBRATO: The string is vibrated by rapidly bending and releasing the note with the fretting hand.

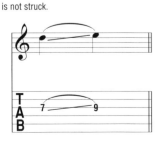

WIDE VIBRATO: The pitch is varied to a greater degree by vibrating with the fretting hand.

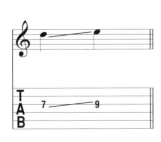

HAMMER-ON: Strike the first (lower) note with one finger, then sound the higher note (on the same string) with another finger by fretting it without picking.

PULL-OFF: Place both fingers on the notes to be sounded. Strike the first note and without picking, pull the finger off to sound the second (lower) note.

LEGATO SLIDE: Strike the first note and then slide the same fret-hand finger up or down to the second note. The second note is not struck.

SHIFT SLIDE: Same as legato slide, except the second note is struck.

TRILL: Very rapidly alternate between the notes indicated by continuously hammering on and pulling off.

TAPPING: Hammer ("tap") the fret indicated with the pick-hand index or middle finger and pull off to the note fretted by the fret hand.

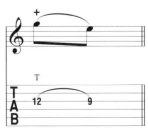

NATURAL HARMONIC: Strike the note while the fret-hand lightly touches the string directly over the fret indicated.

PINCH HARMONIC: The note is fretted normally and a harmonic is produced by adding the edge of the thumb or the tip of the index finger of the pick hand to the normal pick attack.

HARP HARMONIC: The note is fretted normally and a harmonic is produced by gently resting the pick hand's index finger directly above the indicated fret (in parentheses) while the pick hand's thumb or pick assists by plucking the appropriate string.

PICK SCRAPE: The edge of the pick is rubbed down (or up) the string, producing a scratchy sound.

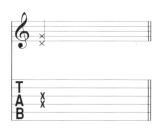

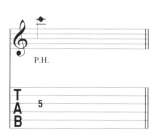

MUFFLED STRINGS: A percussive sound is produced by laying the fret hand across the string(s) without depressing, and striking them with the pick hand.

PALM MUTING: The note is partially muted by the pick hand lightly touching the string(s) just before the bridge.

RAKE: Drag the pick across the strings indicated with a single motion.

TREMOLO PICKING: The note is picked as rapidly and continuously as possible.

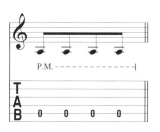

ARPEGGIATE: Play the notes of the chord indicated by quickly rolling them from bottom to top.

VIBRATO BAR DIVE AND RETURN: The pitch of the note or chord is dropped a specified number of steps (in rhythm), then returned to the original pitch.

VIBRATO BAR SCOOP: Depress the bar just before striking the note, then quickly release the bar.

VIBRATO BAR DIP: Strike the note and then immediately drop a specified number of steps, then release back to the original pitch.

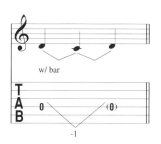

Additional Musical Definitions

(accent)	• Accentuate note (play it louder).
(accent)	• Accentuate note with great intensity.
(staccato)	• Play the note short.
⊓	• Downstroke
V	• Upstroke
D.S. al Coda	• Go back to the sign (%), then play until the measure marked "***To Coda***," then skip to the section labelled "**Coda**."
D.C. al Fine	• Go back to the beginning of the song and play until the measure marked "***Fine***" (end).

Rhy. Fig.	• Label used to recall a recurring accompaniment pattern (usually chordal).
Riff	• Label used to recall composed, melodic lines (usually single notes) which recur.
Fill	• Label used to identify a brief melodic figure which is to be inserted into the arrangement.
Rhy. Fill	• A chordal version of a Fill.
tacet	• Instrument is silent (drops out).
	• Repeat measures between signs.
	• When a repeated section has different endings, play the first ending only the first time and the second ending only the second time.

NOTE: Tablature numbers in parentheses mean:
1. The note is being sustained over a system (note in standard notation is tied), or
2. The note is sustained, but a new articulation (such as a hammer-on, pull-off, slide or vibrato) begins, or
3. The note is a barely audible "ghost" note (note in standard notation is also in parentheses).

GUITAR RECORDED VERSIONS®

RECORDED VERSIONS GUITAR®

HENTIC TRANSCRIPTIONS
H NOTES AND TABLATURE

Guitar Recorded Versions® are note-for-note transcriptions of guitar music taken directly off recordings This series, one of the most popular in print today, features some of the greatest guitar players and groups from blues and rock to country and jazz.

*Guitar Recorded Versions are transcribed by the best transcribers in the business Every book contains notes and tablature. Visit **www.halleonard.com** for our complete selection.*

1344	The Definitive AC/DC Songbook	$39.99
0016	The Will Ackerman Collection	$19.95
0501	Bryan Adams – Greatest Hits	$19.95
0002	Aerosmith – Big Ones	$24.95
2015	Aerosmith – Greatest Hits	$22.95
0603	Aerosmith – O Yeah! (Ultimate Hits)	$24.95
0147	Aerosmith – Rocks	$19.95
0146	Aerosmith – Toys in the Attic	$19.99
0178	Alice in Chains – Acoustic	$19.95
4865	Alice in Chains – Dirt	$19.95
0225	Alice in Chains – Facelift	$19.95
4925	Alice in Chains – Jar of Flies/Sap	$19.95
0387	Alice in Chains – Nothing Safe: Best of the Box	$19.95
0899	All That Remains – The Fall of Ideals	$22.99
1056	All That Remains – For We Are Many	$22.99
0980	All That Remains – Overcome	$22.99
0812	All-American Rejects – Move Along	$19.95
0983	All-American Rejects – When the World Comes Down	$22.99
4932	Allman Brothers Band – Definitive Collection for Guitar Volume 1	$24.95
4933	Allman Brothers Band – Definitive Collection for Guitar Volume 2	$24.95
4934	Allman Brothers Band – Definitive Collection for Guitar Volume 3	$24.95
0958	Duane Allman Guitar Anthology	$24.99
1071	Alter Bridge – AB III	$22.99
0945	Alter Bridge – Blackbird	$22.99
0755	Alter Bridge – One Day Remains	$22.99
0571	Trey Anastasio	$19.95
1013	The Answer – Everyday Demons	$19.99
0158	Chet Atkins – Almost Alone	$19.95
94876	Chet Atkins – Contemporary Styles	$19.95
4878	Chet Atkins – Vintage Fingerstyle	$19.95
0865	Atreyu – A Deathgrip on Yesterday	$19.95
0609	Audioslave	$19.95
0804	Audioslave – Out of Exile	$19.95
90884	Audioslave – Revelations	$19.95
0926	Avenged Sevenfold	$22.95
0820	Avenged Sevenfold – City of Evil	$24.95
91065	Avenged Sevenfold – Waking the Fallen	$22.99
94918	Randy Bachman Collection	$22.95
90503	Beach Boys – Very Best of	$19.95
94929	Beatles: 1962-1966	$24.99
94930	Beatles: 1967-1970	$24.95
90489	Beatles – 1	$24.99
94880	Beatles – Abbey Road	$19.95
91066	Beatles – Beatles for Sale	$22.99
90110	Beatles – Book 1 (White Album)	$19.95
90111	Beatles – Book 2 (White Album)	$19.95
90902	Beatles – The Capitol Albums, Volume 1	$24.99
94832	Beatles – For Acoustic Guitar	$22.99
90137	Beatles – A Hard Day's Night	$16.95
91031	Beatles – Help!	$19.99
90482	Beatles – Let It Be	$17.95
91067	Beatles – Meet the Beatles!	$22.99
91068	Beatles – Please Please Me	$22.99
94891	Beatles – Revolver	$19.95
594914	Beatles – Rubber Soul	$22.99
594863	Beatles – Sgt. Pepper's Lonely Hearts Club Band	$22.99
10193	Beatles – Tomorrow Never Knows	$22.99
590383	Beatles – Yellow Submarine	$19.95
591044	Jeff Beck – Best of Beck	$24.99
590632	Beck – Sea Change	$19.95
591041	Jeff Beck – Truth	$19.99
594884	Best of George Benson	$19.95
592385	Chuck Berry	$19.95
590835	Billy Talent	$19.95
590879	Billy Talent II	$19.95
590149	Black Sabbath	$16.99
590901	Best of Black Sabbath	$19.95
591010	Black Sabbath – Heaven and Hell	$22.99
590148	Black Sabbath – Master of Reality	$16.99
590142	Black Sabbath – Paranoid	$16.99
592200	Black Sabbath – We Sold Our Soul for Rock 'N' Roll	$19.95
00690389	blink-182 – Enema of the State	$19.95
00690831	blink-182 – Greatest Hits	$19.95
00691179	blink-182 – Neighborhoods	$22.99
00690523	blink-182 – Take Off Your Pants and Jacket	$19.95
00690028	Blue Oyster Cult – Cult Classics	$19.95
00690008	Bon Jovi – Cross Road	$19.95
00691074	Bon Jovi – Greatest Hits	$22.99
00690913	Boston	$19.95
00690932	Boston – Don't Look Back	$19.99
00690829	Boston Guitar Collection	$19.99
00690491	Best of David Bowie	$19.95
00690583	Box Car Racer	$19.95
00691023	Breaking Benjamin – Dear Agony	$22.99
00690873	Breaking Benjamin – Phobia	$19.95
00690764	Breaking Benjamin – We Are Not Alone	$19.95
00690451	Jeff Buckley Collection	$24.95
00690957	Bullet for My Valentine – Scream Aim Fire	$22.99
00690678	Best of Kenny Burrell	$19.95
00691077	Cage the Elephant – Thank You, Happy Birthday	$22.99
00690564	The Calling – Camino Palmero	$19.95
00691159	The Cars – Complete Greatest Hits	$22.99
00690261	Carter Family Collection	$19.95
00691079	Best of Johnny Cash	$22.99
00690043	Best of Cheap Trick	$19.95
00690171	Chicago – The Definitive Guitar Collection	$22.95
00691004	Chickenfoot	$22.99
00691011	Chimaira Guitar Collection	$24.99
00690567	Charlie Christian – The Definitive Collection	$19.95
00101916	Eric Church – Chief	$22.99
00690590	Eric Clapton – Anthology	$29.95
00692391	Best of Eric Clapton – 2nd Edition	$22.95
00691055	Eric Clapton – Clapton	$22.99
00690936	Eric Clapton – Complete Clapton	$29.99
00690074	Eric Clapton – Cream of Clapton	$24.95
00690247	Eric Clapton – 461 Ocean Boulevard	$19.99
00690010	Eric Clapton – From the Cradle	$19.95
00690363	Eric Clapton – Just One Night	$24.99
00694873	Eric Clapton – Timepieces	$19.95
00694869	Eric Clapton – Unplugged	$22.95
00690415	Clapton Chronicles – Best of Eric Clapton	$18.95
00694896	John Mayall/Eric Clapton – Bluesbreakers	$19.95
00690162	Best of the Clash	$19.95
00690828	Coheed & Cambria – Good Apollo I'm Burning Star, IV, Vol. 1: From Fear Through the Eyes of Madness	$19.95
00690940	Coheed and Cambria – No World for Tomorrow	$19.95
00690494	Coldplay – Parachutes	$19.95
00690593	Coldplay – A Rush of Blood to the Head	$19.95
00690806	Coldplay – X & Y	$19.95
00690855	Best of Collective Soul	$19.95
00691091	The Best of Alice Cooper	$22.99
00694940	Counting Crows – August & Everything After	$19.95
00690405	Counting Crows – This Desert Life	$19.95
00694840	Cream – Disraeli Gears	$19.95
00690285	Cream – Those Were the Days	$17.95
00690819	Best of Creedence Clearwater Revival	$22.95
00690648	The Very Best of Jim Croce	$19.95
00690572	Steve Cropper – Soul Man	$19.95
00690613	Best of Crosby, Stills & Nash	$22.95
00690777	Crossfade	$19.95
00699521	The Cure – Greatest Hits	$24.95
00690637	Best of Dick Dale	$19.95
00690892	Daughtry	$19.95
00690822	Best of Alex De Grassi	$19.95
00690967	Death Cab for Cutie – Narrow Stairs	$22.99
00690289	Best of Deep Purple	$19.99
00690288	Deep Purple – Machine Head	$17.99
00690784	Best of Def Leppard	$19.95
00694831	Derek and the Dominos – Layla & Other Assorted Love Songs	$22.95
00692240	Bo Diddley – Guitar Solos by Fred Sokolow	$19.99
00690384	Best of Ani DiFranco	$19.95
00690322	Ani DiFranco – Little Plastic Castle	$19.95
00690380	Ani DiFranco – Up Up Up Up Up Up	$19.95
00690979	Best of Dinosaur Jr.	$19.99
00690833	Private Investigations – Best of Dire Straits and Mark Knopfler	$24.95
00695382	Very Best of Dire Straits – Sultans of Swing	$22.95
00690347	The Doors – Anthology	$22.95
00690348	The Doors – Essential Guitar Collection	$16.95
00690915	Dragonforce – Inhuman Rampage	$29.99
00690250	Best of Duane Eddy	$16.95
00690533	Electric Light Orchestra Guitar Collection	$19.95
00690909	Best of Tommy Emmanuel	$22.99
00690555	Best of Melissa Etheridge	$19.95
00690515	Extreme II – Pornograffitti	$19.95
00690982	Fall Out Boy – Folie à Deux	$22.99
00690810	Fall Out Boy – From Under the Cork Tree	$19.95
00691009	Five Finger Death Punch	$19.99
00690664	Best of Fleetwood Mac	$19.95
00690870	Flyleaf	$19.95
00690257	John Fogerty – Blue Moon Swamp	$19.95
00690931	Foo Fighters – Echoes, Silence, Patience & Grace	$19.95
00690808	Foo Fighters – In Your Honor	$19.95
00691115	Foo Fighters – Wasting Light	$22.99
00690805	Best of Robben Ford	$22.99
00690842	Best of Peter Frampton	$19.95
00690734	Franz Ferdinand	$19.95
00694920	Best of Free	$19.95
00694807	Danny Gatton – 88 Elmira St	$19.95
00690438	Genesis Guitar Anthology	$19.95
00690753	Best of Godsmack	$19.95
00120167	Godsmack	$19.95
00690338	Goo Goo Dolls – Dizzy Up the Girl	$19.95
00113073	Green Day – Uno	$21.99
00690927	Patty Griffin – Children Running Through	$19.95
00690591	Patty Griffin – Guitar Collection	$19.95
00690978	Guns N' Roses – Chinese Democracy	$24.99
00691027	Buddy Guy Anthology	$24.99
00694854	Buddy Guy – Damn Right, I've Got the Blues	$19.95
00690697	Best of Jim Hall	$19.95
00690840	Ben Harper – Both Sides of the Gun	$19.95
00691018	Ben Harper – Fight for Your Mind	$22.99
00690987	Ben Harper and Relentless7 – White Lies for Dark Times	$22.99
00694798	George Harrison Anthology	$19.95
00690778	Hawk Nelson – Letters to the President	$19.95
00690841	Scott Henderson – Blues Guitar Collection	$19.95
00692930	Jimi Hendrix – Are You Experienced?	$24.95
00692931	Jimi Hendrix – Axis: Bold As Love	$22.95
00690304	Jimi Hendrix – Band of Gypsys	$24.99
00690608	Jimi Hendrix – Blue Wild Angel	$24.95
00694944	Jimi Hendrix – Blues	$24.95
00692932	Jimi Hendrix – Electric Ladyland	$24.95
00690602	Jimi Hendrix – Smash Hits	$24.99
00691033	Jimi Hendrix – Valleys of Neptune	$22.99
00691152	West Coast Seattle Boy: The Jimi Hendrix Anthology	$29.99
00691332	Jimi Hendrix – Winterland (Highlights)	$22.99
00690017	Jimi Hendrix – Woodstock	$24.95
00690843	H.I.M. – Dark Light	$19.95
00690869	Hinder – Extreme Behavior	$19.95
00660029	Buddy Holly	$22.99
00690793	John Lee Hooker Anthology	$24.99
00660169	John Lee Hooker – A Blues Legend	$19.95
00694905	Howlin' Wolf	$19.95
00690692	Very Best of Billy Idol	$19.95
00690688	Incubus – A Crow Left of the Murder	$19.95
00690136	Indigo Girls – 1200 Curfews	$22.95
00690790	Iron Maiden Anthology	$24.99
00691058	Iron Maiden – The Final Frontier	$22.99
00690887	Iron Maiden – A Matter of Life and Death	$24.95
00690730	Alan Jackson – Guitar Collection	$19.95
00694938	Elmore James – Master Electric Slide Guitar	$19.95
00690652	Best of Jane's Addiction	$19.95
00690721	Jet – Get Born	$19.95
00690684	Jethro Tull – Aqualung	$19.95
00690693	Jethro Tull Guitar Anthology	$19.95
00691182	Jethro Tull – Stand Up	$22.99
00690647	Best of Jewel	$19.95

**AUTHENTIC TRANSCRIPTIONS
WITH NOTES AND TABLATURE**

00690898	John 5 – The Devil Knows My Name	$22.95
00690959	John 5 – Requiem	$22.95
00690814	John 5 – Songs for Sanity	$19.95
00690751	John 5 – Vertigo	$19.95
00694912	Eric Johnson – Ah Via Musicom	$19.95
00690660	Best of Eric Johnson	$22.99
00690845	Eric Johnson – Bloom	$19.95
00691076	Eric Johnson – Up Close	$22.99
00690169	Eric Johnson – Venus Isle	$22.95
00690846	Jack Johnson and Friends – Sing-A-Longs and Lullabies for the Film Curious George	$19.95
00690271	Robert Johnson – The New Transcriptions	$24.95
00699131	Best of Janis Joplin	$19.95
00690427	Best of Judas Priest	$22.99
00690651	Juanes – Exitos de Juanes	$19.95
00690277	Best of Kansas	$19.95
00690911	Best of Phil Keaggy	$24.99
00690727	Toby Keith Guitar Collection	$19.99
00690888	The Killers – Sam's Town	$19.95
00690504	Very Best of Albert King	$19.95
00690444	B.B. King & Eric Clapton – Riding with the King	$22.99
00690134	Freddie King Collection	$19.95
00691062	Kings of Leon – Come Around Sundown	$22.99
00690975	Kings of Leon – Only by the Night	$22.99
00690339	Best of the Kinks	$19.95
00690157	Kiss – Alive!	$19.95
00690356	Kiss – Alive II	$22.99
00694903	Best of Kiss for Guitar	$24.95
00690355	Kiss – Destroyer	$16.95
14026320	Mark Knopfler – Get Lucky	$22.99
00690164	Mark Knopfler Guitar – Vol. 1	$19.95
00690163	Mark Knopfler/Chet Atkins – Neck and Neck	$19.95
00690780	Korn – Greatest Hits, Volume 1	$22.95
00690836	Korn – See You on the Other Side	$19.95
00690377	Kris Kristofferson Collection	$19.95
00690861	Kutless – Hearts of the Innocent	$19.95
00690834	Lamb of God – Ashes of the Wake	$19.95
00690875	Lamb of God – Sacrament	$19.95
00690977	Ray LaMontagne – Gossip in the Grain	$19.99
00690890	Ray LaMontagne – Till the Sun Turns Black	$19.95
00690823	Ray LaMontagne – Trouble	$19.95
00691057	Ray LaMontagne and the Pariah Dogs – God Willin' & The Creek Don't Rise	$22.99
00690658	Johnny Lang – Long Time Coming	$19.95
00690679	John Lennon – Guitar Collection	$19.95
00690781	Linkin Park – Hybrid Theory	$22.95
00690782	Linkin Park – Meteora	$22.95
00690922	Linkin Park – Minutes to Midnight	$19.95
00690783	Best of Live	$19.95
00699623	The Best of Chuck Loeb	$19.95
00690743	Los Lonely Boys	$19.95
00690720	Lostprophets – Start Something	$19.95
00690525	Best of George Lynch	$24.99
00690955	Lynyrd Skynyrd – All-Time Greatest Hits	$19.99
00694954	New Best of Lynyrd Skynyrd	$19.95
00690577	Yngwie Malmsteen – Anthology	$24.95
00694845	Yngwie Malmsteen – Fire and Ice	$19.95
00694757	Yngwie Malmsteen – Trilogy	$19.95
00690754	Marilyn Manson – Lest We Forget	$19.95
00694956	Bob Marley – Legend	$19.95
00690548	Very Best of Bob Marley & The Wailers – One Love	$22.99
00694945	Bob Marley – Songs of Freedom	$24.95
00690914	Maroon 5 – It Won't Be Soon Before Long	$19.95
00690657	Maroon 5 – Songs About Jane	$19.95
00690748	Maroon 5 – 1.22.03 Acoustic	$19.95
00690989	Mastodon – Crack the Skye	$22.99
00691176	Mastodon – The Hunter	$22.99
00690442	Matchbox 20 – Mad Season	$19.95
00690616	Matchbox Twenty – More Than You Think You Are	$19.95
00690239	Matchbox 20 – Yourself or Someone like You	$19.95
00691034	Andy McKee – Joyland	$19.99
00690382	Sarah McLachlan – Mirrorball	$19.95
00120080	The Don McLean Songbook	$19.95
00694952	Megadeth – Countdown to Extinction	$22.95
00690244	Megadeth – Cryptic Writings	$19.95
00694951	Megadeth – Rust in Peace	$22.95
00690011	Megadeth – Youthanasia	$19.95
00690505	John Mellencamp Guitar Collection	$19.95
00690562	Pat Metheny – Bright Size Life	$19.95
00691073	Pat Metheny with Christian McBride & Antonion Sanchez – Day Trip/Tokyo Day Trip Live	$22.99
00690646	Pat Metheny – One Quiet Night	$19.95
00690559	Pat Metheny – Question & Answer	$19.95
00690040	Steve Miller Band Greatest Hits	$19.95
00690769	Modest Mouse – Good News for People Who Love Bad News	$19.95
00102591	Wes Montgomery Guitar Anthology	$24.99

00694802	Gary Moore – Still Got the Blues	$22.99
00691005	Best of Motion City Soundtrack	$19.99
00690787	Mudvayne – L.D. 50	$22.95
00691070	Mumford & Sons – Sigh No More	$22.99
00690996	My Morning Jacket Collection	$19.99
00690984	Matt Nathanson – Some Mad Hope	$22.99
00690611	Nirvana	$22.95
00694895	Nirvana – Bleach	$19.95
00690189	Nirvana – From the Muddy Banks of the Wishkah	$19.95
00694913	Nirvana – In Utero	$19.95
00694883	Nirvana – Nevermind	$19.95
00690026	Nirvana – Unplugged in New York	$19.95
00120112	No Doubt – Tragic Kingdom	$22.95
00690226	Oasis – The Other Side of Oasis	$19.95
00307163	Oasis – Time Flies... 1994-2009	$19.99
00690358	The Offspring – Americana	$19.95
00690203	The Offspring – Smash	$18.95
00690818	The Best of Opeth	$22.95
00691052	Roy Orbison – Black & White Night	$22.99
00694847	Best of Ozzy Osbourne	$22.95
00690399	Ozzy Osbourne – The Ozzman Cometh	$22.99
00690129	Ozzy Osbourne – Ozzmosis	$22.95
00690933	Best of Brad Paisley	$22.95
00690995	Brad Paisley – Play: The Guitar Album	$24.99
00690866	Panic! At the Disco – A Fever You Can't Sweat Out	$19.95
00690939	Christopher Parkening – Solo Pieces	$19.99
00690594	Best of Les Paul	$19.95
00694855	Pearl Jam – Ten	$22.99
00690439	A Perfect Circle – Mer De Noms	$19.95
00690661	A Perfect Circle – Thirteenth Step	$19.95
00690725	Best of Carl Perkins	$19.99
00690499	Tom Petty – Definitive Guitar Collection	$19.95
00690868	Tom Petty – Highway Companion	$19.95
00690176	Phish – Billy Breathes	$22.95
00691249	Phish – Junta	$22.99
00690428	Pink Floyd – Dark Side of the Moon	$19.95
00690789	Best of Poison	$19.95
00693864	Best of The Police	$19.95
00690299	Best of Elvis: The King of Rock 'n' Roll	$19.95
00692535	Elvis Presley	$19.95
00690925	The Very Best of Prince	$22.99
00690003	Classic Queen	$24.95
00694975	Queen – Greatest Hits	$24.95
00690670	Very Best of Queensryche	$19.95
00690878	The Raconteurs – Broken Boy Soldiers	$19.95
00694910	Rage Against the Machine	$19.95
00690179	Rancid – And Out Come the Wolves	$22.99
00690426	Best of Ratt	$19.95
00690055	Red Hot Chili Peppers – Blood Sugar Sex Magik	$19.95
00690584	Red Hot Chili Peppers – By the Way	$19.95
00690379	Red Hot Chili Peppers – Californication	$19.95
00690673	Red Hot Chili Peppers – Greatest Hits	$19.95
00690090	Red Hot Chili Peppers – One Hot Minute	$22.95
00691166	Red Hot Chili Peppers – I'm with You	$22.99
00690852	Red Hot Chili Peppers – Stadium Arcadium	$24.95
00690893	The Red Jumpsuit Apparatus – Don't You Fake It	$19.95
00690511	Django Reinhardt – The Definitive Collection	$19.95
00690779	Relient K – MMHMM	$19.95
00690643	Relient K – Two Lefts Don't Make a Right ... But Three Do	$19.95
00690260	Jimmie Rodgers Guitar Collection	$19.95
14041901	Rodrigo Y Gabriela and C.U.B.A. – Area 52	$24.99
00690014	Rolling Stones – Exile on Main Street	$24.95
00690631	Rolling Stones – Guitar Anthology	$27.95
00690685	David Lee Roth – Eat 'Em and Smile	$19.95
00690031	Santana's Greatest Hits	$19.95
00690796	Very Best of Michael Schenker	$19.95
00690566	Best of Scorpions	$22.95
00690604	Bob Seger – Guitar Anthology	$19.95
00690659	Bob Seger and the Silver Bullet Band – Greatest Hits, Volume 2	$17.95
00691012	Shadows Fall – Retribution	$22.99
00690896	Shadows Fall – Threads of Life	$19.95
00690803	Best of Kenny Wayne Shepherd Band	$19.95
00690750	Kenny Wayne Shepherd – The Place You're In	$19.95
00690857	Shinedown – Us and Them	$19.95
00690196	Silverchair – Freak Show	$19.95
00690130	Silverchair – Frogstomp	$19.95
00690872	Slayer – Christ Illusion	$19.95
00690813	Slayer – Guitar Collection	$19.95
00690419	Slipknot	$19.95
00690973	Slipknot – All Hope Is Gone	$22.99
00690733	Slipknot – Volume 3 (The Subliminal Verses)	$22.99
00690330	Social Distortion – Live at the Roxy	$19.95
00120004	Best of Steely Dan	$24.95
00694921	Best of Steppenwolf	$22.95
00690655	Best of Mike Stern	$19.95

00690949	Rod Stewart Guitar Anthology	$19.99
00690021	Sting – Fields of Gold	$19.95
00690689	Story of the Year – Page Avenue	$19.95
00690520	Styx Guitar Collection	$19.95
00120081	Sublime	$19.95
00690992	Sublime – Robbin' the Hood	$19.99
00690519	SUM 41 – All Killer No Filler	$19.95
00691072	Best of Supertramp	$22.99
00690994	Taylor Swift	$22.99
00690993	Taylor Swift – Fearless	$22.99
00691063	Taylor Swift – Speak Now	$22.99
00690767	Switchfoot – The Beautiful Letdown	$19.95
00690830	System of a Down – Hypnotize	$19.95
00690531	System of a Down – Toxicity	$19.95
00694824	Best of James Taylor	$16.95
00694887	Best of Thin Lizzy	$19.95
00690871	Three Days Grace – One-X	$19.95
00690891	30 Seconds to Mars – A Beautiful Lie	$19.95
00690030	Toad the Wet Sprocket	$19.95
00690233	The Merle Travis Collection	$19.99
00690683	Robin Trower – Bridge of Sighs	$19.95
00699191	U2 – Best of: 1980-1990	$19.95
00690732	U2 – Best of: 1990-2000	$19.95
00690894	U2 – 18 Singles	$19.95
00690775	U2 – How to Dismantle an Atomic Bomb	$22.95
00690997	U2 – No Line on the Horizon	$19.99
00690039	Steve Vai – Alien Love Secrets	$24.95
00690172	Steve Vai – Fire Garden	$24.95
00660137	Steve Vai – Passion & Warfare	$24.95
00690881	Steve Vai – Real Illusions: Reflections	$24.95
00694904	Steve Vai – Sex and Religion	$24.95
00690392	Steve Vai – The Ultra Zone	$19.95
00690024	Stevie Ray Vaughan – Couldn't Stand the Weather	$19.95
00690370	Stevie Ray Vaughan and Double Trouble – The Real Deal: Greatest Hits Volume 2	$22.95
00690116	Stevie Ray Vaughan – Guitar Collection	$24.95
00660136	Stevie Ray Vaughan – In Step	$19.95
00694879	Stevie Ray Vaughan – In the Beginning	$19.95
00660058	Stevie Ray Vaughan – Lightnin' Blues '83-'87	$24.95
00690036	Stevie Ray Vaughan – Live Alive	$24.95
00694835	Stevie Ray Vaughan – The Sky Is Crying	$22.95
00690025	Stevie Ray Vaughan – Soul to Soul	$19.95
00690015	Stevie Ray Vaughan – Texas Flood	$19.95
00690772	Velvet Revolver – Contraband	$22.95
00690132	The T-Bone Walker Collection	$19.95
00694789	Muddy Waters – Deep Blues	$24.95
00690071	Weezer (The Blue Album)	$19.95
00690516	Weezer (The Green Album)	$19.95
00690286	Weezer – Pinkerton	$19.95
00691046	Weezer – Rarities Edition	$22.99
00690447	Best of the Who	$24.95
00694970	The Who – Definitive Guitar Collection: A-E	$24.95
00694971	The Who – Definitive Guitar Collection F-Li	$24.95
00694972	The Who – Definitive Guitar Collection: Lo-R	$24.95
00690672	Best of Dar Williams	$19.95
00691017	Wolfmother – Cosmic Egg	$22.99
00690319	Stevie Wonder – Some of the Best	$17.95
00690596	Best of the Yardbirds	$19.95
00690844	Yellowcard – Lights and Sounds	$19.95
00690916	The Best of Dwight Yoakam	$19.95
00690904	Neil Young – Harvest	$29.99
00690905	Neil Young – Rust Never Sleeps	$19.95
00690443	Frank Zappa – Hot Rats	$19.95
00690624	Frank Zappa and the Mothers of Invention – One Size Fits All	$22.99
00690623	Frank Zappa – Over-Nite Sensation	$22.99
00690589	ZZ Top – Guitar Anthology	$24.95
00690960	ZZ Top Guitar Classics	$19.95

7777 W. BLUEMOUND RD. P.O. BOX 13819 MILWAUKEE, WI 53213

Complete songlists and more at www.halleonard.com
Prices, contents, and availability subject to change without notice.

1112